The Evolving Rationality
of Rational Expectations

An Assessment of Thomas Sargent's Achievements

Inspired by recent developments in science studies, *The Evolving Rationality of Rational Expectations* offers an innovative type of analysis of the recent history of rational expectations economics. In the course of exploring the multiple dimensions of rational expectations analysis, Esther-Mirjam Sent focuses on the work of Thomas Sargent, a pioneer instrumental in the development of this school of thought. The investigation attempts to avoid a Whiggish history that sees Sargent's development as inevitably progressing to better and better economic analysis. Instead, *The Evolving Rationality of Rational Expectations* provides an illustration of what happened to the approach through a contextualization of Sargent's presence in a rich external configuration of people and ideas. The treatment aims to illuminate some of the shifting negotiations and alliances that characterize the rise and shift of direction in rational expectations economics.

Esther-Mirjam Sent is Assistant Professor in the Department of Economics and Faculty Fellow in the Reilly Center for Science, Technology, and Values at the University of Notre Dame. She has published articles in the *Journal of Post Keynesian Economics, Cambridge Journal of Economics, History of Political Economy, Philosophy of Science, Journal of Economic Methodology,* and *Social Epistemology,* among other journals.

Historical Perspectives on Modern Economics

General Editor: Craufurd D. Goodwin, Duke University

This series contains original works that challenge and enlighten historians of economics. For the profession as a whole it promotes better understanding of the origin and content of modern economics.

Other books in the series:

The Evolving Rationality of Rational Expectations

An Assessment of Thomas Sargent's Achievements

Esther-Mirjam Sent
University of Notre Dame

CAMBRIDGE
UNIVERSITY PRESS

PUBLISHED BY THE PRESS SYNDICATE OF THE UNIVERSITY OF CAMBRIDGE
The Pitt Building, Trumpington Street, Cambridge CB2 1RP, United Kingdom

CAMBRIDGE UNIVERSITY PRESS
The Edinburgh Building, Cambridge CB2 2RU, UK   http://www.cup.cam.ac.uk
40 West 20th Street, New York, NY 10011-4211, USA   http://www.cup.org
10 Stamford Road, Oakleigh, Melbourne 3166, Australia

First published 1998

Printed in the United States of America

Typeset in Times Roman 10/12 pt, in Quark XPress™ [AG]

Library of Congress Cataloging-in-Publication Data

Sent, Esther-Mirjam, 1967–

The evolving rationality of rational expectations : an assessment
of Thomas Sargent's achievements / Esther-Mirjam Sent.

p.   cm. – (Historical perspectives on modern economics)

Includes bibliographical references and index.

ISBN 0-521-57164-2 (hardbound)

1. Rational expectations (Economic theory)   2. Sargent, Thomas J.
3. Macroeconomics – Mathematical models.   4. Econometrics.
I. Title.   II. Series.
HB172.5.S46   1998
339'.01'5118 – DC21   97-38884
                                                              CIP

A catalog record for this book is available from the British Library.

ISBN 0 521 57164 2 hardback

Contents

Acknowledgments

Stimulated by an inspiring high school economics teacher, a boyfriend who was an economics major, and a desire to improve the world, I first set foot in the realm of economics at the University of Amsterdam. My Dutch teachers soon made me realize that I would have a hard time improving the world through the use of economics, for they tended to be somewhat critical of economic assumptions and very wary of abstract economic theories. I had one elective during my first year, wanted to take a course that would be outside my desired area of specialization, and decided to take history and philosophy of economics. Well, things did not quite turn out as I expected and I ended up specializing in history and philosophy of economics. As a result, I finished my undergraduate education in the Netherlands with a sense of suspicion about abstraction, mathematization, and simplification in economics and a strong desire to explore alternative approaches. Encouraged by my adviser Neil de Marchi, to whom I am very grateful for rousing my fascination with economics, I set out to continue on this path by enrolling in graduate school at Stanford University. However, much to my surprise, my American teachers, including Thomas Sargent, expressed considerable resistance to the ideas of their Dutch colleagues. In fact, their classes started and ended with the mathematical models my Dutch teachers had criticized so persistently. My questions concerning the justification and interpretation of these models were frequently met with disheartening frowns. Fortunately, my by-then-eroded enthusiasm for economics was rekindled when I had the good fortune to spend a year at the University of Notre Dame, invigorated by Philip Mirowski's never-ending inspiration and verve. This book would have been impossible without his urging and support. In addition, the stimulating discussions during history and philosophy of science reading group meetings at the University of Notre Dame provoked me to look for answers to my questions by making use of sociology of scientific knowledge.

I am very thankful to Kenneth Arrow for allowing me to pursue this study of the sociology of economics and for forcing me, in long discussions, to face the resistances within my research. I was very fortunate to receive valuable and constructive comments on topics related to rational expectations economics from Orazio Attanasio and on questions concerning philosophy and history from John Dupré and Timothy Lenoir. I am very grateful to Jeff Biddle, Daniel Hammond, and Donald Moggridge, who were members of the 1995 Joseph

Dorfman Dissertation Prize committee, and James Henderson, who was president of the History of Economics Society, for awarding the prize for the best 1995 history of economic thought dissertation to the first draft of my manuscript. For helpful discussions, I would like to thank participants of seminars at Duke University, University of Limburg, Loyola Marymount University, McMaster University, Michigan State University, University of Notre Dame, Occidental College, Stanford University, Tinbergen Institute in Amsterdam, Vassar College, and Williams College and attendees of conference sessions at the 1995 and 1996 Allied Social Science Association meetings, 1995 European Conferences on the History of Economics, and 1995 History of Economics Society meetings. Special thanks must go to Jeff Biddle and Warren Samuels, who suffered through my very first seminar presentation on the issues discussed in this book, and to Mary Ann Dimand, Wade Hands, Kevin Hoover, and Arjo Klamer, who sometimes proved to be challenging discussants. I am very grateful to Robert Blattberg, Deirdre McCloskey, Ellen McGrattan, John Meyer, Richard Roll, Herbert Simon, and Neil Wallace for spending time answering my questions. Thomas Sargent deserves my deepest gratitude for providing me with a fascinating book topic and for giving me the stimulating experience of interviewing him. I would also like to thank Craufurd Goodwin, Scott Parris, and two anonymous referees for pushing me to reflect seriously on what I am trying to achieve with my book and whether I am successful at reaching my goals. Finally, I acknowledge the research assistance of Matthew Weagle, Steven Tradewell, Katarina Keller, and Edward Nik-Khah; the research support of the University of Notre Dame's Institute for Scholarship in the Liberal Arts; the help of Anita Marlin in transcribing the interview; and the support of Gregory Kucich.

Portions of this book have appeared in earlier manifestations in *Journal of Post Keynesian Economics, Cambridge Journal of Economics, History of Political Economy,* and *Journal of Economic Methodology.* I thank the publishers of these publications for permission to use this material.

CHAPTER 1

Introduction

Come writers and critics,
Who prophesize with your pen,
And keep your eyes wide,
The chance won't come again,
And don't speak too soon,
For the wheel's still in spin,
And there's no tellin' who,
That it's namin',
For the loser now,
Will be later to win,
For the times they are a-changin'.

The times were changing in the late 1960s. During that period, rational expectations economics started changing the face of macroeconomics. Economists such as Robert Lucas, Thomas Sargent, and Neil Wallace began to dominate the macroeconomics discussion. Notions such as the Lucas critique, the Lucas supply curve, and the Sargent–Wallace policy irrelevance proposition became integral parts of the macroeconomics discourse. As Snippe (1986) notes, "Modern controversy is concerned with the kind of economic performance rational expectations can explain, rather than being concerned with the acceptability of the rational expectations hypothesis as such" (p. 427; also see Klamer 1983, p. 77). By the time I enrolled in graduate school at Stanford University in 1989, rational expectations economics had firmly taken root. Thomas Sargent, one of my teachers, would help me in taking derivatives, multiplying matrices, and solving differential equations but was unwilling to entertain any of my questions about the history and philosophy of rational expectations economics. Snippe concurs: "Those who still attempt to raise doubts about the hypothesis fail to receive much attention or to initiate further debates. This state of affairs may, at least in part, be explained by the ambiguity of the rational expectations assumption" (p. 427). In searching for answers to the questions of why rational expectations economics was developed and what it entailed, I encountered ten different accounts, related to availability of new data or use of new techniques or natural development from existing theories or problems with existing theories or linking of theory and econometrics. These ten stories are discussed briefly.

1.1   Stories about the Rise of Rational Expectations

1.1.1   *Story One: Expiration of the Phillips Curve*

The expiration of the Phillips curve in the 1970s is often credited with dealing a fatal blow to Keynesianism.[1] Positing a trade-off between inflation and output, the Phillips curve was a key element in the Keynesian models. Government policymakers tried to exploit this Phillips curve trade-off in an effort to lower unemployment in the late 1960s to early 1970s by managing aggregate demand and tolerating the inflation that was its consequence. However, the inflationary bias in this economic policy was accompanied by tremendously high unemployment rates in the 1970s. Making use of the rational expectations hypothesis, economists were able to explain that the government actions caused an adverse shift of the Phillips curve, leading to higher inflation, with no benefits in terms of lower unemployment on average (see, e.g., Friedman 1968; Hoover 1988, pp. 23–37; Lucas 1972a, 1972b, 1973; Lucas and Rapping 1969a, 1969b; Phelps 1967; Phelps et al. 1970; Sargent 1987a, pp. 438–46). They showed that the value of the Phillips curve was erased by rapid inflation and people's actions in anticipation of more inflation to come, if markets clear and expectations are rational. Their setup resulted in a vertical Phillips curve in which unemployment is independent of expected inflation rates yet exhibits some expost correlation with actual inflation. Hence, this story attributes the rise of rational expectations to new data that became available as a result of new economic developments. These new data also called into question the effectiveness of economic policy, as we will see in the next account.

1.1.2   *Story Two: Policy Irrelevance*

The consensus following from the confident and apparently successful applications of Keynesian principles to economic policy in the 1960s was undermined by the failure of traditional Keynesian policies in the 1970s. The ensuing observation that government policy did not seem to work, some argue, lent a certain credibility to the rational expectations school's insistence that the government could not fine-tune the economy. Specifically, the rational expectations postulate gave rise to a skeptical attitude about how much economists knew and how much the government could accomplish, and a suggestion that both economists and the government had overreached themselves to society's detriment (see, e.g., Barro 1976; Buiter 1980; Hoover 1988, pp. 65–73; Lucas 1972a, 1972b, 1975, 1976; McCallum 1979a; Sargent and Wallace 1975, 1976). Recognizing the limitations of their profession, rational expectations economists maintained that the economy would basically be stable if it were not subjected to the shocks repeatedly administered by the government. Since nobody understood deeply how the economy responded, they argued that it was best not to try anything fancy. Instead, rational expectations economists claimed that they should recommend policy rules.

In addition, proponents of the rational expectations hypothesis argued that government tinkering could be not only dangerous, as outlined previously, but also ineffective. They replaced the old view that the government could manage the economy through fooling people by the idea that people can foil government policymakers. By taking seriously the observation that people learn from their mistakes, rational expectations economists showed that orthodox prescriptions of economic policy crumbled, since much of the effectiveness of these policies relied on the government's ability to fool people indefinitely. In particular, as people wised up to government scheming to manage the economy, they forestalled the very results that the government sought when it tried to alter the economy's course through fiscal or monetary interventions. In the end, rational expectations economists contended, the interventions would prove worse than useless, because people would change their strategies when the government changed its strategies. Hence, this story also attributes the rise of rational expectations to new data that became available as a result of new policy developments.[2]

Before shifting the narrative with a new story, it should be noted that there is an internal contradiction in using the rational expectations hypothesis for policy recommendations (see, e.g., Lucas and Sargent 1981; Sargent 1984; 1987a, pp. 435–6; 1987c; Sargent and Wallace 1976). If there is a rational expectations equilibrium with optimal policy, then there is no room for improvement in government policy, because the system cannot be influenced. On the other hand, if there is no rational expectations equilibrium with no optimal policy, then there is room for improvement in government policy. However, this presumes that agents' expectations about government policy do not take the policy advice into account properly. Hence, if government policy is believed to have room for improvement, any rational expectations model always misspecifies the economic structure.[3] This raises the question of the purpose of rational expectations economics if policy is supposed to be always optimal. Rather than dwelling on this question here, I will move on to the next story. There the narrative will shift from availability of new data to the use of new techniques.

1.1.3   Story Three: Using Available Techniques

Some claim that economic analysts were often directed by, if not prisoners of, the mathematical techniques that they possessed. These tools influenced the very questions that they asked as well as the way in which they were posed. Specifically, economists learned and used the techniques of intertemporal optimization (e.g., calculus of variations) developed by mathematicians and control scientists more quickly than they did the tools of optimal prediction and filtering of stochastic processes (see, e.g., Sargent 1987a, pp. xvii–xxii; 1987c; 1996a, p. 541; Sent 1998). In the 1950s to early 1960s, much literature was produced in which agents were imagined to solve optimal control problems using the calculus of variations, and therefore using static or adaptive expectations-generating mechanisms. Classical linear prediction theory, the mathematical theory crucial for interpreting distributed lags in terms of economic parameters and incorporating the rational expectations hypothesis in economic models, was developed in the 1940s to 1950s but did not immediately become part of economists' tool kits. However, Peter Whittle published a book in the mid-1960s that conveniently summarized and made more accessible to economists the classical linear prediction theory that was heavily used by rational expectations economists (see, e.g., Whittle 1983). This delay partly explains the lagged effect of Muth's (1960, 1961) contributions (see, e.g., Sargent 1996a, p. 537). Hence, this story attributes the rise of rational expectations to the availability of new techniques. The narrative will shift again with the following two stories which both attribute the rise of rational expectations to attempts to extend existing theories.

1.1.4   Story Four: Restoring Symmetry

The hypothesis of adaptive expectations, which was used heavily up until the late 1960s, postulated that individuals used information on past forecasting errors to revise their current expectations (see, e.g., Begg 1982; Cagan 1956; Friedman 1968; Nerlove 1958). In particular, agents were presumed to rely on mechanistic backward-looking extrapolative rules. As a result, there was an asymmetry among economists, econometricians, and agents, in that adaptive expectations economists and econometricians fit models that forecast better than agents. The reason is that the economists and econometricians were presumed to be fully knowledgeable, whereas the agents were postulated to make systematic forecasting errors period after period. By starting with the idea that individuals were inspecting and altering their own forecasting records just like economists and econometricians in their attempts to eliminate systematic forecasting errors, some argue, the concept of rational expectations was able to banish this asymmetry. It embodied the idea that economists and econometricians, on the one hand, and the agents they are modeling, on the other hand, were placed on an equal footing by postulating that the forecasts made by the agents within the model were no worse than those by the economists or econometricians who had the model (see, e.g., Kantor 1979, p. 1429; Sargent 1987a, pp. 411, 440; 1987c, p. 76; 1993, pp. 21, 39). Whereas the first part of this story deals with the asymmetry among economists, econometricians, and agents, the second part confronts the asymmetry between governments and agents.

Some have argued in addition that the treatment of policy in the Keynesian tradition led inevitably to rational expectations (see, e.g., Keuzekamp 1991; Sargent 1987a, p. xxii). The reason is that Keynesian policy analysis, extending back to Tinbergen, pursued the idea of applying optimal control theory to models in order to make precise quantitative statements about optimal policies. In these policy experiments, the government was imagined to behave precisely as an agent with rational expectations. Therefore, it was only natural that economists would eventually apply these ideas to private agents' decision rules as well as those of the government. Symmetry between government agents and private agents was established by assuming that both types of agents had rational expectations and solved rich dynamic optimization problems that took into account all the constraints that they faced. However, considering themselves just as smart as agents and policymakers, rational expectations economists were led to confront the nullifying effect of their hypothesis on economic policy, as discussed in the second story. Rather than elaborating on this conundrum here, I close by noting that this story argues that rational expectations followed from existing theories. It merely completed the symmetry picture in these theories by including private agents.

1.1.5 Story Five: Optimizing over Information

In addition to the asymmetry among economists, econometricians, private agents, and government agents discussed in the previous story, adaptive expectations treated the separate decision components of private agents asymmetrically. In particular, rational expectations economists argued that the suboptimal use of available information under adaptive expectations was hard to reconcile with the idea of optimization that was the foundation of most economic analysis. Instead, rational expectations economists claimed that since agents were posited as optimizers, it was only natural to presume that they would also form their expectations optimally (see, e.g., Coddington 1975, 1976; Hoover 1988, pp. 15–16; Kantor 1979; Lucas and Prescott 1969, 1971, 1974; Lucas and Sargent 1981, pp. xiv–xvi; McCallum 1979b; Sargent 1982, 1987a, pp. xvii–xxii; 1987b). Hence, some argue that the rational expectations hypothesis was nothing but a direct derivation from the optimization principle extended to the problem of expectations of future events. In particular, optimizing over perceptions implied that agents did the best they could and formed their views of the future by taking account of all available information, including their understanding of how the economy works. If perceptions were not optimally chosen, unexploited utility or profit-generating possibilities would exist within the system. Hence, rational expectations economists insisted on the disappearance of all such unexploited possibilities.[4]

Rational expectations economists contrasted their approach with Keynesian analyses. They argued that economics had to account for the decisions of firms and people in ways that were consistent with the idea of optimizing behavior, because ad hoc assumptions about the actions of firms and people did not sit well with the microfoundations of economic theory. At the same time, they criticized the typical Keynesian assumptions that markets did not clear and that economic agents did not always pursue optimizing strategies, because both implied ad hoc departures from the axiom of rational behavior. Hence, some see rational expectations economics as replacing earlier ad hoc treatments with an approach squarely based on the microfoundations of incentives, information, and optimization. One drawback of the rigorous approach advocated by rational expectations economists was its inability to deal with some of the untidy facts about the real world. Some have countered the argument that the rational expectations idea was not a description of actual behavior with the claim that it could be a rule of good conduct for economic modelers since it was less arbitrary. Hence, this story also attributes the rise of rational expectations to attempts at extending existing theories. The narrative will shift with the following three stories, which attribute the rise of rational expectations to problems with existing theories.

1.1.6   Story Six: Endogenizing Expectations

Though economists had long understood that expectations played a central role in driving the economy and that even the simplest economic theory should say something about how people viewed the future, they lacked a plausible theory of how expectations were formed (see, e.g., Begg 1982; Sheffrin 1983). For example, Keynes (1936, chaps. 12, 15), doubting that expectations could be modeled or measured accurately, brushed the problem aside by taking expectations as given. Furthermore, when Keynes's followers operationalized models of intertemporal decision making, they argued that people made guesses about the future by looking exclusively backward. As discussed in story four, for example, the hypothesis of adaptive expectations postulated that individuals used information on past forecasting errors to revise current expectations (see, e.g., Cagan 1956; Friedman 1968).[5] Whereas story four focused on the ensuing asymmetry among economists, econometricians, and agents, this story highlights the fact that even though people with adaptive expectations were thought to use their own forecasting errors to derive their next forecasts, no widely accepted economic theory was offered to explain the magnitude of the adjustment parameter.

Some argue that rational expectations economics was able to remedy this defect by arguing that guesses about the future must be correct on average if individuals are to remain satisfied with their mechanism of expectations formation (see, e.g., Begg 1982; Janssen 1993, pp. 131–43; Klamer 1983, pp. 13–14; Lucas and Rapping 1969a; Muth 1960, 1961; Sheffrin 1983). The rational expectations hypothesis asserted that the resulting predictions might still be wrong, but that the errors would be random. For if errors followed a pattern, they held information that could be used to make more accurate forecasts. Therefore, when all individual expectations were added together, errors were presumed to cancel out. The reason is that though agents with rational expectations did still make mistakes, they did not make the same mistakes each time. Hence, this story attributes the rise of rational expectations to its ability to deal with the problem of explaining expectations revision under adaptive expectations.

Before moving on to the next story, which focuses on additional problems associated with existing theories, I close this section by noting that some economists have argued that, despite its insistence that expectations should be endogenous, rational expectations economics has dodged the crucial question of how expectations are actually formed (see, e.g., Buiter 1980; DeCanio 1979; Friedman 1979; Lucas 1987, p. 13; Snippe 1986, pp. 428–9; Taylor 1975). One response to this criticism may be that individuals actually used economic models to make sophisticated calculations about the future. Another interpretation of the rational expectations hypothesis may be that people absorbed this information from experts. It may further be argued that the rational expectations hypothesis is of the "as-if" variety, interpreted either in a micro or in a macro sense. Again, there is no room here for discussing these issues in more detail.

1.1.7   Story Seven: Making Public Predictions

Some have argued that the rise of rational expectations may be attributed to its ability to fight the threat of indeterminacy (see, e.g., Grunberg 1986; Grunberg and Modigliani 1954; Hands 1990; Lucas 1976; Lucas and Sargent 1979; Sargent 1987c; Simon 1954). This indeterminacy followed from the realization that it was possible to make both self-falsifying and self-fulfilling predictions about people. This, in turn, was the result of the observation that the formation of mutual expectations about behavior might have very large stabilizing or destabilizing effects for a society (see, e.g., Merton 1936, 1948). Since outcomes depended partly on what people expected those outcomes to be if people's behavior depended on their perceptions, economic systems were thought to be self-referential. This led some to despair that economic models could produce so many outcomes that they were useless as instruments for generating predictions. As a first approximation, many economists abstracted from such difficulties as infinite regress and reflexivity by assuming that people believed and expected whatever the facts were.

Rational expectations, however, was a powerful hypothesis for restricting the range of possible outcomes since it focused only on outcomes and systems of beliefs that were consistent with one another. In particular, a rational expectations equilibrium was a fixed point of a particular mapping from believed laws of motion to the actual laws of motion for the economy. Under rational expectations, correct public predictions could be made because the rational expectations predictions were presumed to be essentially the same as the predictions of the relevant economic theory. Furthermore, the theory necessarily included the expectational response of the agents, and therefore the influence of predictions on behavior of the agents. However, there may still be indeterminacy under rational expectations as a result of bubble equilibria.

Before moving on to the final story that addresses additional criticisms of existing theories, I should note that some have attacked the rational expectations school for equating successful action with successful prediction, for equating success with small statistical error in prediction. They contend that rational expectations were simply predictive. Rather than elaborating on this criticism here, I will reiterate that this story attributes the rise of rational expectations to the problem of making public predictions within the context of existing theories.

1.1.8   Story Eight: Countering Bounded Rationality

Some argue that it is no coincidence that rational expectations theory was born at the same time in the same institution as bounded rationality, namely, in the 1960s at the Graduate School of Industrial Administration (GSIA) at Carnegie Mellon University.[6] Keynesians (Holt, an electrical-engineer-turned-economist, and Modigliani), the prophet of bounded rationality (Simon), the father of rational expectations (Muth, who started his career at Carnegie as a graduate student), and the popularizers of rational expectations (Lucas, Sargent, and Rapping) were all at Carnegie Mellon University during some part of the 1960s (see Simon 1982d, p. 486; 1991, p. 250).

Initially, the atmosphere among these adversaries was congenial. For example, Holt, Modigliani, Muth, and Simon (1960) collaborated on the Planning and Control of Industrial Operations project, which consisted of developing and applying mathematical techniques to business decision making. Modigliani left Carnegie in 1960 for MIT and later recalled the cordial ambiance (see Klamer 1983, p. 119). Muth left in 1964 and did not have much of a direct impact on his colleagues (see Klamer 1983, pp. 120, 225). In addition, Lucas joined the department in 1963 and collaborated with Rapping on work in the Chicago tradition.

The atmosphere slowly started to turn sour during the late 1960s. Simon began to feel more and more alienated and was dismayed that the new faculty that had been recruited had little taste or talent for empirical research that did not start (and sometimes end) with formal model building (see Simon 1991, pp. 249–50, 270–1). The escalating conflicts eventually caused Simon to leave the GSIA for the Psychology Department at Carnegie (see Simon 1991, pp. 167, 251). Interestingly enough, though Simon and Muth had both participated in the Planning and Control of Industrial Operations project, Simon saw the strong assumptions underlying their project as an instance of satisficing (see Simon 1982c, p. 113; 1991, p. 167), whereas Muth saw this special case as a paradigm for rational behavior under uncertainty (see Muth 1960, 1961; Simon 1991, pp. 486, 250, 270–1). Some argue that Muth, in his announcement of rational expectations, explicitly labeled his theory a reply to the doctrine of bounded rationality. Though his proposal was at first not much noticed by the economics profession, it later caught the attention of Lucas, a new young assistant professor at the GSIA.[7]

This story continues with attempts to show that some form of bounded rationality in the form of learning may converge to the rational expectations equilibrium (see, e.g., Blume, Bray, and Easley 1982; Bray 1982, 1983; Bray and Kreps 1987; Frydman 1982; Frydman and Phelps 1983; Sargent 1993). In addition, incorporating dynamics in the form of learning may solve some of the problems associated with the static rational expectations equilibrium. For instance, a system with learning agents could be used to select an equilibrium path, to modify the sharp predictions that arise in some rational expectations models, to analyze regime changes, and to compute rational expectations equilibria.

Hence, this story may also be interpreted as attributing the rise of rational expectations to problems with existing theories, though it has focused more on the sociology than on the theory. Before shifting the narrative to econometric considerations, I should note that there was not only a split between Simon and the neoclassical economists at the GSIA, but also antagonism within the neoclassical faction. Though Sargent was at Carnegie for a while, for instance, he was associated with the non-Chicago faction and as a result did not interact much with Lucas (Klamer 1983, pp. 33, 60–1, 225).

1.1.9   Story Nine: Restricting Distributed Lags

Some argue that rational expectations research was popularized mostly by time series econometricians, who were looking for methods that could be used for restricting the parameters of the lag distributions in their econometric models in the late 1960s (see, e.g., Hansen and Sargent 1991a; Klamer 1983, pp. 58–80). These econometricians were confronted with theoretical models that analyzed individual behavior in a context without uncertainty and randomness. At the same time, since they treated their data probabilistically, they had to add uncertainty and randomness to the theoretical models. Rather than dealing with uncertainty and randomness as afterthoughts, they felt that these elements ought to be made an integral part of economic theories by endowing agents with rational expectations.

According to this story, then, rational expectations modeling began as an attempt at incorporating uncertainty and randomness in optimizing economic theory and using the outcome to understand, interpret, and restrict the distributed lags that abounded in the decision rules of dynamic macroeconometric models. For time series econometricians, rational expectations modeling promised to tighten the link between theory and estimation. Both theorizing and econometrics confronted uncertainty and randomness from the start. In addition, the objects produced by the theorizing were exactly the objects in terms of which econometrics was cast. The final and most telling step in that research effort was the insight that optimizing dynamic economic theory could deliver cross-equation restrictions across the distributed lags in decision rules, on the one hand, and equations for the motion of the variables that appeared in agents' objective functions, on the other hand. Rather than discussing these technical details here, I move on to the final story, which focuses on linking theory and method through the use of vector autoregressions rather than distributed lags.

1.1.10   Story Ten: Incorporating Vector Autoregressions

This final story attributes the rise of rational expectations to the belief that it allowed a connection between vector autoregressions and economic theory. Vector autoregressive models were developed during the 1970s to provide compact summaries of the properties of the data within a given sample (see, e.g., Hoover 1988, pp. 167–85; Klamer 1983, pp. 22–4; Sargent and Sims 1977). Although the initial driving force behind these models consisted of an interest in exploring time series with advanced econometric techniques and with a minimum of economic theory, vector autoregressive models ultimately outperformed the earlier large-scale simultaneous equation models in forecasting. Large Keynesian econometric models came under additional attack as a result of the Lucas critique[8] and Sargent's discovery of observational equivalence.[9] In response, many econometricians started putting much greater priority on representing the data relative to the theory and limiting the guidance of theory to the selection of the variables and the lag length (see, e.g., Hickman 1972; Sims 1980a; Zellner and Palm 1974).

Some argue that rational expectations modeling was able to revive theory by showing that vector autoregressions were not necessarily atheoretical and could provide a statistical setting within which the restrictions implied by theoretical models could be imposed (see, e.g., Hansen and Sargent 1991a; Hoover 1988, pp. 187–92; Sargent 1981a). In particular, rational expectations economists exploited cross-equation restrictions to connect the vector autoregressive parameters of decision rules with the theoretical parameters of taste, technology, and other stochastic environments. Since this approach disentangled the parameters governing the stochastic processes that agents faced from the parameters of their objective function, it was a safeguard against the Lucas critique and Sargent's observational equivalence. A major problem with this strategy was that it was difficult to carry out successfully as a result of the highly nonlinear nature of the restrictions.

1.1.11 Evaluation of Stories

Although the reader is referred to the cited sources for a more thorough discussion of the stories and though there may be other stories, the brief outline indicates that there are many different, not necessarily independent, perspectives on the rise of rational expectations.[10] The first two stories focus on data as the driving force. In particular, story one argues that rational expectations arose out of the expiration of the Phillips curve and story two emphasizes policy irrelevance. Story three concentrates on the availability of new techniques that were employed in calculating rational expectation equilibria. The following two stories concentrate on rational expectations economics as a natural extension of existing theories. In particular, story four focuses on how it eliminated asymmetry among economists, econometricians, and agents and between government agents and private agents. Story five argues that rational expectations economics extended the optimization principle to the problem of expectations. The next three stories emphasize how rational expectations dealt with problems associated with existing theories. Story six attributes the rise of rational expectations economics to its ability to endogenize expectations. Story seven concentrates on how the problem of making public predictions may be solved by the rational expectations hypothesis. Story eight claims that rational expectations economics was developed in direct opposition to bounded rationality. The final two stories concentrate on how rational expectations economics sought to connect economic theories and econometric models. Whereas story nine discusses how rational expectations theory may restrict distributed lags, story ten attributes the rise of rational expectations economics to its ability to incorporate vector autoregressions. It should be noted that the ten stories are neither mutually exclusive nor mutually exhaustive. In fact, they may be overlapping and to some extent mutually reinforcing. In many cases, they amount to varied aspects or perspectives on a complicated subject, many of which could be comfortably held by one and the same person, as we will see in the story that is the focus of this book.

Before moving on to the story that will be the focus of the following chapters, I should note that the upsurge of the rational expectations hypothesis is often linked to the rise of new classical economics. However, a quick consultation of some textbooks on new classical economics does not help much in clarifying the stories about the rise of rational expectations. According to Klamer (1983), the

rational expectations hypothesis is undoubtedly the most salient characteristic of new classical economics. Rational expectations and new classical economics are commonly taken as synonyms, but this interpretation is probably incorrect. Rational expectations does not necessarily separate new classical economists from the others. The policy ineffectiveness proposition and the issue of equilibrium modeling have turned out to be more controversial. Nevertheless, rational expectations is a crucial assumption in new classical models. (p. 13)

Hoover (1988) replaced the policy ineffectiveness proposition with the importance of real factors when he asserted that

[t]hree tenets are keys to the new classical doctrine. First, agents' real economic decisions . . . are based solely on real, not nominal or monetary, factors. Second, agents are, to the limits of their information, consistent and successful optimizers, i.e. they are continuously in equilibrium. Third, agents make no systematic errors in evaluating the environment, i.e. they hold rational expectations. (pp. 13–14; also see Snowdon, Vane, and Wynarczyk 1994, pp. 188–95)

And Kim (1988) referred to new classical economics as equilibrium business cycle theory and added incomplete information as an assumption. According to Kim, the "equilibrium business cycle theory has three fundamental components: (a) an optimization foundation in a general equilibrium context, (b) the natural rate hypothesis, or the neutrality of money, and (c) the incomplete information assumption" (p. 6).

## 1.2	Focus on Sargent's Story

Why was rational expectations theory developed? Was it because certain data became available? Was it because rational expectations economics relied on new techniques? Was it because the hypothesis followed naturally from existing theories? Were there certain flaws in existing theories? Did rational expectations economics link theory with econometrics? An additional question is how rational expectations are defined. What does it mean for agents not to make systematic mistakes? Do they use econometric models such as distributed lags or vector autoregressions? Do they use theoretical models such as those developed in general equilibrium theory or game theory? Do agents converge to the rational expectations equilibrium through learning? Is the rational expectations hypothesis descriptive or is it of the "as-if" variety? Is it a micro or a macro concept? Janssen (1993) observed, "Although the notion of rational expectations has been in the economics profession for more than thirty years now, there is still no consensus about the motivation for using the notion in macroeconomics" (p. 131).

The many stories about the rise of rational expectations economics and the various interpretations of the rational expectations hypothesis strengthen the argument that there is no generic science. In an attempt to show that the treatment of rational expectations had multiple aspects, the following chapters focus on one economist, Thomas Sargent, who has been instrumental in the development of the field. Robert Townsend accurately remarked, "Sargent is an important person for many economists these days, through his writing as well as through personal contact" (Klamer 1983, p. 82). Furthermore, Klamer concurred that "[t]he prominence of Sargent among new classical economists is unmistakable. ... [H]e has had a profound influence on theoretical and empirical discourse in new classical economics" (p. 58). Rather than looking at Sargent's accomplishments from the perspective of orthodox philosophy of economics or conventional history of economic thought, this book employs a novel approach to search for the stories Sargent is likely to have told at the time he made certain contributions to rational expectations economics. Rather than analyzing rational expectations economics at a general level, the following chapters try to understand the specific alternatives available to Sargent, the choices he made, and the consequences of those decisions. They show that even the treatment of rational expectations by this one particular economist had many faces.

Before outlining the approach used in the following chapters, I should explain why I have written an entire book on Sargent. Like so many others, I chose economics as a major because I wanted to improve the world. However, my undergraduate education in the Netherlands instilled in me a sense of suspicion about abstraction, mathematization, and simplification in economics, which led me to question whether I could ever achieve my goal through the use of economics. This concern did not diminish during my graduate education in the United States. In fact, it increased as a result of the classes I took from Thomas Sargent. He would help me in taking derivatives, multiplying matrices, and solving differential equations, but was unwilling to entertain any of my questions about abstraction in rational expectations economics. In response, my interests gradually switched from attempting to improve the economy to trying to understand economists in general and Sargent in particular. Why was it that my concerns seemed to be so different from Sargent's? Why did he not seem to be bothered by the same things? What was he trying to achieve with his rational expectations economics? I have to confess that I started out feeling different from and being hostile to Sargent in my first attempts at answering these questions. However, throughout the course of writing this book, I have come to see myself as more similar to Sargent. Whereas Sargent is attempting to model the actions of economic agents, I am trying to understand the conduct of economists. Therefore, we are both trying to capture human behavior. We turned out to be fascinated by very similar things, struggling with very similar issues, and having very similar concerns. I will return to this in the concluding chapter.

The framework of analysis used in this book is inspired by the increased interest of science studies scholars in scientific culture and practice (see, e.g., McMullin 1992; Mulkay 1979; Pickering 1992), where culture is defined as a heterogeneous multiplicity of skills, tools, social relations, concepts, models, theories, and so on, and practice involves cultural extension. At this point, there would be little disagreement about the claim that the social dimensions of science must be taken seriously. However, science studies scholars have taken the extra step of viewing science as constitutively social.[11] Challenging the older assumptions that "properly" executed science reflected the world of nature and that general criteria existed for assessing scientific knowledge claims, science studies approaches looked closely at the ways in which scientists constructed their accounts of the world and at the ways in which variations in social context influenced the formation and acceptance of scientific assertions. They argued that fact and theory, or observation and presupposition, were interrelated in a complex manner and that the empirical conclusions of science must be seen as interpretative constructions, dependent for their meaning on and limited by the cultural resources available to a particular social group at a particular point in time. Similarly, they claimed that criteria for assessing scientific knowledge claims were always open to varied interpretations and were given meaning in terms of particular scientists' specific intellectual commitments, presuppositions, and objectives. Hence, the recent developments in science studies were united by a common rejection of philosophical apriorism coupled with a sensitivity to the social dimensions of science.

My analysis of Sargent's work, therefore, is based on the idea that his contributions were shaped by his conceptual, experimental, and sociotechnical practices. The approach is different from that of methodologists, who would want to evaluate the scientific character of Sargent's work and are faced with the problems that the cognitive/technical resources of scientists are open to continual change of meaning and that universal standards are lacking. This want of universal standards is reflected by the fact that many disagreements in economics stem from root-and-branch differences of view, not just on economics, but also on politics, and in temperament and social attitudes. Since there is conflict over what makes for good research in economics, these disagreements cannot be resolved by appealing to certain facts about the world. Furthermore, most scientists are almost entirely isolated from trends in methodology, and, if they have any view at all, it is to dismiss methodology as irrelevant to the practice of science.

The following chapters offer an innovative type of analysis of the recent history of rational expectations economics neglected by previous historians of economic thought. By developing a highly focused historical study of Sargent's research, the analysis attempts to avoid a Whiggish history that sees Sargent's development as an inevitable progress to better and better economic analysis. Rather than following currently existing research in describing what rational expectations was, the following chapters provide an illustration of what happened to it through a contextualization of Sargent's presence in a multifaceted configuration of people and ideas. Rather than supplying post hoc rationalizations, this book develops a historical analysis of some of the shifting negotiations and alliances that went into the rise of rational expectations economics. In particular, the following chapters generally start from the standards Sargent himself imposed. They show that Sargent's shifting interests were the driving force behind his different interpretations and justifications of rational expectations. I should note that interests are not meant to carry an ominous connotation here but simply reflect the lack of universal standards for science.

As discussed in more detail in the following chapters, the main theme in Sargent's work was the attempt to develop a universal economic science by establishing a tie between neoclassical economic theory and econometrics. In particular, interviews and publications evidence Sargent's *interest in conceptual integrity of theory and method.* For instance, in his interview with Arjo Klamer (1983), he said: "This question about the relationship between theories and time-series has guided my studies. I try to learn both about theories and time-series econometrics with a purpose. I get particularly excited when I see possibilities of merging the two" (p. 64).[12] Furthermore, in the introduction to one of his best-known textbooks, Sargent (1987a) wrote: "[O]ne of the main substantive economic motivations of my own studies has been to understand the connections between economic theories and econometric tests of those theories" (p. xix). Sargent's desire to establish a link between theory and method should be distinguished from more "philosophical" goals such as "unification." Instead, Sargent's search was driven by more narrow technical concerns. This is confirmed by Klamer's (1983) interviews with Alan Blinder and James Tobin. According to Blinder, Sargent is "a sort of tinkerer, playing an intellectual game. He looks at a puzzle to see if he can solve it in a particular way, exercising these fancy techniques. That's his thing, so to speak" (p. 159). And Tobin evaluates Sargent's motivation in the following way: "It is a good point but a very difficult one to implement. . . . I understand, though, why it is exciting for young people in the profession. It is challenging; it provides new mathematical problems" (pp. 107–8). However, rather than relying on how others perceive Sargent's motivation, the following analysis starts from Sargent's own attempts to connect theory and method. Though I can give no causal explanation of Sargent's formulation of his particular goal, it will gain meaning as the following chapters illustrate that he tried to extend and combine the particular resources that were available to him. For instance, he said: "I tried to figure out the relationship between time-series and economic models. At the time I started the links weren't formal" (Klamer 1983, p. 60). Finally, I would like to refer readers who believe that Sargent's interests here are characterized as narrowly technical without any political considerations to Klamer's (1983) interview with Sargent, where he said that rational expectations economics is "certainly not politically motivated. It is technically motivated" (p. 80).[13]

Whereas Sargent's scientific culture can be characterized as an attempt to satisfy his interest in conceptual integrity, his scientific practice can be viewed as the creative extension of this conceptual net to fit new circumstances.[14] This extension was influenced both by the technical aspects of Sargent's scientific knowledge and by his relationship with other scientific actors, and it was accomplished through a process of open-ended modeling and analogy. As the discussion that follows will illustrate, this process could develop in a number of ways and had no determinate destination. On the one hand, Sargent could be seen as tentatively seeking to extend culture in ways that might serve his interests rather than in a way that might not, where his interests should themselves be seen as situated in and subject to change through practice. Modeling typically aims at producing associations in which a plurality of projected elements are aligned in some way, but the achievement of such associations is not guaranteed in advance. On the other hand, then, Sargent's interests served as standards against which the products of such extensions, Sargent's new conceptual nets, could be assessed. As we will see, encounters with resistances, which arose in practice to the achievement of goals, set in train a process of accommodation.

In his interview with Klamer (1983), Sargent described this process in the following way:

My published work is just a record of my learning. I'm sharing it with people so they won't make the same mistakes that I did. It's been a painful and slow process. My work is like a journey, a journey of discovery. . . . That's basically the philosophy of doing it. When we do research, the idea is that you don't produce a finished product. You produce an input. You write a paper in the hope that it will be superseded. It's not a success unless it's superseded. Research is a living process involving other people. (p. 74)

The phases in this process may be divided into free moves, forced moves, resistances, and the dialectic of resistance and accommodation, as will be discussed in detail later.

For Sargent, the first leg of his journey of discovery consisted of deciding what economic theories and econometric methods he would try to connect: "[M]y own process of learning the subject has continually mixed technical tools and economic models" (Sargent 1987a, p. xix). These initial steps I label Sargent's *free moves*. In this phase, social, cultural, and political resources from society at large entered into the very form and content of Sargent's scientific claims and played a significant part in their acceptance. The following chapters sometimes establish the connection between Sargent's research and the wider society by means of direct social contact between Sargent and others. In addition, they illustrate that the link can also arise in a more diffuse way through Sargent's ability to select from and interpret resources generally available to him during a specific period. By emphasizing the wider social, cultural, and political context, Sargent's free moves illustrated that his economics of a particular place and time was a reflection of the prevailing institutional structures and the popular ideologies. Though Sargent was influenced by his environment in making his initial decisions, he exercised choice and discretion in this phase. Another characteristic of these free moves was that he made them in a direct attempt to serve his interest in conceptual integrity of theory and method. However, these were tentative and revisable trials that carried no guarantee of satisfaction of Sargent's interests. In addition, the free moves may be seen as the source of the open-endedness in his scientific practice. Since Sargent's free moves to connect certain theories and methods were disparate, the exact nature of the connection was unknown in advance. This brings us to a discussion of the forced moves.

The second segment in Sargent's journey, then, consisted of facing the consequences of the economic theories and econometric models he had attempted to connect. For instance, Sargent (1987a) indicated that "[m]ore often than not, once [a] tool was possessed, it became clear how a further class of economic models or phenomena could be studied" (p. xix).[15] These consequences of Sargent's initial steps are labeled his *forced moves*. Since the forced moves revealed how his scientific culture further directed his plans and intentions, Sargent surrendered agency in this phase. As the following chapters illustrate, these forced moves elaborated Sargent's choices in ways often beyond his control as a result of existing conceptual, experimental, and sociotechnical practice. As a result of the intertwining of his free moves and the associations or extensions of culture, the outcome of Sargent's particular modeling sequences was thus at once structured by choice but not determined by it. Although Sargent selected and interpreted both social and cognitive/technical formulations with his free moves at particular instances, both kinds of resource acquired their specific meanings as they were combined in the sequence of informal interaction plus formal demonstration through his forced moves. Hence, Sargent negotiated not only the meaning of his own and his colleagues' actions, but also the assessment of knowledge claims in the process of elaboration.

Sargent (1987a) acknowledged that although the forced moves followed from the free moves, he could not predict the outcome: "While this was a natural step, it was not an easy one to take or to see fully the consequences of" (p. xviii). Furthermore, to continue the journey metaphor, Sargent encountered obstacles in his attempt to reach the destination of conceptual integrity. In his interview with Parkin (1996), he conceded: "Economists build models that help predict and intervene to improve economic affairs. During this process, we also learn about our limits to predict and intervene" (p. 650).[16] These barriers are labeled *resistances* here. Using his motivation as a standard against which he assessed the forced moves, the following chapters show that Sargent was unable to establish conceptual integrity of theory and method in this phase because of the temporal emergence of resistances. These resistances were situated in the context of the free and forced moves that Sargent made. Furthermore, they were plastic, and any of them may be modified, as we see in the final phase of Sargent's journey of discovery.

His encounters with resistances led Sargent (1987a) to embark on a new journey with different economic theories and econometric methods: "In this learning process, the desire to understand a particular economic model or phenomenon often prompted my learning to use some mathematical tool or other" (p. xix). This final phase had its roots in Sargent's *dialectic of resistance and accommodation.* Faced with a failure to satisfy his interests as a result of his resistances, Sargent was led to accommodate them by tinkering with the elements of the structure he had built up as a result of his free and forced moves. In his interview with Klamer (1983), he said: "[O]bjections are important for me. I think about them all the time but don't let them stop me" (p. 75).[17] For Sargent, as we will see, accommodation involved getting around his resistances by making and breaking alliances. In particular, he could either transform his interests or engage in a trial revision of prior free moves or ignore the forced moves and resistances. Pickering (1995a, p. 52) stressed three aspects of accommodations: First, they must be seen as situated with respect to particular goals and resistances. Second, they are made in real time.[18] Finally, an element of contingency enters into accommodation. This phase, then, further captured the open-endedness of Sargent's modeling and the openness of future extensions, which had no determinate destination.

Though the framework of interests, free moves, forced moves, resistances, and accommodation is closely linked to Sargent's own interpretation of his journey of discovery, it was originally developed by Pickering and Stephanides (see Pickering 1992, 1993, 1995a, 1995b; Pickering and Stephanides 1992),[19] who employed it to picture physics as a mangle of practice in which emergent human and nonhuman agency engaged by means of a dialectic of resistance and accommodation.[20] Why would I use this approach? Once we abandon previous notions of universality and progress, it becomes possible to tell many stories about the history of economic thought. The following chapters structure the discussion in terms of the concepts of interests, moves, and resistances to capture the many components of Sargent's extension of his culture and the constantly changing concept of rational expectations that resulted in his research. This framework for the analysis of practice as it happened "forced" me to focus on the specifics of Sargent's practice by taking its difficulty and temporality seriously. Moreover, there are close ties between the way I analyze economists and the way economists analyze economic agents, as will be discussed in more detail in the concluding chapter. Furthermore, the framework can be connected with Sargent's own evaluation of his research, as argued in the previous paragraphs. Though the distinction between free and forced moves is very subtle, what is important for my analysis is that Sargent's dialectic of resistance and accommodation is far from subtle. Before moving on to a discussion of the contents of the following chapters, I highlight two characteristics of the approach used in this book, which not only balances human and nonhuman agency but also gives an account of the emergent structure of Sargent's research.[21]

First, the framework argues for a so-called posthumanist decentering of the human subject. Next to Sargent, there is also a role for nonhuman agency: tools, concepts, models, and so on. The following chapters model Sargent as an agent doing things in the world, a world consisting of data, theories, and techniques that "fought back" when he attempted to control it. While Sargent made free moves in an attempt to satisfy his interests, he was not in full control, as witnessed by the resistances called forth by the forced moves. Elaborations with respect to the data, theories, and techniques used unveiled the difficulties Sargent encountered in serving his interests. As a result, the framework captures both the structure and the contingency of Sargent's research. The structure follows from the insight that the world could only resist Sargent by virtue of his moves to achieve his goals. The contingency follows from the realization that Sargent's attempts at accommodation through new moves to achieve his goals evolved reciprocally as a result of the emergence of resistance. The interlinking of human and nonhuman agency points to the importance of a culturally situated historicism.

Second, the framework captures the temporally emergent structure of Sargent's research. Sargent was oriented to the future goal of achieving conceptual integrity of theory and method that did not exist at that time. In his attempts to satisfy his interests, the nonhuman agency that Sargent encountered was temporally emergent in practice, because its exact shape was not known in advance, needed to be explored, and gave rise to problems that Sargent had to solve. That is, it did not arise from some features that were already present, but emerged in Sargent's scientific practice. As a result of the temporal emergence of resistances and accommodation, Sargent's different interpretations of rational expectations were temporally specific. Therefore, a serious analysis of the temporality of Sargent's practice further points to a historicist understanding of Sargent's scientific knowledge. Hence, his journey of discovery was located in real-time history, neither free of nonhuman agency nor predetermined.[22]

These two characteristics, the mix of human and nonhuman agency and the temporality of practice, justify my writing about a living economist. As an agent not involved in the process, I can follow Sargent through real-time practice. I can track the interlinking of human and nonhuman agency in and the temporal emergence of the structure of Sargent's practice. Of course, after the fact, Sargent can and does offer highly persuasive technical accounts of why (his) rational expectations economics has developed in specific ways. Yet, for the purposes of real-time accounting, the substance of such retrospective accounts is one aspect of what needs to be analyzed. It would be antithetical to my framework to bow to Sargent and project his retrospective account backward in time as part of my explanation. As Sargent is led to reflect on his own agency, I can understand his practice as a mixing of human and nonhuman agency. Furthermore, I can track the emergence of different interpretations of rational expectations in Sargent's published and unpublished books and articles, using contemporaneous interviews whenever available. Though aware of these tendencies to post hoc rationalizations by agents involved in the process, I did decide to give Sargent the opportunity to respond to my analysis in the interview that constitutes Chapter 6, as discussed in more detail in the outline that follows.

1.3   Outline

Using the approach outlined in the previous section, the following chapters aim to exemplify and explore how the interplay of free and forced moves resulted in the emergence of resistances in Sargent's attempts to satisfy his interests and how he consequently attempted to accommodate those. The analysis uses Sargent's dialectic of resistance and accommodation to provide an evaluation of rational expectations economics from an insider's perspective by tracking the real-time practice in which Sargent simultaneously negotiated and constituted several interpretations and justifications of the concept(s) of rational expectations in contemporary macroeconomic theory. In particular, Sargent's research is discussed in four case studies, each organized around a discrete set of free and forced moves, that capture nearly all of his work from his graduation in 1968 to the present. In each case study, Sargent's goal of achieving conceptual integrity of theory and method involved deciding which theory and method to employ and how to connect the two. Furthermore, Sargent's changing free moves to certain economic theories and particular econometric models are shown to be influenced by his community and to result in different justifications and interpretations of rational expectations as forced moves. The case studies further illustrate that Sargent had several ways of dealing with the resistances that followed from his free and forced moves.

Chapter 2 focuses on the tensions among probabilism, determinism, and randomness in philosophy, neoclassical economics and econometrics, and Sargent's work in the late 1960s to early 1970s, while comparing and contrasting these tensions. In this context, we revisit story six, about endogenizing expectations, and story nine, about restricting distributed lags. Chapter 3 shows how Sargent tried to fit vector autoregressions into his framework in the late 1970s to early 1980s and how he ended up with a very restricted environment as a result of his reliance on convenient engineering conceptions in his search for neoclassical dynamics. In this chapter, we encounter story two, about policy irrelevance; story three, about using available techniques; story seven, about making public predictions; and story ten, about incorporating vector autoregressions. Chapter 4 discusses several manifestations of symmetry in Sargent's analysis in the early to mid-1980s. In this context, we revisit story four, about restoring symmetry, and story five, about optimizing over information. When symmetry threatened to be broken, Sargent changed his tentative choices and embraced the idea of learning with bounded rationality. Chapter 5 braids the two narratives of (free and forced) moves and learning in Sargent's work in the late 1980s to early 1990s. In this setting, we encounter story eight, about countering bounded rationality.

Chapter 6 contains an interview with Thomas Sargent. Though this may satisfy the reader who feels that I should give Sargent the opportunity to respond to the issues raised in this book, I should warn her that since Sargent has made different moves on different occasions, as discussed in the four case studies, his interpretation and justification of rational expectations are historically specific. For instance, Chapter 2 analyzes how he used an econometrically motivated interpretation of rational expectations with a focus on restricting distributed lags, and Chapter 3 shows that he subsequently changed his emphasis to restricting vector autoregressions. Chapter 4 argues that Sargent later moved to a theoretically motivated interpretation of rational expectations within a general equilibrium framework. Finally, Chapter 5 indicates that he eventually tried to show convergence to rational expectations through learning with adaptive expectations or artificial intelligence. Furthermore, Sargent has given different perspectives on the rise of rational expectations, as will be discussed in Chapter 4. For instance, he has argued both that rational expectations economics led to general equilibrium modeling (see, e.g., Klamer 1983, p. 66) and that the general equilibrium discipline led to rational expectations modeling (see, e.g., Parkin 1996, p. 651; Sargent 1993, p. xxi). In addition, Sargent has also argued that both general equilibrium economics (see, e.g., Sargent 1996a, p. 536) and rational expectations macroeconomics (see, e.g., Klamer 1983, p. 64) followed from econometric modeling techniques.[23] Therefore, though the interview sheds some light on the questions Sargent faced, his current answers will depend partly on his current moves. In addition, it is only natural for Sargent to want to rewrite his own history by providing post hoc rationalizations of his moves. This is related to the Faraday effect, coined after Faraday's observation that he would describe his own results "not as they were obtained, but in such a manner as to give the most concise view of the whole" (Munz 1985, p. 96). Rather, what is more relevant to the narrative here is how Sargent would have assessed these issues as he was confronted with them.

Before moving on to the first case study, I would like to make one comment and one disclaimer. First, I have tried to use as much concurrent material as was available for each period. My research was complicated by the fact that Sargent's private correspondence is not (yet) available. It was facilitated by the fact that some of his teachers, colleagues, and students were willing to answer some of my questions. However, their current reconstructions may be just as historically specific as Sargent's post hoc rationalizations. In addition, some of his teachers, colleagues, and students were unwilling to answer my questions because they were reluctant to talk about a living economist "behind his back." Furthermore, for reasons of propriety in discussing a living economist, I decided to refrain from appealing to Sargent's personal life in my analysis. Second, having been trained in the representative agent tradition, I initially thought this study would provide a deeper understanding of rational expectations economics in particular and macroeconomics in general. Though the ebb and flow of Sargent's interests, moves, resistances, and accommodations capture the very local and contextual forces that helped constitute the field of rational expectations macroeconomics in a way not attempted by previous historians of economics, I now realize that this analysis is only the first step in that direction and that the next phase consists of similar analyses of the work of Robert Lucas, Christopher Sims, and Neil Wallace, among others. In fact, Pickering (1995b) sees the mangle of practice as extending beyond the work of individual scientists to the wider organization of science. This study is just the best I can do in the limited space I have available, and I encourage readers to "thicken" the history described here. With this in mind, we are now ready to examine the evolution of Sargent's views.

CHAPTER 2

Accommodating Randomness

Fate, Time, Occasion, Chance and Change? To these
All things are subject but eternal Love.

Percy Bysshe Shelley, *Prometheus Unbound*

In this chapter, I focus on the story Sargent is likely to have told when he was trying to use rational expectations economics in the late 1960s to early 1970s. An argument is made for his interest in achieving what he would regard as conceptual integrity of the determinism in neoclassical economic theory and the randomness in econometrics. This involves providing a narrative of how he came to the idea of rational expectations and what he had to relinquish to be able to put his initial interpretation of the concept to use. However, before focusing on Sargent, it is important to consider the context within which he developed his ideas. The case study focuses on the tensions among probabilism, determinism, and randomness in philosophy, neoclassical economics and econometrics, and Sargent's work, comparing and contrasting these tensions. The intent is to braid the two narratives of, on the one hand, free and forced moves and, on the other hand, probabilism, determinism, and randomness. Section 2.1 gives a brief analysis of the general relationships among probabilism, determinism, and randomness; 2.2 discusses its treatment in neoclassical economics and econometrics. Section 2.3 looks at the free and forced moves made by Sargent in an effort to dissolve the tensions among probabilism, determinism, and randomness.

2.1 Probabilism, Determinism, and Randomness

What does determinism in neoclassical economic theory signify? What is meant by randomness in econometrics? The first steps in our narrative journey take us to the general relationships among probabilism, determinism, and randomness. We need to jump this hurdle to gain perspective on its treatment in economics, which is discussed in the following section, and by Sargent, covered in the third section.

A general vernacular definition of *determinism* is that the future is fixed in one unavoidable pattern, and different forms of determinism give different explanations of why and how this is the case (see, e.g., Dupré 1993; Earman 1986; Weatherford 1991). The form that is relevant to the discussion here is physical determinism – also known as causal or scientific determinism – which holds that natural laws are strictly determinative of future consequences.[1] Many philosophers – probably most philosophers – reject determinism. There are, of course, many reasons for this rejection. The obvious rejoinder to this determinism is that laws are not deterministic. The usual form of these arguments is that scientists have established that some events, in particular at the microlevel, are not inevitable and unique consequences, but are the random expression of a probability distribution. The present state limits the probability of future outcomes, but does not determine a definite fixed result. Defenders of determinism have several moves available to them. The simplest is that there must be some more fundamental theory that would show how probability distributions were just approximations to the fully determined events beneath the surface. A second rejoinder is that even if microevents are undetermined, the same is not true at the macrolevel.

What happens if we leave determinism and wander into the world of *indeterminism?* The first departure from extreme causal regularity maintains a complete and exceptionless causal nexus, but one in which the laws are generally not deterministic, but probabilistic. Laws are still as universal as underdeterminism, but now they decree only the range of possible events and the (precise) probabilities of their occurrence. Using the language of economics, I label this view *randomness.*[2] Leaving many scientists and most economists behind, we can take the journey into an indeterministic world one step further by asking why we should believe that there are any such precise probabilities if there is typically no way of determining probabilities affecting a specific case.[3] There might only be probabilities relative to some set of specified factors, but no general convergence toward a precise probability as more and more factors are considered. This possibility raises the further prospect that the degree of convergence on precise probabilities might vary considerably from one case to another and leads to the conclusion that the degree of causal structure in different parts of the world may be quite variable. Going along this path, the final destination of our trip would be the extreme possibility of *complete randomness,* which implies that the probability of an event is quite independent of any antecedent events (Dupré 1993).

Where do we encounter scientists on our journey from determinism to indeterminism (Gigerenzer and Murray 1987)? At first, the deterministic understanding of science ignored randomness and did not permit uncertainty or variability. Then, the introduction of probabilistic ideas resulted in a transition from a purely deterministic understanding of science to an understanding in which probabilistic ideas became indispensable at the level of theory construction and method. For the social sciences they make it possible to explain social trends and to make short-range predictions, whereas in the physical sciences they allow the study of irreversible dynamics and provide a way to show the lawlike behavior of some natural phenomena, as in quantum mechanics.

Although *probabilistic ideas* have become central and indispensable for science, the interpretation of probability has been and continues to be one of the most contentious areas in philosophy of science. So as not to become entangled in this debate, I will only briefly touch on the relationship between probabilism and determinism in some of these renditions.[4] The *classical* theory, which is a historical entity rather than a current contender, defines probability in terms of ratios of equipossible alternatives. Therefore, it functions properly only when nothing is known about the way the system to which it is applied actually works. In that case, knowledge is based on ignorance. By viewing probabilities as a measure of partial ignorance, and therefore dealing with cases in which we are uncertain rather than with uncertainty in the world, the classical theory is consistent with an underlying determinism. The a priori theory characterizes probability as a measure of the logical support for a proposition on given evidence, while viewing this relation as completely determinable. It sees probability as a formal, logical property of the way we think and speak about the world. Since the a priori theory is logical rather than ontological, it remains silent on the topic of determinism. *Relative frequency* theories interpret probability as (the limit of the) relative frequency of appearance of one (infinite) class in another. By counting actual cases and extrapolating the frequency, probability is seen as an empirical, measurable property of the actual physical world. Thus, relative frequency theories make no pronouncements about determinism. I argue in subsequent sections that neoclassical economists and Sargent tend to favor this interpretation of probability, if they make any statements about the formalism of stochastic models at all. The *subjectivist* theory defines probability as the degree of belief of a given person in a given proposition at a specific time; the probability beliefs of a rational individual must be consistent and governed by the calculus of probability. By dealing with beliefs rather than things, we are again discouraged in our search for revelations about ontology or determinism.

Scientists defend the use of probabilistic ideas because they allow them either to accommodate determinism or to tame randomness. First, there is a clear role for probabilism when chance is an irreducible part of the natural phenomena that are being investigated. This is an *ontic* interpretation. Second, there is still use for probability theory in a truly deterministic world. According to the *epistemic* interpretation, probability theory must be incorporated because there is error in our measurements or because we are ignorant of some of the variables affecting the data we are collecting. Likewise, in the large number of cases in which instability occurs, so that minute variations in the initial conditions lead to large variations in the effect, it is unlikely that we could have practical, nonprobabilistic predictions even if we were quite certain that the physical interactions were themselves completely deterministic.

Finally, I started this section with a physical understanding of determinism. I end it with an evaluation of the defense probabilism that departs from the realist accounts on which the ontic and epistemic explanations are based. The *pragmatic* interpretation does not require the scientist to be a realist, as it is not interested in the nature of reality. It is concerned in the first place with empirical prediction and conceptual integrity. Empirical prediction requires the use of probabilistic ideas. Once these are introduced at the level of method through statistics, conceptual integrity requires them to be introduced at the level of theory construction as well.

Having analyzed the general relationships among probabilism, determinism, and randomness, we are now ready to discuss their treatment in economics.

2.2   Probabilism, Determinism, Randomness, and Economics

Our next hurdle on the road leading to a perspective on Sargent's work is the analysis of how probability and statistics eventually made their way into economics. However, even though statistical thinking originated in the social sciences around the early nineteenth century, when it was perceived as the numerical science of society, its acceptance in mainstream economics was somewhat delayed (Mirowski 1989b, 1990). The first two generations of neoclassical theorists were reluctant to use concepts of randomness because they were mostly looking for purely deterministic explanations. It may be argued that with the rise of econometrics, neoclassical economists finally admitted some randomness into their theories. However, the stochastic terms were merely appended to the existing theory and did not result in a fundamental reconceptualization of economic theory. Moreover, these stochastic concepts had little or no theoretical justification. Neoclassical economists did not want to commit themselves to any *error term justification.* Since this topic requires a separate narrative, I can only provide a very brief general overview before discussing the rise of econometrics (for more, see Mirowski 1989b, 1990).

According to the epistemic interpretation, the stochastic concepts were due to errors in observation, faulty data, or ignorance of some of the variables affecting the data being collected. This rationalization can be interpreted as errors-in-equations or errors-in-variables. However, the problem with the errors-in-variables justification is that error is not confined to the single dependent variable, making it hard to settle on the correct method to model these equations. According to the ontic interpretation, a large number of independent and individually insignificant causes impinge upon a stable, deterministic neoclassical structure. The problem here is that the central limit theorem argument might have more than one possible outcome, as we witness shortly. Finally, according to the sampling justification, which might be labeled pragmatic, variables are the realization from a stochastic population. The rationalization preferred by econometricians is discussed in this section and the interpretation favored by Sargent in the following section.

What kind of statistics made its way into economics? By the end of the nineteenth century, statistics became identified with inferring conclusions from historical data; in the twentieth century, inferential statistics became widely used and was soon institutionalized as the single method of inference from data to hypothesis. With the rise of econometrics, economists became confident that the standards of scientific demonstration had now been objectively and universally defined.[5] Regression analysis became their standard statistical tool (see Mirowski 1989b, 1990). Linking to the earlier general discussion of the formalism of stochastic models, the *interpretation of probability* is hardly ever mentioned in econometrics, and, if it is discussed at all, the relative frequency theory is favored by alluding to Fisherian or Neyman–Pearson statistical theory, which is based on the notion of repeated sampling or experimentation (see, e.g., Amemiya 1985, pp. 81–2; Anderson 1971, p. 3; Feller 1971, pp. 1–25; Judge et al. 1988, pp. 11–13).[6] Furthermore, with respect to the *error term justification,* the presence of disturbances is commonly rationalized by some mixture of random sampling from a population and an epistemic or ontic interpretation of the influence of omitted variables, without an analysis of the implications of these different renditions (see, e.g., Amemiya 1985; Judge et al. 1985, 1988).

Economists often use the method of least squares to test or estimate their basic regression model. The testing and estimation methods in econometrics rely on knowledge of the probability distributions of the variables, and the assumption that the disturbances or the variates underlying them have a finite variance is important in justifying the use of least squares. The Gauss–Markov theorem states that if the disturbances follow a distribution with finite variance, then the least squares estimator has the minimum variance of all linear unbiased estimators. The classical central limit theorem states that the sum of a large number of independently distributed variates, each of which follows a distribution with finite variance, will tend to be normally distributed. This permits the use of the usual t and F tests and implies that least squares is the maximum likelihood estimator. According to Amemiya (1985), the least squares estimator is so popular "because many sophisticated testing procedures have been developed under the normality assumption (mathematical convenience) and because statisticians have put undue confidence in the [classical] central limit theorem (rationalization)" (p. 71). Now, if the underlying variates follow a distribution with *infinite variance,* the assumptions of the classical central limit theorem fail to hold and the disturbances will not be normally distributed. Thus, the applicability of normal distribution theory for hypothesis testing is lost. Moreover, that part of the Gauss–Markov theorem that demonstrates the minimum variance or efficiency property of least squares is no longer applicable.

Distributions with infinite variance tend to have thick or heavy tails, implying that large values or outliers will be relatively frequent. This means that sample variances grow unpredictably and without bound with increases in the sample size. Because the least squares technique minimizes squared deviations, it places relatively heavy weight on outliers, and their presence can lead to estimates that are extremely sensitive. If the variance does not exist, it is obviously impossible to obtain a meaningful variance estimator and the least squares estimator will not possess its usual minimum variance property. This in turn implies that the conventional F and t tests on the coefficients could be very misleading. If the error distribution is so thick-tailed that the mean and the variance do not exist, then the least squares estimator cannot be unbiased because its mean will also not exist. The possibility of nonnormal distributions in general has led to the development of alternative estimation techniques that, relative to least squares, place less weight on outliers. These methods come under the general heading of robust estimation (see, e.g., Amemiya 1985, pp. 70–9; Judge et al. 1985, pp. 822–46; Judge et al. 1988, pp. 887–90). However, I show shortly that there are problems accompanying distributions with infinite variance that remain unresolved.

Since its debut in late eighteenth-century error theory, the normal distribution has acquired so many applications in so many disciplines that it has indeed become a "mere" technique. However, certain conditions must hold for the distribution to be applicable. Normal distributions are members of the *family of stable distributions,* which form a four-parameter class of functions. The laws in this family were introduced by Paul Lévy, whose name was given to this class of distributions, in 1925.[7] Lévy showed that the only possible limiting distribution for sums of independent identically distributed random variables was a stable Lévy distribution, which is sometimes referred to as "stable Paretian" in the economics literature. Stable laws were initially met with reserve from mathematicians in probability theory, apparently because they found very few applications. This changed with the work by Mandelbrot, who sketched the use of stable laws in certain economic models, in the 1960s (see, e.g., Mandelbrot 1963a, 1963b). The appearance of stable laws in certain socioeconomic models increased the interest in them and led to the belief that the role of stable laws would grow in the future, especially in the areas of economics, sociology, and biology (Zolotarev 1986, p. viii). In economics, there was a lively interest in Lévy stable distributions in the 1960s to early 1970s.[8] However, by the mid-1970s, almost all references to the Mandelbrot program in the econometrics literature and in the neoclassical theory literature disappeared. Since others have provided a detailed history of the treatment of Lévy stable distributions, I do not dwell on this topic here (Mirowski 1989b, 1990).

An important characteristic of the class of Lévy stable distributions is that they are stable or invariant under addition. A variate Z with density $f(Z; B_Z)$ is said to be stable if, when another variate Y that is independent of Z and has the same form of density $f(Y; B_Y)$, perhaps with $B_Z \neq B_Y$, is added to Z, the result is to produce a variate $X = Z + Y$ obeying the same probability law $f(X; B_X)$, with some B_X. That is, the sum of independent symmetric stable variates with some characteristic exponent will also be distributed according to a symmetric stable distribution with the same parameter. This stability property is often suitable for the purposes of model building and statistical analysis. In addition, the stable distributions possess a domain-of-attraction property that generalizes the classical central limit theorem. Stable distributions are the only distributions that serve as the limiting distributions in standard central limit theorems. The fact that a stable distribution can be thought of as an attractor is a useful property if a random variable is thought of as representing a linear combination of a large number of independently distributed variates.

Since Lévy stable distributions are encountered in limit theorems for sums of independent and weakly dependent random variables, the theory of limit theorems for sums of independent random variables can be used to solve the problem of approximating these distributions. This theory was roughly completed only in the 1930s (Zolotarev 1986, pp. 3–6). An analysis of the limit behavior of distributions carried out by the end of the eighteenth century by Laplace and Gauss led to the application of the first, and as it later turned out, most important distribution in probability theory and its uses – the normal distribution.[9] Lévy made the first step in the direction of analyzing a wider variety of limit distributions. There is an abundance of different forms for expressing the characteristic functions of stable laws.[10] The variants of expressions in the literature for the characteristic functions $g(t)$ have the form

$$g(t) = \exp\left(it\gamma - \lambda\varphi(t,\, \alpha,\, \beta)\right) \qquad (2.1)$$

where α is the characteristic exponent, and the functions β, γ, and λ are, respectively, the generalized asymmetry, shift, and scale characteristics of the distribution. The parameter α controls tail thickness, where a smaller α gives thicker tails. Lévy proposed the best known form of expression for the logarithm of the characteristic functions of stable distributions, which is

$$\log g(t) = \lambda \left(it\gamma - |t|^{\alpha} + it\omega_A(t,\, \alpha,\, \beta)\right) \qquad (2.2)$$

where the real parameters vary within the limits $0 < \alpha \leq 2$, $-1 \leq \beta \leq 1$, $-\infty < \gamma < \infty$, $\lambda > 0$ and

$$\omega_A(t, \alpha, \beta) = \begin{cases} |t|^{\alpha-1} \beta\tan\left(\dfrac{\pi\alpha}{2}\right) & \text{if} \quad \alpha \neq 1 \\[2em] -\beta\left(\dfrac{2}{\pi}\right)\log|t| & \text{if} \quad \alpha = 1 \end{cases} \tag{2.3}$$

When the parameter $\beta = 0$, the distribution is symmetric, since β is a skewness parameter. If the parameters $\alpha = 2$, $\gamma = \mu$, and $\lambda = \sigma^2/2$, then the resulting characteristic function is Gaussian, which is the only distribution that can be fully characterized by its two moments. The only density of a distribution with finite variance corresponds to the value $\alpha = 2$. If $\alpha \leq 1$, the mean is not identified, and if $1 < \alpha \leq 2$, the mean is finite, but the second and higher-order moments are infinite. The classical central limit theorem, which is a special case, restricts the outcome to normality by imposing the condition that each of the constituent random variables has finite variance. Explicit expressions for the density functions of the family of stable distributions were known only in three cases: the Gaussian, the Cauchy ($\alpha = 1$, $\beta = 0$), and the binomial ($\alpha = 1/2$, $\beta = 1$, $\gamma = 0$, $\lambda = 1$).

The application of stable laws was the focus of a series of publications by the American mathematician Benoit Mandelbrot (1963a, 1963b) in the 1960s. Mandelbrot was responsible for introducing the problem of constructing statistical estimators of stable laws into mathematical statistics (Zolotarev 1986, pp. 217–9). According to Zolotarev (1986), it

can be seen from many publications, both theoretical and applied, that Mandelbrot's ideas have more and more won the recognition of [statistical] experts. In this way the hope arose of confirming empirically established principles in the framework of mathematical models and at the same time clearing up the mechanism for the formation of these principles. (p. 54)

Mandelbrot argued that mathematical statistics can be of little help in the empirical determination of parameters of stable distributions, since these methods are based mainly on such assumptions as the availability of an explicit form of the density function, the existence of some particular number of moments, and so on. In the best case, stable distributions have only one moment of integral order (if $\alpha < 2$), and, therefore, estimators could not depend on any moments higher than the first. Only in a few cases are there explicit expressions for their density or distribution functions that would enable us to concretize the algorithms for estimating the parameters, and, therefore, precise statements about the sampling behavior of estimators could generally not be written down. The question of indirectly investigating the analytic properties of stable distributions thus arose.

To illustrate that the search for algorithms meeting the requirements of contemporary theory, that is, estimators that are unbiased, efficient, and so on, at least in the asymptotic sense, continues, a short survey of this literature is in order. DuMouchel (1971) developed a parameter estimation method with the properties of maximum likelihood estimation.[11] Fama and Roll's (1971) fractile method, based on easily calculable functions of sample order statistics, was further generalized by McCulloch (1986). A sample characteristic function was used by the method of moments of Press (1972); the methods of Paulson, Holcomb, and Leitch (1975); and the iterative regression-type method of Koutrouvelis (1980, 1981).[12] Recent studies compute various transforms of the characteristic function.[13] What all these methods have in common is that they face trade-offs among computational complexity, implementation difficulties, consistency, biasedness, and efficiency. Although their theoretical properties are well established, the lack of analytical closed-form expressions for most stable density functions has been a major source of difficulty in applications. There is not a general estimation method for the parameters of stable laws and there is not much theory of statistical inference for stable laws.

Mandelbrot sketched the use of stable laws in certain economic models and suspected that in the situations that were characteristic of economic variates (where $1 < \alpha < 2$), variances are infinite and analytic expressions cannot be written down (Mirowski 1989b, 1990). Mandelbrot's (1987) historical analysis of the *two stages of theoretical indeterminism* alerts us to the threatening nature of stable laws for neoclassical economics.[14] The first stage of indeterminism was an attempt to introduce probability theory into economics by the partitioning off of the causal deterministic aspects from the stochastic disturbances. The latter was subordinated to the former by a resort to the classical central limit theorem. As we have seen, this can be consistent with a world that is either physically deterministic or to a certain extent random. How could precise probabilities be determined? Sufficiently fat tails cause the variance to become infinite, and the classical central limit theorem necessarily becomes invalid. Later on, the mean itself fails to converge, and the law of large numbers becomes invalid as well. This is where we enter Mandelbrot's second stage of indeterminism, which was marked by the exploration of those areas in which the distinction between theoretical determinism and physical indeterminism became blurred.[15]

This second stage of indeterminism began to attract the attention of scholars working in economics in the 1960s to early 1970s, including the leading actor in our narrative. Investigations showed how certain variates conformed to stable Lévy distributions, Monte Carlo studies were mounted to place some bounds on sampling behavior, and attempts were made to link estimation to the formalisms of linear programming. For example, Sargent, together with Robert Blattberg, published a paper in 1971 studying the performance of various estimators where the disturbances follow distributions that have fatter tails than does the normal distribution (Blattberg and Sargent 1971). Blattberg and Sargent worked on the paper during the late 1960s when Sargent was a young assistant professor at Carnegie Mellon University and Blattberg was a student at that institution.[16]

Blattberg and Sargent began by investigating the consequences of the assumption that the disturbances follow a member of a class of symmetric stable Lévy distributions, defining these by the log characteristic function

$$\log \phi_u(t) = i \, \delta \, t - |\sigma t|^\alpha \tag{2.4}$$

This expression corresponds to the one given earlier, where now $\beta = 0$ as a result of the limitation to symmetric distributions, and where t is a real number, α is the characteristic exponent, δ the location parameter, and $|\sigma|^\alpha$ the scale parameter. Blattberg and Sargent noted that if $\alpha = 2$, the distribution is normal with mean δ and variance $2|\sigma|^\alpha$. If $\alpha = 1$, the distribution is Cauchy with central tendency δ and semiinterquartile range σ. Also, as before, when α is less than 2, only integral moments of order less than α exist. Hence, for α less than 2, the variance is infinite, although the mean exists provided that α is strictly greater than 1.

Blattberg and Sargent subscribed to Mandelbrot's suspicion that in the situations characteristic of economic variates, variances are infinite and analytic expressions cannot be written down. Since the assumption of finite variance occupies an important role in the analysis of stable distributions, Blattberg and Sargent (1971) argued that "the accumulating body of evidence which suggests that many economic variables are best characterized as having infinite variances acquires special relevance" (p. 501). Or, that in view of "the body of evidence which suggests that many economic variables have infinite variances, the standard use of the [classical] central limit theorem to support the assumption that the [disturbances] . . . are normally distributed thus actually suggests the weaker condition that the [disturbances] . . . follow a stable distribution" (p. 502).

Blattberg and Sargent proceeded by investigating the performance of two types of estimators that had been suggested in the context of stable distributions. The first type is the best (minimum dispersion) linear unbiased estimator where disturbances are distributed according to a symmetric stable distribution. This estimator, which includes ordinary least squares as a special case, is consistent and unbiased. The second is the estimator that minimizes the sum of absolute errors (MSAE). This one is consistent and probably unbiased.[17] Blattberg and Sargent mounted Monte Carlo studies to place some bounds on the sampling behavior of stable Lévy distributions. They presented the results of some sampling experiments designed to assess the performance of these estimators, with a focus on their relative efficiencies.

Blattberg and Sargent (1971) found results that indicate that the MSAE estimator performs sufficiently well that it deserves further study and elaboration, for in "conjunction with the Monte Carlo results . . . the large body of evidence suggesting that many economic variables are best described as being generated by non-Gaussian stable distributions makes the case in favor of MSAE estimation very strong" (p. 509). They also argued that "it seems fairly clear that the relative superiority of MSAE over OLS will hold for many fat-tailed distributions of disturbances that are not stable" (p. 509) and that the relatively good performance of the MSAE estimator in the presence of disturbances with very fat tails, taken together with "the evidence on the widespread existence of Paretian variables in economics" (p. 510), can be used to give alternative explanations of existing results.

Blattberg and Sargent mentioned Roll's (1970) study as part of the increasing evidence of the importance of infinite variances. *Richard Roll* completed his dissertation on the efficient market model applied to U.S. Treasury bill rates in March 1968 and received a Ph.D. from the University of Chicago with Eugene Fama as his principal adviser. Although Roll's book was published in 1970, it was only a minor revision of his dissertation, which had been published in 1968.[18] At Chicago, he had participated as a student in the rapidly developing field of finance. He and his fellow graduate students in finance constituted a very exciting intellectual group under the guidance of Merton Miller and Eugene Fama in finance and Henri Theil and Arnold Zellner in econometrics.[19] His first academic job was at Carnegie Mellon University, where he arrived from Chicago in September 1967. His dissertation was widely circulated in manuscript form in 1968 and was read by most of the Carnegie economists at that time.[20] Roll knew about the work on stock market prices with infinite variance, since there were many people at Chicago working on those topics, including Fama, and because Mandelbrot had visited Chicago a few times.[21] The first applications in economics of the stable Lévy family of distributions were concerned with data on stock market prices (see, e.g., Mandelbrot 1963a, 1963b; Fama 1965).[22] Roll was curious whether this family applied to interest rates as well. He met both Blattberg and Sargent at Carnegie Mellon University and discussed Lévy stable distributions with them.[23]

Roll's (1970) study used data on internal rates of return on U.S. Treasury bills to find the term structure hypothesis that fits the data best and to use its implications in market efficiency tests. Roll noted that since inferences drawn from parametric tests depend on the underlying probability functions, it is necessary to check the empirical distributions of the variables to be tested for conformity to known probability laws. He also argued that the distributions are of interest in their own right. Under the efficient market assumption, interest rate changes reflect an accumulation of new information between successive periods. According to Roll, this accumulation was the sum of many small, independent pieces of information, that is, the sum of many individually unimportant random variables.[24] As before, it follows from the generalized central limit theorem that if a sum of independent random variables with common distribution tends toward any limiting distribution, that distribution will be a member of a stable class. Thus, if interest rate changes obey any probability law, they will likely conform to a stable distribution. If the empirical frequencies fit no members of the stable class, then (1) there are not many independent pieces of information arriving at the market each period, or (2) the process has no limiting distribution, or (3) marked differences exist among the distributions of the individual pieces of information.

To determine whether his set of data fit a stable distribution well, Roll wrote out a characteristic function for Lévy stable distributions and estimated the characteristic component, α; the scale parameter, s; the location parameter, δ; and the index of skewness, using Fama and Roll's (1971) fractile method.[25] Roll used these estimates in a goodness-of-fit test. He noted that, as before, when $\alpha = 2$ (the Gaussian distribution), s^2 is one-half the variance, and when $\alpha = 1$ (the Cauchy distribution), s is the semiinterquartile range. Roll found that, with a large degree of confidence, most of the distributions of interest rate changes had α significantly lower than 2 and thus were nonnormal. Indeed, the upper limit of the simulation range suggested that most of the α's were significantly lower than 1.5. Most of Roll's estimates of scale followed regular patterns and he found no evidence of asymmetry in the empirical distributions. His goodness-of-fit test results were somewhat less favorable to the hypothesis of symmetric stable distributions, but Roll showed that the discreteness of the data undermined the credibility of the χ^2 goodness-of-fit test. However, this discreteness should not, according to Roll, affect statistical methods that do not require the data to be split in classes, and in these cases the evidence was strong that the theory of symmetric stable distributions can be useful. This evidence consisted of (1) the generalized central limit theorem, (2) empirical measures of skewness that showed that the empirical distributions were symmetric, and (3) empirical evidence that although χ^2 values were high as a result of discrete data, they were minimized by the particular member of the stable family chosen (i.e., by the empirically determined value of $\hat{\alpha}$ and $\hat{s}$).

Roll concluded that symmetric stable distributions were evidently better models of the data distributions than were any other continuous distributions and were probably more useful than any discrete model. According to Roll (1970), the "cost of introducing discrete (and more complex) distributional models such as Markov models, probably outweighs the benefits in changed inferences one can reasonably expect to obtain" (p. 81). Consequently, he used the theory of stable probability laws for statistical inference. Roll's use of the concept of *costs* here is endowed with greater significance in the next section by comparing it with Sargent's interpretation.[26]

Roll suggested further research as an appendage to his work and mentioned Sargent's (1968) examination of interest rate sequences with spectral methods. Roll knew of the recent work on spectral analysis of economic time series and was curious about its applicability to his interest rate sequences.[27] However, he was unaware of Mandelbrot's (1963b) demonstration that spectral analysis is heavily compromised in the presence of Lévy stable distributions, since two time series can be identical in the long run even if the structures are vastly different. On the one hand, time series with very long dependence and finite variance would exhibit a characteristic spectrum, a hyperbolic spectral density $S'(f) \sim f^{\alpha-2}$ with $1 < \alpha < 2$. In this case spectral analysis might be useful in trying to diagnose the presence of long dependence, but it cannot be used to decompose a time series into a sum of periodic harmonic components, as the separate periodicities have no actual existence. Thus, there may actually be nothing to estimate. On the other hand, time series with infinite variance would have – in effect – a white spectrum. That is, the spectrum would be flat and the same as a pure Gaussian spectral density, so many cases would cover the "typical spectral shape" of an economic time series.[28] Furthermore, as spectral analysis deals exclusively with second moments, it is clearly best suited for use with normal or Gaussian processes because all information about such processes is contained in their first and second moments (see Granger and Hatanaka 1964, pp. 69–70).[29]

As discussed in the following section, this general analysis of probabilism, determinism, and randomness in economics helps provide a perspective on Sargent's early incentives.

2.3 Probabilism, Determinism, Randomness, and Sargent

Sargent decided to study economics because he liked it in college and was also truly curious about what causes depressions (Klamer 1983, pp. 58–80). Furthermore, he saw economics as an interesting combination of subjects that allows an analytical analysis of policy issues. Sargent (1996a) recalled that the "late 1960s were good times to be a young macroeconomist" (p. 536). He left the University of California at Berkeley with a medal for the most distinguished scholar in the class of 1964 and subsequently earned a Ph.D. from Harvard University in 1968. Sargent's dissertation analyzed time series of interest rates. His thesis adviser, *John Meyer*, had previously revealed in an important study of investment decisions that the minimum sum of absolute error (MSAE) estimator had outperformed least squares in forecasting (Glauber and Meyer 1964, pp. 222–31). Interest in this estimator had been rekindled in the mid-1950s by proofs that the problem involving a minimization of absolute values could be transformed to the standard linear programming form.[30] Meyer had attributed his results to sensitivity of the model specification combined with peculiarities of the forecast period and had made no mention of stable Lévy distributions, as he was then unaware of their existence.[31] In a footnote, Blattberg and Sargent (1971, 501n) thanked Meyer for his helpful comments and argued that the reason MSAE outperformed least squares in his study might lie in the presence of stable Lévy distributions. They speculated whether their results might "provide an explanation of the rather remarkable outcome of an important experiment involving MSAE and several least-squares-based estimators recently reported by Meyer and Glauber" (p. 509). Their explanation of the results was that "they flow from the property of the MSAE estimator established above, its relatively good performance in the presence of disturbances with very fat tails" (pp. 509–10) and that this "provides a possible reason for the better performance of the MSAE predictor in Meyer and Glauber's study" (p. 510).

In an interview, Sargent said that his dissertation "was not very good" (Klamer 1983, p. 60) because he did not comprehend how to relate time series and economic models.[32] He "didn't know enough about time series and . . . didn't know enough about theory to do things satisfactorily, but . . . did recognize that the link between them wasn't satisfactory" (p. 60). Sargent said, "[When] I was a second- or third-year graduate student, I did not understand the connection between theories and statistical tests. I assumed it was because I didn't have a firm enough grasp of the subject. But as I learned more and more, I realized that the connection wasn't there" (pp. 63–4). He started thinking about time series very seriously after graduate school:

I read lots of books on time series. I tried to figure out the relationship between time-series and economic models. At the time I started, the links weren't formal. You would write down static models, models that weren't even stated in probabilistic or dynamic terms, and then apply time-series procedures. But these models weren't really in any shape to confront time series. (p. 60)

Sargent's interest in conceptual integrity of neoclassical theory and econometrics sheds light on the fact that he was troubled by the unclear link between time-series econometrics and the models that were then being used:

What I mean by the links not being clear is that often the models that we used had no randomness in them. They analyze individual behavior in a context in which there is no uncertainty, but they treated the data probabilistically, thus adding randomness. That procedure is not a tight one, not even an understandable one. The statistical model you're using implies that there is an environment in which there's uncertainty, whereas the economic model that you're using assumes that away. The hunch is, and it's a hunch that turned out right, that it's not just a matter of adding a random term. If there really is uncertainty, it ought to change the way you think about individual behavior. But it's not only the uncertainty, it's also the dynamics. (pp. 63–4)

How do agents, economists, and econometricians deal with uncertainty? Sargent noticed that in econometrics empirical prediction requires the use of probabilistic ideas. Once these are introduced at the level of method, conceptual integrity requires that they be introduced at the level of theory construction as well. Recall that this is the pragmatic interpretation of the transition to probabilism.

Sargent's first publications dealt with the analysis of time series for interest rates; there we witness his first free moves in his search for what he would regard as conceptual integrity. He chose to approach the problem from the *perspective of time-series econometrics* and the *term structure of interest rates,* by looking at the relationships among interest rates on various instruments and by using spectral and cross-spectral analysis to study the behavior of the series and the relationships among them at various components of oscillation (Sargent 1968). He used the same tools to assess the strength of the interdependence between short and long rates (Dobell and Sargent 1969; Frost and Sargent 1970) and to determine the importance of price expectations to the relationship between nominal and real interest rates (Sargent 1969).

I should note that the time-series econometricians who adopted the rational expectations hypothesis during the late 1960s to early 1970s focused on distributed lags. According to Hansen and Sargent (1991a), "the hypothesis of rational expectations has invaded economics from a variety of sources. . . . But in macroeconomics, the first invaders were time-series econometricians, who in the late 1960s were seeking methods of restricting the parameters of lag distributions in their econometric models" (p. 1).[33] For models with one dependent and one explanatory variable, the distributed lag will look like this:

$$y_t = \alpha + \beta_0 x_t + \beta_1 x_{t-1} + \cdots + e_t \qquad (2.5)$$

where the variable x is assumed to be independent of the stochastic process e_t at all times.

Since he started from the viewpoint of time-series econometrics, Sargent was led to emphasize the *role of probabilism and randomness.* If statistical knowledge is the best that is accessible to us, then empirical prediction requires the introduction of probabilities. Thus, Sargent chose to rest content with certain kinds of probabilistic explanations rather than seeking to pursue complete determinism. He adopted the techniques of econometrics and with them the reigning interpretation of probability and randomness of the econometrics community. Because he did not change the techniques and was mostly silent on the interpretation of probability and randomness, this course can be seen as a forced move. Therefore, as follows from the discussion of econometrics in the previous section, he was led to favor the relative frequency theory by an allusion to classical statistical theory and to rationalize the disturbances by some mixture of random sampling from a population and an epistemic or ontic interpretation of the influence of omitted variables.

Sargent encountered *Lévy stable distributions* and the associated problem of constructing statistical estimators in his early work on interest rates. This initial choice was again further elaborated by his immediate scientific community and its practices. Roll had shown that some interest rates follow a member of the class of Lévy stable distributions, had suggested extending his work by Sargent's examination of interest rate sequences with spectral methods, and had discussed these issues with his colleague Sargent and his student Blattberg, at Carnegie Mellon University. Furthermore, Lévy stable distributions promised to explain why MSAE outperformed least squares in Sargent's thesis adviser's study of investment decisions.

Through his analysis of time series for interest rates, Sargent also became aware of the role of expectations, because orthodox neoclassical theory stated that they influence the relationship between spot and forward rates, nominal and real rates, and short- and long-term rates. Furthermore, expectations, or more specifically *rational expectations,* provided Sargent with an answer to how conceptual integrity might be achieved – the question that has guided his studies – as they allowed him to introduce probabilistic ideas at the level of theory construction as well. His focus on econometrics let Sargent enter Mandelbrot's first stage of indeterminism, by introducing probability theory while retaining the classical central limit theorem. He considered rational expectations a more elegant way to establish a link between the randomness of time-series econometrics and the determinism of neoclassical models. Notice that Sargent made yet another free move by limiting his analysis to *neoclassical economic theory.* If he had chosen the treatment of determinism in another economic theory, he would have faced different forced moves and resistances in his attempts to satisfy his interests.

The concept of adaptive expectations was criticized in the 1960s for fitting models that forecast better than agents, as it allows individuals to make systematic forecasting errors period after period. This was an obstacle in Sargent's search for conceptual integrity. The hypothesis of adaptive expectations postulates that individuals use information on past forecasting errors to revise current expectations. Objections to the hypothesis included, first, that it is entirely backward-looking, and that all mechanistic backward-looking extrapolative rules allow the possibility of systematic forecasting errors for many periods in succession. Critics argued that the suboptimal use of available information is hard to reconcile with the idea of optimization, which is the foundation of most microeconomic analysis. Second, no widely accepted economic theory was offered to explain the magnitude of the adjustment parameter. Some economists sought to meet these objections by using the concept of rational expectations, by taking the idea that individuals should not make systematic errors as their point of departure (Begg 1982). Expectations are rational when they depend, in the proper way, on the same things that economic theory says actually determine that variable. Econometric methods can then be used to estimate the economic model. Since Sargent had started from the viewpoint of econometrics, he was led to choose an *econometrically motivated interpretation of the concept of rational expectations,* which involved treating the econometrician and the agents in the model in a symmetric fashion.

It is important to note that the rendition of rational expectations differs among its proponents, and that even Sargent later changed his interpretation of the concept. As we see here, Sargent started by combining rational expectations with statistical models; however, the following chapter discusses how he subsequently combined the concept first with IS-LM models that incorporate non-Keynesian assumptions and then with atheoretical vector autoregressive models. The connection between rational expectations and general equilibrium models is analyzed in Chapters 3 and 4, and Chapter 5 examines the links among rational expectations, bounded rationality, and artificial intelligence. Looking back at the "rational expectations revolution," Sargent (1996a) wrote, "The victory of rational expectations owes to its beauty and its utility: the economy with which it eliminates what we had thought were free variables – peoples' expectations about endogenous variables – while adding no free parameters, but bringing instead cross-equation and cross-frequency restrictions" (p. 542). Note that the first component resonates with the theme of this chapter, that for Sargent conceptual integrity in the late 1960s to early 1970s required an econometric interpretation of people's expectations. The second component resonates with the theme of the following chapter, that for Sargent conceptual integrity in the late 1970s to early 1980s required a link between general equilibrium theory and rational expectations that resulted in cross-equation restrictions. Also note that "beauty" and "utility" are in the eye of the beholder. In the framework used here, their interpretations depend on motivations and moves.

After this short digression, let me sum up the argument so far in this section. Sargent was initially motivated to establish a link between econometrics and theoretical models. He made tentative choices in the form of free moves – taking time-series econometrics as given and wanting to link it with the determinism of neoclassical economic theory, focusing on interest rates, and using the concept of rational expectations to establish a tie – to satisfy his interests. Furthermore, he used his motivation as a standard for assessing other potential extensions of the conceptual network. The existing conceptual, experimental, and sociotechnical practices of Sargent's scientific community further elaborated his tentative choices, in the form of forced moves – the econometric interpretation of probabilism and randomness, the importance of Lévy stable distributions, and the econometrically motivated interpretation of rational expectations. Furthermore, the forced moves introduced a resistance in Sargent's attempts to satisfy his interests. For most members of the family of Lévy stable distributions, precisely the ones that were characteristic of economic variates, Mandelbrot's second stage of indeterminism looms on the horizon. Sargent had entered the first stage of indeterminism by introducing probability theory at the level of not only method but also theory construction, while still resorting to the classical central limit theorem. However, the second stage of indeterminism, with its blurred distinction between theoretical determinism and physical indeterminism, was considered off-limits by Sargent, since the econometrically motivated interpretation of rational expectations required the availability of statistical estimators. When stable laws entered the scene, econometricians and agents would run into problems with the construction of statistical estimators, since the upshot of stable laws is that almost all techniques of modern econometrics are useless and would have to be discarded. Rather than relinquishing the econometrically motivated interpretation of rational expectations, Sargent gave up Lévy stable distributions with infinite variance, without explicit justification.

Why did Sargent *relinquish the theory of Lévy stable distributions with infinite variance?* Why did he not pursue the indirect investigation of the analytical properties of alternative statistical estimators? Only a few explicit discussions of Lévy stable distributions can be found in his publications. In a paper on Macaulay's test, Sargent (1971a) took up Roll's suggestion of extending his study of the efficient market model applied to U.S. Treasury bill rates with an examination of interest rate sequences with spectral methods.[34] He used Roll's data to illustrate how the tools of spectral and cross-spectral analysis might be used to implement tests of the expectations theory of the term structure (p. 401n). Sargent wanted to inspect the accuracy of the expectations implicit in the yield curve and explored the adequacy of the accurate forecasting hypothesis in explaining the term structure of U.S. Treasury bill rates in the 1950s. He proposed to test the accurate forecasting hypothesis by using the phase of the estimated cross-spectrum between one-week and n-week bills to estimate the parameter of the following model, which expresses the hypothesized lead as a function of angular frequency w

$$\phi_n(w) = b_n w \tag{2.6}$$

where $b_n = (0 + 1 + \cdots + (n - 1)/n)$ periods, w is the angular frequency expressed in radians per time period, and $\phi_n(w)$ is the phase of the cross-spectrum between the yield to maturity on n-period and one-period bills. The accurate forecasting version of the expectations hypothesis implies that n-period rates lead one-period rates by $(0 + 1 + \cdots + (n - 1)/n)$. Sargent's procedure was to estimate the phase diagram of the cross-spectrum between n-period and one-period bills and then to use it to estimate b_n. Now, for "the purposes of empirical implementation, a stochastic term must be added to the right side of [the above] equation. . . . This term is present for several reasons. First, it incorporates the possibility of an error in the specification. . . . The use of the estimated phase, which is itself a random variable, provides another reason for including a stochastic term. . . . This is the standard errors-in-variables cause for the presence of a stochastic term" (pp. 401–2).[35] If uncertainty is so central to theorizing, we would expect lengthy discussions on it. Instead, this is one of the few *explicit discussions of the justification of the error term* by Sargent. Recall that the first interpretation is the epistemic version of errors-in-equations. Also note that the problem with the second, errors-in-variables, justification is that error is not confined to the single dependent variable, making it hard to settle on the correct method to model these equations. Sargent assumed that the random term follows a distribution with finite variance, thus taming indeterminism by assuring the availability of an explicit form of the density, and thereby ignoring the accumulating body of evidence mentioned in Blattberg and Sargent and the conclusions Roll drew from this data set.

Sargent did allow for heteroscedasticity of the disturbances and got rid of the inefficiency that follows from heteroscedasticity by applying least squares to a transformed equation, which amounts to using the generalized least squares estimator. However, this estimator is efficient provided that the variances of the random terms are finite, such that the classical central limit theorem and the Gauss–Markov theorem hold. In the case of infinite variance, as Blattberg and Sargent had shown, the MSAE estimator might be more efficient than (generalized) least squares (also see Taylor 1974). Estimating his model, Sargent (1971a) found some elements of accuracy in the forecasts impounded in the yield curve for Treasury bill rates in the 1950s. However, his empirical results cast rather serious doubt on the utility of the very restrictive version of the expectations hypothesis used in his study. He attributed these somewhat negative results to the severely strict nature of the requirement that he had imposed on the yield curve in his statement of the accurate forecasting hypothesis: "Our procedure in this paper, which is admittedly very extreme, amounts to assuming that the variance of the [disturbances] is so small that the [difference between the actual value and the minimum mean squared error forecast] can be neglected" (p. 409). Thus, Sargent's analysis not only assumed that the variance of the random terms was finite, it further required an especially small variance. Sargent ascribed his negative results to the latter assumption and did not mention the consequences of dropping the first one. He showed in an appendix the potential implications of replacing the assumption that forecasts are accurate with the one that forecasts are unbiased, thus introducing a symmetric treatment of the econometrician and the agents in the model, and thereby establishing a link between the econometric model and the theoretical one. *This is where we witness the first appearance of the econometrically motivated concept of rational expectations in Sargent's analysis of the term structure of interest rates.* Sargent's avoidance of the problems associated with Lévy stable distributions led to his first interpretation of rational expectations, thereby allowing the agents in the model to use the same techniques as econometricians. This suggestion would serve his interest in conceptual integrity of theory and method by making the agents in the model use the same kinds of unbiased forecasts as econometricians calculate.

In a subsequent publication, Sargent (1972) took up the suggestion in the appendix to the paper discussed previously. This study reported some tests of two hypotheses about the behavior of the term structure of interest rates. The first is the expectations hypothesis, which states that forward rates of interest are forced into equality with the short rates that investors expect in subsequent periods. Sargent combined this with the second hypothesis that the expectations are rational in the sense that investors' expectations are equivalent to the optimal forecasts of statistical theory for a certain specified class of econometric models. Being naive autoregressive schemes, the statistical models that he assumed as representative of the interest rate had no analytical economic content. Notice again the econometric motivation underlying Sargent's rendition of rational expectations. According to Sargent, much sharper tests of the expectations hypothesis were made possible by also invoking the second hypothesis. He argued that the requirement that available information be used efficiently was much weaker than the requirement that expectations be very accurate. Whereas the first hypothesis had been subjected to many empirical tests, it had only rarely been tested within the framework of the second hypothesis. Sargent (1972) noted that the "most notable exception is Roll's excellent study of the behavior of U.S. Treasury Bill rates" (p. 74n) and claimed that his paper was closely related to Roll's. However, Roll's analysis was

considerably broader than the one included here, being based on his extensive work on capital-market equilibrium theory. In addition, his empirical tests . . . do not assume that bill rates are covariance stationary. Instead, Roll argues that the evolution of bill rates is more adequately described by assuming that they are drawn from one of the stable distributions with infinite variance. While that specification is certainly an interesting one, abandoning the assumption of covariance stationarity has its costs. (pp. 75–6)[36]

Imposing covariance stationarity and ignoring stable distributions with infinite variance assured that the algorithms for estimating the parameters can be concretized, a prerequisite for the introduction of rational expectations.

Notice that Sargent used the language of costs to argue for relinquishing stable distributions with infinite variance.[37] Recall from the previous section that Roll also used the concept of costs to make an argument for the use of the theory of stable probability laws for statistical inference. Why were they able to give different interpretations of costs? The reason lies in the different motivations and moves of Roll and Sargent. Roll was interested in checking the empirical distributions of the variables to be tested for conformity to known probability laws because inferences drawn from parametric tests depend on the underlying probability functions and because he considered the distributions to be of interest in their own right. Through the intertwining of free and forced moves with this motivation, Roll stressed the costs associated with relinquishing stable distributions. Sargent was interested in using an econometrically motivated interpretation of rational expectations to achieve conceptual integrity.

Since this idea of rational expectations hinged on the existence of algorithms for estimating the parameters, Sargent emphasized the costs associated with allowing for stable Lévy distributions with infinite variance. This suggests that the metaphor of cost in the context of scientific research has no universal meaning.[38]

As a short digression, note that some social science scholars have commented on this use of economic metaphors for economic science:

It has always struck me that in a social science like economics, the practitioners of the discipline have showed a marked preference for the philosophy they produced themselves, to the almost complete neglect of what was going on "outside." I guess something similar is happening in physics, which has always been the paradigmatic science for economics. (Callebaut 1993, pp. 193–4)

Still, economists were not on their own, since even some philosophers of science have appealed to certain economic metaphors for the final attainment of rationality (see, e.g., Bartley 1990; Goldman and Shaked 1991; Kitcher 1993; Laudan 1984, 1987; Radnitzky and Bartley 1987; Radnitzky and Bernholz 1987). According to Latour, philosophers "have the equivalent of rationality, which is the best allocation of resources – a typical American myth. It's a completely American myth of economists: the optimization of resources, and now of disputes" (Callebaut 1993, p. 315). However, the analysis of the different interpretations of costs by Roll and Sargent illustrates that it may be difficult to use economic metaphors as a serious analytical device in the process of research.[39]

Sargent (1972) tried to show that if the assumption of covariance stationarity is retained, a wide variety of empirical work can be interpreted as testing both hypotheses about the term structure of interest rates. He started out by assuming that the probability distribution function of the spot one-period rate was "independent of calendar time. That is all. The process need not be normal. It can even be stable Paretian, having infinite variance, provided that its mean exists (which rules out Cauchy processes). It need not be linear" (p. 76). However, he did not stop there, but continued to assert that it is "interesting to explore the implications of further restricting the probability distribution" (p. 78). He assumed that the one-period spot rate follows a discrete (covariance) stationary stochastic process with finite variance, since it is "the more restrictive (but still very general) version of the model . . . that seems to be implicit in some of the best empirical work on the term structure" (p. 80). Furthermore, this version guaranteed that the parameters can be located empirically, a precondition for the application of rational expectations as the optimal forecasts of statistical theory:

[M]any empirical models of the term structure can be rationalized within the [more restrictive] framework. . . . Yet while all those studies can be rationalized in a general way by appealing to this framework, the tests that they have reported make no use at all of the second of our hypotheses – that forecasts incorporate information efficiently. (p. 85)

Sargent tested the general version of the model by estimating the spectrum of increments in the forward-rate sequence and reporting F-statistics. He found that the data tend to disconfirm this broader version of the model. However, as was previously discussed by Blattberg and Sargent (1971), if the underlying variates have infinite variances, then the use of the usual t and F tests is not permitted. The more restrictive version of the model, which assumed that stationary spot rates follow a stationary process with finite variance, was tested by calculating the spectral densities of forward-rate sequences. Sargent found that data also tend to disconfirm this version of the model.

In the paper discussed previously, Sargent analyzed the key implications of the rational expectations theory of the term structure of interest rates for sequences of forward interest rates: "Some of these implications were spelled out by Roll (1970) and tested against data by Roll (1970) and Sargent (1972)" (Sargent 1979a, p. 133n). However, the theory also had ramifications for the regression of current and past short-term rates. In a paper published in 1979, Sargent (1979a) analyzed these implications by estimating the vector autoregression of long-term and short-term rates.[40] He did not check the probability distributions for his data, which might be part of the accumulating body of evidence mentioned by Blattberg and Sargent in 1971.

What happened since this publication is that by the mid-1970s almost all references to stable Lévy distributions in economic variates disappeared and that the earlier enthusiasts, among them Fama and Blattberg, abandoned the analysis of stable Lévy distributions. Since a full account of the rise and fall of stable distributions has been provided elsewhere (see Mirowski 1989b, 1990) and is beyond the scope of this chapter, which focuses on the people relevant to Sargent's narrative, I briefly mention two views on the disappearance of these distributions. Some argued that they were abandoned because of empirical evidence that mixtures of distributions were leptokurtotic and that estimated characteristic exponents increased as the data were either randomized or aggregated. This suggestion that thick tails were not actually caused by non-Gaussian stable laws but simply by nonconstant parameters of finite variance laws convinced many to relegate stable laws to the back burner, arguing that thick tails were the consequence of mixing normal distributions with different parameters.[41] For instance, Clark (1973) developed a finite variance lognormal alternative to the infinite variance stable model (also see, e.g., Hsu, Miller, and Wichern 1974). However, his reformulation in terms of a subordinated stochastic process model with finite variance was marred by undesirable features.[42] In addition, Mandelbrot (1973) commented on Clark's paper, "I am sensible in my belief that stability in Paul Lévy's sense is a feature both convenient mathematically and illuminating of reality, so that to achieve it one should learn to live with infinite variance" (p. 157). Hence, others claimed that the threat of Lévy stable distributions, which would require econometrics to search for algorithms for estimating the parameters, was averted by ignoring them, without a direct critique of the earlier findings of infinite variance. They argue that the strict deterministic stance of neoclassical theory seems incommensurable with economic variates following distributions that do not guarantee the existence of algorithms for estimating parameters (Mirowski 1989b, 1990).

Sargent's (1979a) paper gave a compact formula for the restriction on the bivariate vector autoregression of the long-term rate and the short-term rate that is implied by the rational expectations theory. As Mandelbrot (1963b, pp. 403, 415) had argued, the very practice of fitting vector autoregressions acts to filter out low-frequency variances and outliers, thus effectively "prewhitening" the data and taming the stochastic processes. In a sense, a preoccupation with rational expectations theory thus obstructs the ability to "see" the full range of stochastic possibilities. Sargent (1979a) assumed that

the process of first differences [of the one-period rate and the *n*-period rate] . . . is a second-order jointly stationary, indeterministic stochastic process. Among other things, this means that the covariances between [the two first differences] . . . exist and are independent of time *t;* it also means that the variances . . . exist and are not dependent on *t*. (p. 134)

This implied that a bivariate autoregressive representation for the process exists. Now that the idea of rational expectations had taken firm root, Sargent no longer bothered to justify the assumption that the variances are finite. As I argued earlier, Sargent's avoidance of the problems associated with Lévy stable distributions led to his first econometrically motivated interpretation of rational expectations. If variances existed and were independent of time *t,* then expectations could be interpreted as the linear least squares forecast of the random variable based on information available at time *t*. Under the assumption that the process of disturbances was bivariate normal, maximum likelihood estimation was equivalent to estimating each equation by least squares. Using these assumptions and insights, Sargent found no strong evidence for rejecting the rational expectations restrictions. He did note that it "should be emphasized that the theory predicts that none of the representations estimated . . . will be invariant with respect to an intervention that alters the stochastic processes facing agents and thereby alters the second-order characteristics of the distributions of yields" (p. 143). Hence, if variances were infinite rather than finite, the representations would change – they might not even be available. Furthermore, expectations could no longer be interpreted as the linear least squares forecast. That part of the Gauss–Markov theorem that demonstrates the minimum variance or efficiency property of least squares is no longer applicable. Also, the assumptions of the classical central limit theorem fail to hold and the least squares estimator is no longer the maximum likelihood estimator.

Sargent's textbooks contained very few discussions of Lévy stable distributions. Most of his theoretical analyses originated after he had restrained his earlier consideration of many members of the family of Lévy stable distributions and had equated rational expectations with the least squares forecast. The only explicit reference in the first edition of *Macroeconomic Theory* to his earlier discussions of infinite variance is found in Sargent's discussion of liquidity preference as behavior toward risk (Sargent 1979d, pp. 146–53). He argued for the use of stable distributions, since they facilitate the analysis and are the only distributions that serve as limiting distributions in central limit theorems. Because he wanted to establish a link between his discussion of liquidity preference as behavior toward risk and Tobin's "mean variance analysis," which requires the variances to be finite, Sargent further restricted his analysis to normal distributions. What led Sargent to restrict his discussion to distributions with finite variance in this instance was not the desire for a connection between time series and theoretical models, but the wish to establish a link between his study and Tobin's analysis. In the second edition of *Macroeconomic Theory,* Sargent added an explicit discussion of normal distributions when he analyzed investment under uncertainty (Sargent 1987a, pp. 391–7). The use of the special case of a multivariate normal stochastic process guarantees that rational expectations can be used to establish a connection between econometric models and theoretical ones. Sargent further required the variances to be sufficiently small to assure the desired settings for employment. The only explicit reference in *Dynamic Macroeconomic Theory* to his earlier discussions of infinite variance is found in his use of the recursive structures to which dynamic programming is applicable in constructing theories of asset prices (Sargent 1987b, pp. 93–5). Sargent mentioned Roll's work as an important early empirical application and went on to assume the existence of explicit expressions for the density function. However, if Roll's finding of the likelihood of a nonnormal distribution is accepted, then the existence of explicit expressions for the density is not warranted.

2.4   Conclusion

Probabilistic ideas attempt to find a solution to the problem of the tension between randomness and determinism. Statistical probabilities have now been widely embraced as a way for searching of a larger order, by not only inferring conclusions from data but also inferring from data to hypothesis. If probability is interpreted as an artifact of human ignorance, then determinism is saved. Statistical probabilists just rest content with probabilistic explanations rather than seeking to pursue complete determinism. Probabilistic ideas have become central and indispensable for this species of science, on the level of either theory construction or method.

The rise of econometrics symbolized the introduction of probabilistic ideas into the method of economics, with regression analysis as the standard statisti-

cal tool in neoclassical econometrics. This is Mandelbrot's first stage of indeterminism. Testing and estimation methods in econometrics generally rely on
knowledge of the probability distributions of the variates. Lévy stable distributions are useful in econometrics, since random variables are thought of as representing a linear combination of a large number of independent or weakly dependent variates. If the random variables follow a member of the family of Lévy
stable distributions, an explicit expression for the density function and algorithms for estimating the parameters might not be available. This is Mandelbrot's second stage of indeterminism. Most econometric techniques ignore the
problems with constructing statistical estimators under stable laws, primarily
by privileging the method of least squares to test or estimate its basic regression model. This requires the distribution of the random variables to be Gaussian and hence assures the existence of an algorithm for estimating the parameters. Randomness is tamed by assuming that variances are finite. Hence, one
reading of neoclassical econometrics is that it is a set of techniques forged to
attempt a reconciliation between the strict deterministic stance in neoclassical
theory and the apparent stochastic nature of economic variates.

The main theme in Sargent's work is trying to achieve that conceptual integrity of method and theory. He was dissatisfied by the fact that the statistical
models that were being used imply randomness in the economy, whereas the
neoclassical economic models assumed that away. The free moves Sargent initially made to serve this interest consist of taking time-series econometrics as
given and trying to link it with the determinism of neoclassical economic theory, focusing on interest rates, and using the concept of rational expectations to
establish a tie. Whereas these free moves stressed the agency of Sargent in the
extension of the conceptual network, this agency is surrendered in the forced
moves. The latter consisted of the econometric interpretation of probabilism
and randomness, the importance of Lévy stable distributions, and the econometrically motivated interpretation of rational expectations. This symbolized
the introduction of probabilistic ideas into the theory of economics. Whereas
Lévy stable distributions previously only threatened neoclassical econometrics,
they could now also compromise economic theory based on rational expectations. Sargent dealt with this resistance by silently relinquishing stable laws
rather than neoclassical econometrics or rational expectations, without extensive justification.

Whereas this chapter discusses Sargent's first attempts at trying to connect
economic theory and econometrics through an econometrically motivated interpretation of rational expectations, the following chapters focus on how his
interpretation changed as a result of altered circumstances and different free
moves.

CHAPTER 3

Accommodating Prediction

They will get it straight one day at the Sorbonne.
We shall return at twilight from the lecture
Pleased that the irrational is rational

Wallace Stevens, *It Must Give Pleasure*

The concept of rational expectations starts from the idea that individuals should not make systematic mistakes. Agents are not stupid; they learn from their mistakes and draw intelligent inferences about the future from what is happening around them. Although econometricians were the first promoters of rational expectations, their initial focus on methods for restricting the parameters of lag distribution subsequently changed to restricting vector autoregressions. Whereas the previous chapter indicated how Sargent tried to use rational expectations to restrict distributed lags, in this chapter we witness how Sargent, influenced by a change in his econometric environment, tried to use rational expectations to restrict vector autoregressions. The times are the late 1970s to early 1980s, the places are the University of Minnesota at Minneapolis and the University of Chicago, and the supporting roles are performed by Neil Wallace, Christopher Sims, and Lars Hansen.[1] Before continuing Sargent's saga, section 3.1 gives some background information on controversies over the possibility of prediction in economics. Section 3.2 analyzes Sargent's attempts to predict by adopting vector autoregressions "without too much a priori theory." Section 3.3 addresses the resistances Sargent encountered as he tried to put this idea to use. Section 3.4 discusses his efforts to combine vector autoregressions with general equilibrium theory. Section 3.5, as you might expect, discusses the resistances Sargent subsequently encountered. Section 3.6 puts Sargent's analysis in a wider perspective by connecting it with engineering mathematics.

3.1   The Problem of Prediction

As we saw in the previous chapter, Sargent experimented with Lévy stable distributions with infinite variance for a while but abandoned them without explicit justification. When variances are infinite, mathematical statistics can be of little help in the empirical determination of parameters, since these methods rely on such assumptions as the availability of an explicit form of the density function. If economic agents are supposed to use the relevant economic theory to make predictions, the help of these particular methods of mathematical statistics is crucial. However, the availability of econometric techniques is a necessary, but not a sufficient condition for predictability. This leads me to the topic of this chapter.

Predictability is one of the fundamental manifestations of symmetry in physics. According to Rosen (1990, pp. 288–90), it is one of the components of the dual foundation of science, along with reproducibility. In physics, predictability means that among the phenomena investigated, order can be found,[2] and from that order laws can be formulated, predicting the results of new experiments. Then theories can be developed to explain the laws.[3] When expressed in terms of experiments, predictability means that it is possible to predict the results of new experiments. Of course that does not often come about through pure inspiration, but is usually attained by performing experiments, fine-tuning them, studying their results, finding order, and formulating laws. That predictability is symmetry can be seen as follows: The symmetry is manifest in that for any experiment and its result, the experiment and its result obtained by changing the experimental input have the same relation as the original experiment and result.

As discussed in the following section, Sargent adopted vector autoregressions to determine the predictive power of each variable for each of the others. In this structure each variable was treated symmetrically, being explained by lagged values of itself and other variables in the system. The question is why he adopted such structure and the answer can be found in convenience, a central theme of this chapter. This raises another question, though, which is where this convenience comes from. I argue that Sargent adopted convenient techniques from engineering.

If we move beyond the realm of experiments, predictability might conflict with time asymmetry (Gans 1990; Hawking 1988). In the Newtonian mechanistic conception of the universe, time flows along independently of what occurs within the universe – time is a symmetrical entity that can drift in any direction. However, from our own individual viewpoint, time seems to flow in one direction only, toward the future. We only remember the past, and the future is uncertain. The deterministic view of nature cannot adequately explain this phenomenon. Furthermore, the second law of thermodynamics is a principle that states that order will always, eventually, turn to disorder. The reverse is (almost) never the case. Thus, there exists an asymmetry with regard to time in that it can move only in one direction, away from the past. Other instances of time asymmetry in the natural sciences include the collapse of the wave function of quantum mechanics and the increasing complexity of evolution.

Yet, even if there really is a completely deterministic and unified theory, "it would presumably determine our actions. And so the theory itself would determine the outcome of our search for it! And why should it determine that we come to the right conclusions from the evidence? Might it not equally well determine that we draw the wrong conclusion? Or no conclusion at all?" (Hawking 1988, p. 12). As social scientists have begun increasingly to recognize, human beliefs and expectations, not just the facts about which people have beliefs and expectations, are crucial to understanding human behavior. Questions of the reactions of human actors to communications from their fellow actors are of great importance in the social sciences. In particular, the formation of mutual expectations about behavior may have very large stabilizing or destabilizing effects for a society. Hence, awareness of or belief in various social theories will affect behavior. If society is determined by the theory of social scientists, then would not that theory itself be the product of society? If this reflexivity is defined as a relation between the forecaster and at least one other individual whose expectations and actions are to some extent affected by the prediction, then we enter the phenomenal domain of infinite regress and reflexivity of public predictions, which are often seen as phenomena especially relevant to and even characteristic of the social sciences.[4]

It is possible to make both self-defeating and self-fulfilling claims about people. A self-defeating prediction may be correct when privately formulated but, when published, is falsified through the change in expectations and actions of the agents who totally or partially believe it. Whatever the final truth about social facts, there is no denying some self-fulfilling element in shared expectations guided by public prediction. That is implicit in the definition of social action as action that takes account of the behavior of others and is thereby oriented in its course, as is seen when one looks at the actions of several agents together. Where each is guided by the expectation about others also so guided, the outcome is a function of what it was expected to be.

The problem of self-defeating and self-fulfilling public prediction has a long history in philosophy of science and in social science (see Grunberg 1986; Hands 1990). Prediction as a primary goal of science was intimately linked to the positivist movement, in order to absolve itself of "metaphysics."[5] Prediction is often seen as one of the main goals of economics, in its attempt to be the most quantitative of the social sciences and make policy recommendations.[6] During the mathematization of economics and the introduction of probability theory to economics in the 1920s, prediction was seen as an indication of objectivity. As a first approximation, economists abstracted from such difficulties as infinite regress and reflexivity by assuming that people believe and expect whatever the facts are. In that way theorists need not worry about what people's beliefs and expectations are. However, once one goes beyond this first approximation, the difficulties loom large.

In 1944, von Neumann and Morgenstern threw some light on the problem of infinite regress in the formation of mutual expectations about behavior. Reflexive predictions and infinite regress entered the stage again in 1954, with the work of the Keynesian theorists Emile Grunberg and Franco Modigliani, who gave an existence proof for the claim that social scientists could predict both publicly and correctly even when the agent's reaction to public prediction is taken into account. Grunberg and Modigliani showed that a public prediction will not necessarily alter the behavior of the relevant agents in such a way as to falsify a prediction that would have been privately correct. According to Modigliani, "people had been saying that economists cannot forecast, because when they do, something different happens as people react to those forecasts. We say that economists can forecast, even if you take the reaction of people into account" (Klamer 1983, p. 125). In the same year, Herbert Simon also demonstrated that it is possible, in principle, to make public predictions within the social sciences that will be confirmed by the events, by proving that reactions to published election predictions can be accounted for so that appropriately adjusted election predictions can avoid being self-destructive.[7] Simon (1982c) claimed that his "paper was stimulated by conversations with [Grunberg and Modigliani] about their work, and amounts to a generalization of their result with the help of some simple topology" (p. 405).[8]

Some have argued that the papers by Grunberg, Modigliani, and Simon were precursors to the general concept of rational expectations (see Hands 1990).[9] Grunberg, Modigliani, and Simon were concerned with showing that under certain conditions – presuming expectations based on some version of neoclassical theory – correct public predictions could be made even when those predictions influenced the behavior of the agents. However, Modigliani said: "I must confess that that article with Grunberg . . . [is] written with tongue in cheek, to really make fun of my colleagues. The article with Grunberg does not say people anticipate government policy and therefore render it ineffective" (Klamer 1983, p. 125). According to Simon (1982c), this work "falls far short of stating the full rational expectations thesis . . . but shows that the problem to which that thesis is addressed was in the Pittsburgh air as early as 1954" (p. 405). Rational expectations put the conditions for correct public predictions at the center of the stage. Under Muth's definition, rational expectations are informed predictions of future events and are essentially the same as the predictions of the relevant economic theory, which necessarily includes the expectational response of the agents. Public predictions are possible precisely by considering the relevant theory in making the prediction. Furthermore, not only will a public prediction have no substantial effect, it will simply have no effect at all. Hence, if agents have rational expectations, the correct public predictions can still be made, but this is not relevant to the problem that concerned Grunberg, Modigliani, and Simon, since the behavior of the agents is not affected by the predictions.

One of the central tenets of the rational expectations community, known as the "Lucas critique," is that rational agents consider policy rules in forming expectations and that therefore an econometric model that predicts the impact of a change in policy will err because of the way the policy change affects the behavior of economic agents. This is strictly a problem of econometric prediction under different policy rules. Whereas Grunberg, Modigliani, and Simon were concerned with models in which a correct private prediction could be made, the Lucas critique starts with the presumption of a correct private prediction and finds a solution in a rational expectations model. Rational expectations theorists likewise wanted to call a halt to the regress. Under rational expectations, the economic agents use the relevant economic theory to make predictions. A collection of agents is solving the same optimum problems and the solution of each agents is consistent with the solution of other agents.[10]

Sargent agreed with the claim that rational expectations solved the problem of prediction:

In economic affairs, the way that the future unfolds from the past depends partly on how people expect it to unfold from the past. Economic systems can thus be described as self-referential, because outcomes depend partly on what people expect those outcomes to be. This self-referential aspect of economic systems gives rise to enormous theoretical problems of indeterminacy (i.e., multiple equilibria) when people's expectations are left as "free variables" that are not restricted by economic theory. To fight that threat of indeterminacy, economists have embraced the hypothesis of rational expectations. (Marcet and Sargent 1992, p. 139)[11]

For Sargent (1987c), "Rational expectations is an equilibrium concept that can be applied to dynamic economic models that have elements of self-reference. . . . That is, a rational expectations equilibrium is a fixed point of the mapping from a perceived law of motion to an actual law of motion" (pp. 76–7; also see Sargent 1987a, pp. 409n, 411).[12] Interestingly, Sargent was unaware of this attribute of rational expectations during a 1971 meeting at the Minneapolis Fed. In response to the question whether he and Wallace had heard about fixed point theorems being applied to differential equations, Sargent (1996a) answered, "We hadn't, and neither had we understood how to adapt Grunberg and Modigliani's (1954) argument" (p. 537n).

Sargent eventually did use the fixed point argument, partly because he was interested in making predictions. As outlined before, Sargent's *interest* lies in *conceptual integrity of theory and method.* Now, why would he want this? Well, ultimately, the conceptual integrity would allow him to make predictions:

But why should anybody want to interpret time-series data as representing the results of interactions of private agents' optimizing choices? The answer is not that this way of modeling is aesthetically pleasing, although it is, nor that modeling in this way guarantees an analysis that implies no role for government intervention, which it does not. The reason for interpreting time series in this way is practical: potentially it offers the analyst the ability to predict how agents' behavior and the random behavior of market-determined variables will change whenever agents' constraints change, as when policy interventions or other changes in the environment occur. (Sargent 1981a, p. 215)[13]

Notice the use of the adjective "practical" here. I would argue that the interpretation of this adjective is not universal, but depends on a scientist's motivations and moves to satisfy those interests. Also note the stress on changes in the environment. When Sargent's environment changed, he had to account for agents' reactions to changes in their environment. As witnessed by the preceding excerpt, Sargent did not look for conceptual integrity of any theory and any method. Instead, he decided to focus on a particular kind of theory and a particular kind of method.

For Sargent (1987a),

Stochastic processes provide a natural context in which to formulate the problem of prediction. . . . The linear prediction problem is of interest to macroeconomists for at least two reasons. First, macroeconomists are interested in modeling the behavior of agents who are operating in dynamic and uncertain contexts. Typically, the hypothesis of utility or profit maximization ends up confronting these agents with some version of a prediction problem that they must solve in order best to achieve their objectives. . . . Second, macroeconomists are interested in using their own models of economic time series . . . in order to predict the future conditional on the past. When the econometric model occurs in the form of a vector version . . . it is said to be a vector autoregression. Linear prediction theory applies directly to such a model. (p. 241)

The vector autoregressive (VAR) model was designed especially to forecast (see, e.g., Anderson 1979). It tried to overcome many of the defects of the structural approach by relying on statistical regularities. Whereas the structural approach attempted to use economic theory and historical data to simulate the structure of the economy as a system of equations, vector autoregressions were not based on economic theories at all. Whereas the large national econometric models were successful in the 1950s to 1960s, their performance hit rock bottom in the 1970s: They did not successfully predict and could not explain the simultaneous high inflation and unemployment rates.[14] Vector autoregressions, however, seemed capable of producing forecasts that were, compared to the standard kind, more accurate, more frequent, and cheaper. Vector autoregression is a straightforward, powerful statistical forecasting technique that can be applied to any set of historical data. In the following section, I provide some evidence for this claim from Sargent's perspective.

3.2 Sargent's Version of VAR without Theory

By the mid-1970s, Sargent had moved to the University of Minnesota and the idea of rational expectations had taken firm root in his community. He said in his interview with Klamer (1983), "At Minnesota I have a very supportive environment" (p. 77). Sargent was surrounded by economists who were using the concept of rational expectations, taking the idea that individuals should not make systematic errors as their point of departure. The interpretation of the concept of rational expectations differed among its proponents, and even some of the individual economists changed their renditions. In his interview with Arjo Klamer (1983), Sargent said: "I was really influenced by a number of colleagues such as Neil Wallace and Chris Sims at the University of Minnesota. I was learning from Sims, even before I went to Minnesota, by reading his papers. Neil Wallace really taught me macroeconomic theories" (p. 60).[15]

Inspired by Wallace, Sargent continued to make the *free move* to *rational expectations*.[16] In Sargent and Wallace's (1975) collaborations, "the public's expectations are assumed equal to the objective (mathematical) expectations" (p. 242), and "the mathematical expectation [is] calculated using the model . . . and all information assumed to be available" (pp. 246–7; also see Sargent and Wallace 1976, pp. 204–5). Sargent and Wallace combined the idea of rational expectations with economic models. In particular, Sargent made the *free move* to *IS-LM models with non-Keynesian assumptions* (see, e.g., Sargent and Wallace 1975, 1976).[17] This combination of free moves resulted in the famous "policy ineffectiveness proposition," which is that systematic, and therefore anticipatable, monetary policy would have no real effects even in the short run.[18] In Sargent and Wallace's (1975) words: "It turns out that the probability distribution of output . . . is independent of the particular deterministic money supply rule in effect" (p. 241). Furthermore, "[i]n order for the monetary authority to induce fluctuations in real output, it must induce unexpected movements in the price level. . . . There is no systematic rule that the authority can follow that permits it to affect the unexpected part of the price level" (p. 249). A year after the publication of their original policy ineffectiveness proposition, Sargent and Wallace (1976) even went so far as to assert, "There is no longer any serious debate about whether monetary policy should be conducted according to rules or discretion. Quite appropriately, it is widely agreed that monetary policy should obey a rule" (p. 199).

Since the *policy ineffectiveness proposition* followed from the intricate interplay of free moves, it would be a *forced move* in the framework used here. It is forced rather than free since the development of this proposition was not directly related to Sargent's attempts at satisfying his interests. Whereas the popular press immediately caught on to this idea (see, e.g., Guzzardi 1978; Lee 1984), Sargent did not consider it central to his work. Sargent (1981a) wrote that the appeal of rational expectations is not "that modeling in this way guarantees an analysis that implies no role for government intervention, which it does not" (p. 215). He said in an interview:

The neutrality [or policy ineffectiveness] proposition was an important element in my work six or seven years ago, but not recently. . . . Both Neil and I have talked about building other kinds of models. Some people, however, took that model seriously. They, therefore, took the neutrality proposition more seriously than we did. (Klamer 1983, p. 70)[19]

Sargent did not take the policy ineffectiveness proposition as seriously as others because he was "not really interested in politics" (Klamer 1983, p. 80).[20] Therefore, he felt that rational expectations economics is "certainly not politically motivated. It is technically motivated" (p. 80). However, it should be noted that Sargent's political views changed during his career. In the same interview with Klamer, he said: "When I came out of Berkeley and Harvard I had a really naive view of what the government could accomplish. It was my own fault, but I was very pro-intervention. . . . I distanced myself from that" (p. 80). One of the reasons Sargent distanced himself from his earlier convictions was that he served for a time in the Pentagon, where he "came to understand more clearly the limitations of government actions" (p. 62) and realized that "[t]he people in Washington aren't all that much smarter than anybody else" (Sargent quoted by Guzzardi 1978, p. 74).[21] I should note that though readers may be interested in how Sargent's political views played into his models, I will follow Sargent in discussing his more technical motivation behind rational expectations economics.

Hoover (1988, pp. 73–4) lists three objections that were raised by new classical economists to the model that Sargent and Wallace used.[22] First, the model's asset structure was too simple. Second, the choice of the level of money stock should be related to the choice of policy with respect to deficits and the stock of bonds. Third, one should address the dynamic problem of policy strategies rather than individual independent policy actions. Since these objections were not raised by Sargent and Wallace, I would not label them resistances. Furthermore, they were not directly linked to Sargent's interest in conceptual integrity of theory and method. However, Sargent and Wallace (1981), not unaware of these criticisms, did seek to accommodate some of the objections by incorporating general equilibrium notions such as the link between monetary and fiscal policy. In particular, they assumed that "monetary and fiscal policy are coordinated in a certain way" (p. 1). As it turned out, the model based on these additional assumptions generated very nonmonetarist conclusions about the conduct of monetary policy from apparently monetarist assumptions. Sargent and Wallace concluded, "Nothing in our analysis denies the possibility that monetary policy can permanently affect the inflation rate under a monetary regime that effectively disciplines the fiscal authority" (p. 7).[23]

What was different in Sargent and Wallace (1981) is that in earlier articles the Fed was seen as freely choosing its money growth rate, whereas in this article endogenous constraints on its reaction function were derived. Therefore, we witness Sargent's changing his *free moves* to *a general equilibrium framework*. However, although Sargent and Wallace were moving toward that framework, it still was not a full-fledged general equilibrium framework in the sense used by Lucas. In fact, Sargent looks back at his work with Wallace with some embarrassment: "One of the important moments of discovery was learning how to construct a rational expectations equilibrium. Neil and I very clumsily learned how to do that using homemade techniques. It wasn't till later that we discovered that Lucas was doing it in a more general, elegant way" (Klamer 1983, p. 74).[24] Before analyzing the connection between Lucas's research and that of Sargent and Wallace, we must first discuss the free moves, forced moves, and resistances on the method side of Sargent's search for conceptual integrity.

What is free and what is forced? Why do I call the subsequent moves to IS-LM with non-Keynesian assumptions and a general equilibrium framework free, and the one to the policy ineffectiveness proposition forced? Sargent made free moves in an attempt to satisfy his interest in establishing a connection between theory and method. However, since the policy ineffectiveness proposition was not immediately linked to his interests, it was a forced move. It followed from the free move he made to IS-LM with non-Keynesian assumptions in a direct attempt to connect theory and method. Since this analysis of free and forced moves focuses on theories, the picture needs to be completed by addressing the method side of Sargent's work during this period. There we discover that resistances on the method side of his work also led him to move toward a general equilibrium framework.

Here, Sargent's inspiration came from Sims and the revival of time-series analysis in engineering. Sargent and Sims were fellow graduate students at Harvard University in the 1960s and fellow professors at the University of Minnesota in the 1970s.[25] According to Sargent:

Learning from Chris Sims about time series and about Granger–Sims causality and how that fits in was fun. . . . Very early on I had a hunch that Chris's stuff would fit in with rational expectations, maybe because Granger's criterion was about prediction. It turned out that there's an intimate connection between Granger causality and rational expectations in a whole number of directions. . . . It was increasingly fun to see how these things merged. (Klamer 1983, p. 74)

The fun arose from the fact that time-series analysis combined with rational expectations promised to allow Sargent to serve his interest in linking theory and method. Of course, Sims was not on his own. In fact, Sargent and Sims's wider intellectual environment had changed. According to Hansen and Sargent (1991a), "the hypothesis of rational expectations has invaded economics from a variety of sources. . . . In the late 1970s the focus of attention changed from restricting distributed lags to restricting vector autoregressions" (p. 1).[26]

A process y_t is called a vector ARMA (p, q) process if

$$y_t = \Theta_1 y_{t-1} + \cdots + \Theta_p y_{t-p} + v_t + A_1 v_{t-1} + \cdots + A_q v_{t-q} \qquad (3.1)$$

where

$$\Theta_n = \begin{bmatrix} \theta_{11,n} & \cdot & \cdot & \cdot & \theta_{1k,n} \\ \cdot & \cdot & & & \cdot \\ \cdot & & \cdot & & \cdot \\ \cdot & & & \cdot & \cdot \\ \theta_{k1,n} & \cdot & \cdot & \cdot & \theta_{kk,n} \end{bmatrix}, \quad n = 1, \ldots, p$$

$$A_n = \begin{bmatrix} \alpha_{11,n} & \cdot & \cdot & \cdot & \alpha_{1k,n} \\ \cdot & \cdot & & & \cdot \\ \cdot & & \cdot & & \cdot \\ \cdot & & & \cdot & \cdot \\ \alpha_{k1,n} & \cdot & \cdot & \cdot & \alpha_{kk,n} \end{bmatrix}, \quad n = 1, \ldots, q$$

and v_t is k-dimensional vector (or multivariate) white noise defined by $E[v_t] = 0$, $E[v_t v_t'] = \Sigma_v$ (positive definite), and v_t and v_s are independent for $s \neq t$.[27] The process y_t is called a vector AR(p) process if $q = 0$; that is,

$$y_t = \Theta_1 y_{t-1} + \cdots + \Theta_p y_{t-p} + v_t \tag{3.2}$$

and y_t is called a vector MA(q) process if $p = 0$; that is,

$$y_t = v_t + A_1 v_{t-1} + \cdots + A_q v_{t-q} \tag{3.3}$$

In the late 1970s, influenced by Sims and the change in focus in the econometrics community, Sargent made the *free move* to restricting *vector autoregressions* on the method side.[28] Again, this move is free since it promised to satisfy his interest in conceptual integrity. As in the previous chapter, Sargent ended up with an *econometrically motivated interpretation of rational expectations* following from the intricate interplay of his interests and free moves. Rather than handling distributed lags, agents with rational expectations now fit vector autoregressions. Rather than solving structural models, agents model "without pretending to have too much a priori economic theory" (Sargent and Sims 1977) or "using methods not based on explicit economic theories" (Sargent 1979b).[29]

Where did this invasion of time-series econometrics come from? According to Sargent (1987a), in his "learning process, the desire to understand a particular economic model or phenomenon often prompted my learning to use some mathematical tool or other" (p. xix). The relevant techniques here were the tools of time-series econometrics. In his interview with Klamer (1983), Sargent mentioned his attraction to applied mathematics: "I didn't start taking formal math until after I went to Minnesota. Then I started taking classes again, essentially because the students knew more math than I did. I still take classes. . . . Once I can apply math, I like it" (p. 76; also see Parkin 1996, p. 651).[30] Although the theoretical background for time series was developed in statistics, the main applications arose in communication engineering, as discussed in detail in section 3.6. Sargent (1987b) called these techniques "the 'language of applied macroeconometrics' or at least one dialect" (p. xx). He claimed that in the sense that "the language that macroeconomists speak has changed . . . there has been a rational expectations revolution" (p. xxii).[31] This language of applied macroeconometrics was borrowed from engineering. Hence, engineering conceptions of the world dominated Sargent's quest for a more scientific macroeconomics. Engineers, however, are not theorists; they just want to get the bridge built, the noise suppressed, the job done. I will continue Sargent's story for now and elaborate the engineering roots of his time-series tree in section 3.6.

Structural estimation was the dominant econometric method until the 1970s. It was based on the belief that different economic theories could be tested decisively and that effective policies for changing an economic system could be designed. According to Sargent (1996a), "By the late 1960s, macroeconomic models were influential, big, and econometrically advanced" (p. 536). However, although the statistical theory for structural estimation was (and is) a major intellectual achievement, empirical experience with large structural macromodels had been less satisfactory. Sargent (1979b) argued that "[u]ntil recently, the most popular method of estimating vector autoregressions was to apply classical simultaneous equation estimators to the structural model that presumably underlay the vector autoregression" (p. 9). And, "[t]here is a presumption that these more efficient estimates produced by a simultaneous equation estimator will lead to better predictions when the vector autoregression is used for forecasting" (p. 10).

During the 1970s, shock waves rolled through the econometrics community and hopes collapsed when it turned out that very naive alternative methods, such as simple time-series models, could outperform the traditional structural econometric models in forecasting.[32] A growing number of studies compared the forecasting quality of the large macromodels to a new generation of time-series models and often showed that the large-scale simultaneous equation models predicted no better than the naive models (see, e.g., Cooper and Nelson 1975; Hickman 1972; Litterman 1979; Nelson 1972). Sargent and Sims (1977) noted that studies "show that for some series, univariate autoregressions provide better out-of-sample projections than multivariate models of the standard type, but there are some series for which standard multivariate models do provide better out-of-sample predictions" (p. 70n). Furthermore, econometricians came to believe that the economy experienced major shocks that began to invalidate the forecasts from the large structural macromodels. The period of rapid economic change led econometricians to respecify and reestimate their systems constantly.

Another shattering development during the 1970s was the argument underlying what has become known as the Lucas critique. In a paper first circulated in 1973, Lucas (1976) noted that if the estimated coefficients of observable equations implicitly contain policy parameters that have entered through their role as predictors of the future, these parameters will change when a new policy is adopted (see Sargent 1979b, p. 8).[33] Hence, parameter estimates derived under old policies are inappropriate in simulating new policies. The only use of such equations lies in predicting the future, provided that existing policy rules are maintained. The major fault of structural estimation was alleged to be the "incredible" nature of the restrictions that were used.[34] According to Sargent (1979b), "Alternatives to the structural models have been sought because of increasingly compelling suspicions that the a priori restrictions used in existing structural models are not implied by good dynamic economic theory and that the interpretations and policy conclusions based on those faulty a priori restrictions are worth little" (p. 8).[35] Many of these models were already believed to be implausible on the basis of tests of their overidentifying restrictions, which must also cast doubt on the exactly identifying restrictions.

Sargent (1979b) lamented,

Were there agreement that the a priori restrictions . . . are approximately correct, there would be no quarrel with the preceding case for using existing structural estimators as devices for estimating vector autoregressions for use in unconditional forecasting. However, over the last decade or so it has become increasingly evident that dynamic economic theories typically do not lead to prior information . . . of the kind described above. (p. 10)

Referring to a paper he wrote with Lucas (Lucas and Sargent 1979), Sargent (1979b) claimed that it argues "that dynamic economic theory gives rise to restrictions of a very different form than those that are currently implemented or even implementable in existing computer econometric procedures" (pp. 10–11). He concluded, "The upshot is that there is little reason from good dynamic theory to believe that the restrictions . . . imposed by existing structural macroeconometric models are even approximately correct. As Sims has described the situation, the identifying restrictions used in existing macroeconometric models are 'incredible'" (p. 11).

Lucas and Sargent's (1979) response to all these developments is now related in their own words. They concluded that the predictions of Keynesian models

were wildly incorrect and that the doctrine on which they were based is fundamentally flawed are now simple matters of fact, involving no novelties in economic theory. The task now facing contemporary students of the business cycle is to sort through the wreckage, determining which features of that remarkable intellectual event called the Keynesian revolution can be salvaged and put to good use and which others must be discarded. (p. 1)

They "establish that the difficulties are fatal: that modern macroeconomic models are of no value in guiding policy and that this condition will not be remedied by modifications along any line which is currently being pursued" (p. 2).

This raises the question of whether theory should be abandoned altogether. Sargent (1979b) wondered out loud "whether there are alternatives to the standard simultaneous equation modeling procedures that can be used to restrict the dimensionality of the free parameter space in vector autoregressions" (p. 11). Some econometricians, like Sargent and Sims (1977), responded to the evidence that naive time-series models frequently appeared to offer better forecasting performance than econometric models by focusing on representing the data relative to the theory.[36] Some economists, like Zellner and Palm (1974), suggested that time-series models were a good "representation" of big Keynesian econometric models.[37] Others, like Hansen and Sargent (1980), tried to synthesize structural estimation and time-series analysis by showing that time-series models were not necessarily atheoretical. Is it a coincidence that Sargent's name seems to appear almost everywhere? Undoubtedly, part of this has to do with the focus of this book. However, a more important role is played by the fact that Sargent's attempts to satisfy his interest in conceptual integrity frequently caused him to be a major player in developments in both theory and method. I argue that Sargent's focus in his collaborations with Sims was on time-series analysis as a method, but that subsequent resistances led him to focus on the linking of this analysis with theory in his collaborations with Hansen.[38] I start by elaborating Sargent and Sims's "atheoretical" analysis.

I have mentioned that in the 1970s the focus in time-series analysis changed to vector autoregression, which is a multivariate time-series model. However, I have neglected to explain what vector autoregression was all about. I outline its use in economics here and trace its roots to engineering in section 3.6 (see Epstein 1987, pp. 205–22; Hoover 1988, pp. 197–209; Kim 1988, pp. 99–103). Vector autoregression, which concerns a special stochastic process, was one strand of the response to the evidence that began to accumulate in the 1970s.[39] It was a kind of modern time-series model that provided a compact summary of the properties of the data within a given sample by regressing a vector of variables on its own past values and the past values of the other variables. This regression was used to determine the predictive power of each variable for each of the others. In this structure each variable was treated symmetrically, and explained by lagged values of itself and other variables in the system.[40] There were no exogenous variables and no identifying conditions, and the only roles of theory were to specify the variables that entered into the model and to determine the lag length.[41] Sargent (1979b) argued that "a major alternative was initiated by Sims and is directed at introducing restrictions on vector autoregressions which are frankly admitted at the outset to have no formal basis in dynamic economic theory" (p. 11).[42] The purposes of exploring time series with advanced econometric techniques and with a minimum of economic theory were to forecast and to acquire information to motivate theoretical assumptions. According to Sargent, "the idea is to estimate vector autoregressions with many free parameters and to introduce restrictions not directly motivated by economic theory but rather aimed simply at forecasting better, that is, delivering estimators with small mean squared errors" (p. 8).

Sims, one of the pioneers of vector autoregressions, believed that theoretical restrictions in statistical inference should be kept to a minimum. Hence, Sargent and Sims (1977) illustrated "the application of a certain class of time series model to macroeconomics. One motivation for this application is our suspicion that existing large-scale macroeconometric models represent, to an extent not admitted in the statistical theory applied to them, 'measurement without theory'" (p. 45).[43] It is interesting to note that whereas Koopmans and the Cowles Commission had earlier used this suspicion to argue against the methods of Mitchell and the National Bureau of Economic Research (NBER), this argument was now used by Sargent and Sims against attempts of the Cowles Commission to estimate structural models. Sargent and Sims viewed the identifying restrictions as hypotheses to be tested as critically as available data and statistical techniques will allow, and they used little theory in a search for stable patterns in data. The essence of Sims's approach was to forecast the joint movements of selected macroeconomic variables without tracing the causes back to microeconomic factors (see Sargent 1979b, p. 8). In order to forecast, vector autoregression relied only on regularities in the historical data, and very little on economic theories. Models using this technique were therefore likely to capture historical relationships better than models tied to inadequate economic theories. Models in which the data unfolded the story did not have to deal with the complicated problem of identifying the econometric system. Furthermore, since vector autoregression was based on stylized statistical regularities rather than economic theories, it could easily be used to forecast with whatever data were available. A vector autoregressive model could be used to predict several periods into the future, to analyze unexpected shocks to the economy, and to estimate the probability of future events.

Before vector autoregressions start sounding as if they were too good to be true, I should stress that they could not be used to analyze the impact of alternative government policies, since such policy regime shifts required the derivation of identifying restrictions. Sims agreed with Lucas that the identifying restrictions adopted in most large-scale econometric models were "incredible," but tried to steer clear of the Lucas critique by arguing that true changes of regime were few and far between (see, e.g., Hoover 1988, pp. 185–97). If policy choice could be described as a continuous revision of plans, then policy regime shifts were irrelevant and the exact identification of an econometric system was unnecessary. As long as the regime was constant and, hence, we were restricted to normal policy-making, Sims believed, reduced forms were adequate to provide policy advice. He proposed vector autoregressions to systematize the haphazard manner in which reduced forms were specified and estimated. Sargent (1979b) also acknowledged, "While vector autoregressions can't be used to predict the effects of changes in policy feedback rules, they can be used to characterize the response to unexpected shocks in policy and other variables" (p. 13); and a "final use of vector autoregressions is to make probabilistic statements about events in the future which depend on complicated features of sample paths" (p. 14).

The basic building block of this "atheoretical macroeconometrics" or "letting the data speak" was Granger causality, which was defined by Granger in his 1969 paper (for a thorough technical analysis, see Hoover 1988, pp. 168–209).[44] A variable Y causes a variable X by Granger's criterion, if the error variance of X conditional on all past values of all variables is less than the error variance of X conditional on all past variables except Y. If X causes Y and Y causes X, then there is feedback between X and Y. Sims developed a statistical test for Granger causality and demonstrated that a variable X is strictly exogenous with respect to a variable Y if and only if Y does not Granger-cause X. If in addition X Granger-causes Y, then X is said to be causally prior to Y (see Sims 1972, 1977). A test of exogeneity in this sense was particularly relevant to determine the possible existence of feedbacks in policy control problems. Sims (1972, 1977) applied tests of Granger causality to analyze incremental predictability. These tests told whether or not the current value of a variable carried any information about future values of another variable once the second variable's past was taken into account. These descriptions could then be used to formulate a theoretical model.

There has been quite a bit of confusion as to whether Granger causality was "true" causality (see, e.g., Hoover 1988, pp. 168–76). Sargent (1977b) admitted, "Granger's definition of a causal relation does not, in general, coincide with the economist's usual definition of one: namely, a relation that is invariant with respect to interventions in the form of imposed changes in the processes governing the causing variables" (p. 216; also see Sargent 1977a, p. 61). Instead, Sargent stressed the link between Granger causality and exogeneity. According to him, the "important thing that Sims showed is the coincidence of the condition 'y doesn't Granger-cause x' with the condition 'there exists a representation (a model) in which x is strictly econometrically exogenous with respect to y'" (p. 216; for a formal discussion, see Sargent 1987a, pp. 317, 322–3). Hence, in Sargent's opinion, the "true" contribution of Granger causality lay in its link with exogeneity and not in its representation of causality: "Sims' test is potentially an extremely important diagnostic device for checking on the quality of assumptions about strict econometric exogeneity. . . . From this point of view, it is irrelevant whether or not Granger's definition of causality agrees with the way we ordinarily like to use the word cause" (p. 217). Sargent wanted to use the word "cause" in his own definition as a matter of "convenience." I argue in the following sections that he relied heavily on convenience in his attempts to accommodate prediction.

Once the "causal" ordering of the variables had been established, the next step was to use statistical or graphical techniques to indicate the implied quantitative interrelationships among the variables. The relevant techniques here were innovation accounting and impulse response analysis (see, e.g., Sims 1980a, 1980b). These techniques were driven by stochastic shocks but were not intended to analyze even a component of these shocks in terms of policy regime shifts or structural changes. The purpose was instead to trace out the reaction of a vector stochastic process to a random impulse, under the unstated assumption that the behavior of the system was not sensitive to the underlying economic origin or nature of the shock. These techniques could be used in forecasting and in providing a descriptive guide to the formulation of good theoretical models (see Appendix 3A).

Innovation accounting summarized the main channels of influence in the system. An innovation in a variable was its unanticipated component; it was the difference between its actual and predicted value when the predicted value was calculated through an estimated equation. Under certain conditions on the coefficient matrices, the vector autoregressive system could be written in moving-average form. From this representation, the variance of each variable in a vector autoregressive system could be decomposed into the variances of variables included. Innovation accounting then attributed each variable's total variance to each of the variances of variables in the system. Impulse response analysis described the system's response to a shock. The idea of the impulse response technique was to investigate the way in which the innovation in one variable influenced the time series of the other variables. In the moving-average representation of the vector autoregression, each variable was a function of the orthogonal innovations in the system. The impulse response function tabulated the response of a variable at date $t + s$ to the innovation in another variable at date t for all positive s.

Sargent and Sims (1977) explained innovation accounting in the following way: "The innovation in an element of a vector stochastic process is the difference between the element's current value and the best forecast of the current value available last period – the one-step ahead forecast error" (p. 72). Furthermore, "innovations and the system's typical response to them will not remain fixed under changes in the list of variables unless all nonpassive variables remain in the system" (p. 73). Sargent and Sims also noted that the "notion of an 'innovation' . . . is tied to theory based only on first and second moments or else to an assumption of normality" (p. 72n).[45] However, Sims was well aware of the sensitivity of his results to the assumption of normality:

Sims quickly points out, however, that a high order autoregressive system with a few degrees of freedom "makes interpretation of the tests difficult." He cites sensitivity of the F tests to non-normality. This issue is of great importance since the system likely contains a root of modulus near unity. In this case the true finite sample distribution of the estimators is unknown. (Epstein 1987, p. 211)

Given his interest in conceptual integrity of theory and method, when Sargent made the free move to vector autoregressions, he was led to the *forced move* of using the acquired statistical information to *construct a theoretical model.* According to Sargent, the "atheoretical" approach of macroeconomics should be used to motivate theoretical assumptions. There are three pieces of evidence for this claim. Exhibit one is a paper by Sargent and Wallace (1973) that was subsequently further elaborated by Sargent (1977a), exhibit two a joint project by Sargent and Sims (1977), and exhibit three a paper by Sargent alone (1976a).

Although most of the combined research of Sargent and Wallace dealt with theories, some of it was more empirical. However, they always kept an eye out for conceptual integrity of theory and method. In one instance, Sargent and Wallace (1973) used tests of Granger causality to find out whether adaptive expectations schemes in Cagan's (1956) model of hyperinflation were rational. Cagan had conducted a famous study of the monetary dynamics of hyperinflation under the assumption of autoregressive expectations. Whereas autoregressive expectations had been frequently seen as incompatible with rational expectations, Sargent and Wallace (1973) sought to show that Cagan's autoregressive scheme may coincide with rational expectations. They

described two ways to build a model of hyperinflation in which expectations are rational. ... In [the first] system, money creation "causes" inflation, in the sense of Granger, while inflation does not "cause" money creation. In such a system, adaptive expectations schemes like Cagan's are not rational. The second model is one in which Cagan's adaptive expectation mechanism is a rational one to employ. (pp. 337–8)

Sargent and Wallace concluded, "conditions exist under which adaptive expectations are fully rational. One essential condition is the presence of feedback from inflation to subsequent rates of money inflation. Such feedback appears to have been present in at least several of the hyperinflations" (p. 349).[46] Hence, they advocated one model over another because of its ability to explain the Granger-causal structure exhibited in the data.

Subsequently, Sargent (1977a) aimed "to complete a task begun by Wallace and me" (p. 60) by engaging in "an exercise in applying vector time-series models" (p. 61). The motivation he provided for this exercise gives us another peek at his interests. Having made the free move to rational expectations, he tried to incorporate Cagan's work into his theoretical framework: "One way of justifying imposing rational expectations on Cagan's model is that it enables one to specify a complete model of the inflation–money creation process in a very economical way" (p. 60). However, conceptual integrity required incorporating Cagan's work into his econometric framework as well. According to Sargent, "a more important reason for using the hypothesis of rational expectations to complete Cagan's model is that doing so delivers an econometric model that is seemingly consistent with the exogeneity (or 'causal') structure exhibited by the money creation–inflation process during the seven hyperinflations studied by Cagan" (p. 60). He concluded, "since changes in the stochastic process for money creation are supposed to produce predictable changes in the stochastic process for inflation, money 'causes' inflation" (p. 62).

The second piece of evidence is that in his collaboration with Sims, Sargent also kept stressing the economic models leading to vector autoregressions. Sargent and Sims (1977) stated, "Thus, it would be a mistake to regard the techniques that we describe as being useful solely for pursuing measurement without theory" (p. 48; also see pp. 50, 52). They "indicate how index models seem to be a natural statistical setting in which to study such macroeconomic models" (p. 55) and "show that results from 'non-structural' models of our type may be open to some interesting economic interpretations" (p. 71). Clearly, they were aware of the fact that the NBER had been defeated by the Cowles Commission in the "measurement without theory" controversy.[47] They concluded: "Some of the conclusions developed in the model seem solid, in part because they are non-controversial. . . . [T]he model appears without 'coaching' in the form of a priori constraints to generate conclusions with interesting economic interpretations" (p. 70). Finally, Sargent (1977b) rationalized his work with Sims "as part of the process of turning up empirical regularities, regularities that theorizing should attempt to explain" (p. 216).

In his own work, finally, Sargent (1976a) used tests of Granger causality between policy and price variables and the unemployment and interest rate in an attempt to generate unconditional forecasts and, more importantly, to decide how best to apply rational expectations in a classical macroeconometric model for the United States: "One reason for estimating the model is to produce a simple device capable of generating unconditional forecasts. . . . But a more important reason is that as part of the estimation process the hypotheses underlying the model are subjected to empirical testing" (p. 207).[48] Sargent tried to let the data speak for themselves without imposing theoretical structures on them and thought that his tests of Granger causality constituted a naive but powerful formulation of the hypothesis that there is a natural rate of unemployment. According to Sargent, the "chief novelty of this paper is its formulation of a drastic, statistical definition of the natural unemployment rate hypothesis. That definition is not dependent on any particular macroeconomic structural model" (p. 208), and "From Granger's paper, a direct statistical test of that hypothesis is available" (p. 217). In this paper, Sargent also alluded to the developments in the 1970s mentioned earlier: "The tests of the natural-rate hypothesis implemented here differ substantially from the usual one. . . . This usual test has been harshly criticized on theoretical grounds and furthermore is subject to the purely econometric objection that economic time-series data usually yield very little information about 'long-run' magnitudes" (p. 214).

This is not the end of the story, since Sargent encountered new *resistances* as a result of his decision to focus on vector autoregressions without theory.

3.3   Resistances to VAR without Theory

Although economists have come up with a number of criticisms of vector autoregressions (see Epstein 1987, pp. 205–22), the more important question is whether Sargent was bothered by any of these limitations. Well, Sargent mentioned one minor and one major *resistance*. The minor problem was that Sims's test was a necessary but not a sufficient condition for establishing *strict exogeneity*. In fact, when attacked on these grounds, Sargent (1979c) replied

that for x to be strictly exogenous in a particular equation . . . it is necessary but not sufficient that y fails to Granger cause x. This is enough to make Sims' test useful for testing the null hypothesis that x is exogenous with respect to y in a particular equation. The power of the test is somewhat diminished but not destroyed by the fact that it is possible to fail to reject the hypothesis in "infinite" samples, even when it is false. (p. 407)

Furthermore, Sargent hinted at working on a way out of this resistance:

Occasions do arise in which economic theory . . . places sufficiently strong restriction on the lag distributions in x_t that stronger tests for strict econometric exogeneity than Sims' become applicable. In particular, Hansen and Sargent . . . describe stronger tests for exogeneity that apply in certain rational expectations models that impose overidentifying cross-equation restrictions on the lag distributions on x. (p. 407)[49]

I am moving ahead of myself, though, since the ways Sargent sought to overcome the several resistances are the topic of the next section. Before embarking on that narrative, I want to address the major problem Sargent identified.

Sargent found another *resistance* in *observational equivalence,* which is closely linked to the identification problem. Since the vector autoregressive model relied on observed regularities not traced to underlying behavior and the structure of the complete system was not taken into consideration, the reliability of the model was not known and vector autoregressions were likely to produce misleading forecasts.[50] In particular, vector autoregressions were not able to deal with structural policy changes. It was not at all clear how the effects of instruments available to the policymaker would be quantified without imposing meaningful economic assumptions to identify relevant parameters. The solution developed by advocates of vector autoregressions was to interpret policy as the addition of a known "innovation shock" to the reduced-form disturbance for a particular variable in the current period. Their response to the Lucas critique was to argue that regime changes were rare and that in their absence reduced-form estimation was sufficient for policy analysis. This implied that the shocks were assumed to have constant effects regardless of the state of the system. Only if policy were seen as an "innovation shock," if the government were seen as a "shock" rather than a part of the market "structure," could it be incorporated into the system. This solution was not for Sargent for he did not believe that regime changes were rare.

What did Sargent mean by observational equivalence? Recall that Sargent (1976a) tried to use Granger causality to support the natural rate hypothesis. In the same year, however, his defense turned out to be weak when he learned that both models compatible with the natural rate hypothesis and models incompatible with it could generate the same vector autoregressive relations (see Appendix 3B). Within any policy regime, there were an infinite number of equally accurate representations of the data. If one of these forms were invariant to changes in the policy regime, then the other forms would in general not also be invariant. The natural and nonnatural rate hypotheses generated identical observable consequences and formed the basis for equally good forecasts, as long as the policy regime remained constant.

In Sargent's (1976b) words: "Here I point out that there are always alternative ways of writing the reduced form, one being observationally equivalent with the other, so that each is equally valid in the estimation period" (p. 631). Hence, to "rule on the policy issue thus requires bringing to bear theoretical considerations or doing empirical work of a kind considerably more subtle than that directed solely at estimating reduced forms" (p. 632). Sargent saw links between his discovery of observational equivalence and the so-called Lucas critique. According to Sargent, his "note displays some mechanical equivalencies that force one to stumble upon Lucas' observations about the limits of the usual applications of optimal-control theory to macroeconometric models" (p. 632; also see Sargent 1979b, p. 14).

Sargent (1977a) was well aware that the structure would change with a different policy regime: "If there is a change in the monetary regime, that is a switch in the money supply rule, the economic theory predicts that the Granger-causality structure of the money-inflation process will change" (p. 6). Sargent and Sims (1977) noted, "[B]ecause we interpret these equations as asserting a 'good fit,' they are not, like the equations of a standard simultaneous equations model, unaltered by changes in the choice of left-hand-side variable" (p. 50). Sargent (1979b) warned that "users of [vector autoregressions] must acknowledge from the start that they are vulnerable to Lucas' (1976) criticism of econometric policy evaluation methods, and they often must restrict the domain of the questions to which answers are sought if Lucas' criticism is not to be operative" (p. 8). Hence, vector autoregressions could be used for unconditional forecasting but were useless for formulation of policy recommendations (see Sargent 1979b, p. 8; 1977b, p. 215). They could only be used to achieve vacuous attributions of conceptual integrity of theory and method.

Sargent was particularly disturbed by his discovery of observational equivalence because he wanted to use his conceptually complete economic models for making policy recommendations (see, e.g., Lucas and Sargent 1981, p. xiii). One of the reasons Sargent liked economics was that it dealt with policy issues; he considered it "a nice mix of subjects: it is about people, it relates to policy issues but it also uses technical things, mathematics. It's a way of saying analytical things about virtually every issue in politics" (Klamer 1983, p. 59; also see Sargent 1987b, p. 1).[51] According to Sargent, at the core of the rational expectations revolution was the insight that economic policy does not operate independently of economic agents' knowledge of that policy and their expectations of the effects of that policy (see Guzzardi 1978, p. 73).

As the following section indicates, the dialectic of resistance and accommodation led Sargent to change his free moves. Rather than seeing vector autoregressions as atheoretical econometrics, he tried to combine them with general equilibrium theory in an attempt to escape observational equivalence and restore conceptual integrity of theory and method. He started interpreting vector autoregressions as a reduced form of a system strictly linked to the deep parameters of state variables. When asked in 1982 whether econometrics without much a priori theory was one process in his type of econometrics, he responded: "That's one line. Chris [Sims] has taken that much further than I have, and I respect that line. The other line is the cross-equation stuff and doing econometrics with new dynamic theory" (Klamer 1983, p. 75). He also said that the large-scale models "must be grounded in optimizing behavior. It's a whole new ball game" (p. 67). I consider in the following section why Sargent did not just relinquish vector autoregressions in the face of these resistances and what was involved in his new ball game. Before doing so, I want to speculate a bit on why atheoretical econometrics did not become a dead end for Sims. The answer lies in his interests. When lines of research become unfathomable, it is not because they are "falsified," but because they are impossible to prosecute given the prior context of a project, or interests, in the framework used here.

Contrary to Sargent, Sims did not see why vector autoregressions had to be combined with general equilibrium theory to give it some structure. According to Sims's (1982b) definition of "structure," "a structural model is one which remains invariant under some specified class of hypothetical interventions, and hence is useful in predicting the effects of such interventions" (p. 332). Furthermore, "whether a model is structural depends on the use to which it is to be put – on what class of interventions is being considered" (p. 332). In Sims's relativistic definition of structure, "a true probability model does not exist. Even in natural sciences, if one really looks close enough, there is no such thing and none of the models can be judged as really objective" (p. 332). In other words, "despite the way we sometimes write, we do not estimate parameters which define the truth" (p. 335). Hence, Sims denied the possibility of constructing universally true models; this seems to guarantee his preference for the atheoretical approach to econometric inquiry. Sims suggested that "econometrics can at least be much more scientific if it grounds its models more closely on the aspects of prior beliefs which economists and users of our analysis really do have in common" (p. 337). Moreover, Sims saw practical usefulness as one of the criteria for determining the scientific legitimacy of econometrics. In his view, this usefulness of econometric modeling lay in forecasting performance. So, "loosely restricted multivariate time series models, though often labeled nonstructural, are for practical purposes structural when the object is forecasting" (p. 332). Rather than wanting conceptual integrity, Sims believed that a true econometric model did not exist and was interested in using forecasting performance as a criterion for appraising models. This explains why Sargent ran into resistances when he tried to use vector autoregressions without theory and why Sims continued on this path without much trouble (and theory).

Sims did not give statistical evidence to support his statement that many identifying restrictions in macroeconomic models were invalid, but did give a theoretical example of a particular continuous time model that was formally unidentified if estimated with discrete data (see Sims 1971a). The trouble was that aggregation over time interrupted Granger noncausality patterns that held for continuous time. These considerations seriously limited the applicability of innovation accounting. Sargent argued:

From the viewpoint of interpreting vector autoregressions that are estimated without imposing restrictions from formal economic theories, it would be desirable if the innovations recovered by a vector autoregression could generally be expected to equal either the random shock to agents' information sets, or else some simply interpretable functions of these random shocks. (Hansen and Sargent 1991c, p. 77)

One important setting in which such a connection does not exist is that of aggregation over time. These concerns led Sims to conclude that the econometrician should view the identifying restrictions as hypotheses to be tested as critically as available data and statistical techniques allowed. It led Sargent on another path, though, as we witness shortly.

3.4   VAR with General Equilibrium Theory

Sargent was trying to combine atheoretical vector autoregressions with "economic" theory. Why did Sargent not abandon vector autoregressions in the face of so many resistances as he had Lévy stable distributions? What was the attraction of vector autoregressions for him? His quest for conceptual integrity of theory and method, for development of a language of applied macroeconomics, and for tractable interpretations of rationality was driven by the use of engineering metaphors. Engineering not only provided the tools of vector autoregressions, but also supplied Sargent with devices for linking these atheoretical constructs with theory. In a foreword to a book by the mathematician Peter Whittle, Sargent (1983) wrote:

[S]tatistical theories of prediction and control have assumed an increasing importance in applied fields, especially in engineering and economics. Among economists, this book has attracted a devoted group of readers and users. One reason for this attraction is aesthetic and resides in elegance, cogency, breadth of scope, and insight with which Whittle treats his subject. A more practical explanation is that the book contains tools and results that have proved to be exceedingly useful in constructing models for understanding dynamic economic phenomena. (p. v)

As the following sections show, Sargent's agents could only have rational expectations in a very restricted environment as a result of Sargent's reliance on engineering metaphors. Before moving on to this discussion, I need to explain how Sargent got there. The first steps consist of the free moves Sargent made in an attempt to salvage vector autoregressions on the method side of conceptual integrity.

One response to the shock waves in the 1970s was to use vector autoregressions to ask what can be learned from data alone prior to any theorizing. The trouble was that, according to Sargent's observational equivalence, one cannot distinguish between two reduced forms of new classical and Keynesian models. This problem might be solved by using different regimes to discriminate between the two hypotheses. Sargent (1976b) hinted at possible solutions to the problem of observational equivalence: "Presumably, by estimating reduced forms for various subperiods or countries across which policy rules differed systematically, light can be shed on what way of writing the reduced form remains invariant. . . . Very little satisfactory evidence has yet been assembled" (p. 637). He also sought to remedy this defect in a joint paper with a graduate student from the University of Minnesota, Salih Neftci. Neftci and Sargent (1978) attempted to use different regimes to discriminate between the two hypotheses. They agreed with Sargent's earlier findings that "it seems impossible to test the natural rate hypothesis on the basis of time-series observations on a single economy operating under a single fixed policy regime and fixed processes for other exogenous variables" (p. 315) and followed up on his suggestion "to test the natural rate hypothesis [by] find[ing] periods across which the policy regimes differ and to test for the invariance of alternative models across regimes" (p. 315).[52]

We find further hints of a new direction in Sargent's work in a paper on vector autoregressions published in the late 1970s. In response to the tidal wave of criticism of vector autoregressions, Sargent (1979b) acknowledged that the "techniques described in this article are still in the early stages of development, so they cannot yet be regarded as having proved themselves useful in a wide variety of contexts" (p. 14); he admitted "at the outset that the models will not be capable of analyzing the range of alternative policy interventions which the standard existing macroeconometric models were designed to analyze" (p. 14). "The reason it is not appropriate is to be found in . . . dynamic economic theory" (p. 13; also see Sargent 1977b, p. 216). For Sargent, the solution was a move back to economic theory, because "the range of uses of these [vector autoregressive] models is more limited than the range of uses that would be possessed by a truly structural simultaneous equation model" (p. 14). Rather than agreeing "that in certain contexts structural estimation is possible and desirable," Sargent (1977b, p. 213) moved to make it the central focus of his research. Given that "[m]acroeconometric models have come under increasing attack from theorists precisely because they do not embody the results of coherent general equilibrium theorizing [and that m]acro models are constructed in an ad hoc, piecemeal fashion without any concern for the consistency relations . . . that general equilibrium theory imposes" (p. 215), one way out was to forget about theory altogether and the other was to try to incorporate general equilibrium theory.

This led Sargent (1979b) to the alternative approach of starting from theory and asking how data must be arranged in order to conform to a priori theoretical conjectures:

This line of argument leads one to ask whether there are alternatives to the standard simultaneous equation modeling procedures that can be used to restrict the dimensionality of the free parameter space in vector autoregressions. . . . One main line is much in the spirit of the classical structural or simultaneous equation procedures. The key idea underlying this work is to estimate structural models . . . but to use identifying restrictions . . . that are motivated by dynamic economic theory. (p. 11)

Faced with resistances to his attempt to find conceptual integrity, Sargent sought to get rid of them by incorporating general equilibrium theory in his framework of rational expectations and vector autoregressions. He believed that the true system was composed of such state variables as taste, technology, and policy, so that a model was structural if its equations were strictly linked to the deep parameters of state variables. In this interpretation, a vector autoregression was a reduced form of a system. The general equilibrium framework imposed full theoretical restrictions on the coefficients in the vector autoregression.[53]

To get rid of observational equivalence, therefore, Sargent adopted Lucas's *general equilibrium theory* approach. This is a *free move* because it promised to restore conceptual integrity. I should note that Sargent's general equilibrium theory was not of the Walrasian variety; instead, he used the representative-agent technique (see, e.g., Hansen and Sargent 1996a, pp. 195–6). While Lucas had used general equilibrium theory almost from the start, it took Sargent until the late 1970s to make the free move in this direction. During that time, he spent a year as a visiting professor at the University of Chicago and took two courses from Lucas.[54] "Lucas pointed out that agents' decision rules . . . are predicted by [general equilibrium] economic theory to vary systematically with changes in the stochastic process facing agents" (Hansen and Sargent 1980, p. 91).[55] The realization of the impact of Lucas's insight gave the final blow to Sargent and Wallace's earlier attempts to combine rational expectations with IS-LM models: "[W]e were stunned into terminating our long standing Minneapolis

Fed research project to design, estimate, and optimally control a Keynesian macroeconometric model" (Sargent 1996a, p. 539).[56] Instead, Lucas and Sargent (1981) suggested, "[E]xisting econometric models can be improved by building dynamic models that are motivated by reference to dynamic economic theory, and which impose cross-equation restrictions characteristic of that theory" (p. xx). These observations led Sargent (1981a) to explore the implications "of a single principle from economic theory. This principle is that people's observed behavior will change when their constraints change" (p. 214; also see Sargent 1987b, p. 1). He restricted "things so that the dynamic economic theory is of the equilibrium variety, with optimizing agents and cleared markets" (p. 214).[57] This would allow him to evaluate the effects of systematic policy changes: "The reason for interpreting time series in this way is practical: potentially it offers the analyst the ability to predict how agents' behavior and the random behavior of market outcomes both will change whenever agents' constraints change, as when policy interventions or other changes in the environment occur" (p. 215).

To satisfy his interest in linking vector autoregressions and general equilibrium theory, Sargent availed himself of the concept of *rational expectations,* because "[r]ational expectations modeling promised to tighten the link between theory and estimation, because the objects produced by the theorizing are exactly the objects in which econometrics is cast" (Hansen and Sargent 1991a, p. 3). Besides, "Lucas and Prescott [had done] much to clarify the nature of rational expectations as an equilibrium concept, and also pointed the way to connecting the theory with observations" (Sargent 1987c, p. 76).[58] Rational expectations modeling resulted in vector autoregressions: "This is an attractive assumption because the solutions of such problems are known to imply that the chosen variables . . . can exhibit serial correlation and cross-serial correlation" (Sargent 1981a, p. 215). Furthermore, because the relevant theory was considered in making the prediction, the problem of infinite regress could be circumvented.

Sargent (1987a) summarized these free moves to general equilibrium theory, vector autoregressions, and rational expectations in the following way:

One of the goals of much recent work in rational expectations economics has been to create models whose equilibria are vector stochastic difference equations. In these models, the outcome of the interaction of a collection of purposeful agents is a stochastic process for, say, prices and quantities, whose evolution can be described by a (vector) stochastic difference equation. . . . One goal of this line of research is to acquire the ability to predict how the equilibrium stochastic process (or difference equation) would change in response to hypothetical changes in particular aspects of the environment confronting the agents in the model. (p. 241)

Why were these moves free? Surely, Sargent was not the only one working on these concepts, was he? Well, what characterizes free moves in our framework is the fact that they are made in an attempt to serve interests. That is why Sargent's moves to general equilibrium theory, vector autoregressions, and rational expectations were free. Sargent thought they would allow him to achieve conceptual integrity of theory and method.

Why did Sargent take such a long time to adopt Lucas's interpretation of rational expectations? After all, they had been colleagues at Carnegie Mellon in the late 1960s when Lucas and Rapping were developing their general equilibrium approach to rational expectations. Lucas recalled:

Tom was at Carnegie for a while. That was his first job when he got out of Harvard. I didn't know him too well then. I'll tell you what happened in those days – it's ridiculous in retrospect. There was a kind of Chicago faction and a non-Chicago faction at Carnegie. Mike Lovell . . . was the non-Chicago leader. . . . When Tom came, I associated him with the anti-Chicago group. I thought he didn't show interest in me. We didn't talk very much during the two years he was there. (Klamer 1983, p. 33)[59]

Sargent remembered:

At first, I learned from Lucas mostly by reading his stuff. I first met Lucas at Carnegie-Mellon, but I was way behind him. I didn't really know what he was up to: I didn't completely understand it. . . . I didn't talk to Lucas very much that year. . . . I remember when Lucas and Rapping were writing their paper. I used to talk to Leonard about it, not Bob. I didn't completely understand what they were up to, I don't think they completely understood fully what it meant either. (Klamer 1983, pp. 60–1)

Interestingly enough, it was Mike Lovell who interested Sargent in rational expectations: "I may mention that the one who put me onto rational expectations wasn't Bob Lucas; it was Mike Lovell. . . . [Mike] put me onto the Muth article" (Klamer 1983, p. 61). However, Sargent (1996a) indicated that though Muth's paper had been widely read and admired, it had not been understood well enough because "[m]ost of us were inadequately trained" (p. 537n).[60] Lucas's general equilibrium interpretation only later made Sargent aware of the force of Muth's insights. Before discussion of the forced moves that were part of these steps, the free moves must be elaborated further.

According to Lucas's critique of econometric policy evaluation, reduced forms were not suitable for policy evaluation. According to Sargent's observational equivalence, one could not distinguish between two reduced forms of new classical and Keynesian models. Additional a priori information promised a way out for Sargent, at least for a little while. These restrictions on the parameters in the reduced-form equation following from the incorporation of general equilibrium theory gave rise to so-called cross-equation restrictions. New classical theory could then be tested by comparing the estimates of the model with restrictions with estimates of the model without restrictions.

This is where Lars Hansen helped Sargent. Hansen graduated from the University of Minnesota, where Sargent was a member of the faculty, in 1978 and subsequently collaborated with Sargent on many papers.[61] According to

Hansen and Sargent (1980, pp. 91–2), the implication of Sargent's observational equivalence and Lucas's observation was that instead of estimating the parameters of decision rules, one should estimate the parameters of agents' objective functions and of the random process that they faced historically. This idea was based on the view that econometric estimates would be secure from the Lucas critique only if the theories used to identify them were grounded in well-specified optimization problems. Vector autoregressions could then be interpreted as the reduced form of a traditional structural model (see, e.g., Monfort and Rabemananjara 1990). Hansen and Sargent argued that untestable restrictions could be imposed if they were derived from a well-articulated economic theory. The execution of such an econometric strategy necessarily involved cross-equation restrictions that connected the parameters of decision rules with the deep parameters of tastes, technologies, and other stochastic environments (see Hansen and Sargent 1980, pp. 91–2, 118; 1982, p. 265; 1983b, p. 387; 1996, p. 20). Hansen and Sargent (1980) even went so far as to situate these cross-equation restrictions at the center of rational expectations: "A hallmark of rational expectations models is that they typically impose restrictions across parameters in agents' decision rules and the parameters of the equations that describe the uncontrollable random processes that agents face passively" (p. 118; also see Hansen and Sargent 1981a, p. 127). However, we did not encounter them in Sargent's econometric interpretation of rational expectations; in fact, these restrictions only appeared once the idea of rational expectations was combined with general equilibrium theory.

Cross-equation restrictions can be produced by considering expectations generated by

$$a(L)x_t = 0 \tag{3.4}$$

that are part of the reduced form

$$y_t = a(\lambda)^{-1}\left[1 + \sum_{j=1}^{r-1}\left(\sum_{k=j+1}^{r}\lambda^{k-j}a_k \right)L^j \right]x_t \tag{3.5}$$

Then, changes in the parameters of the process $\{x_t\}$ will alter the parameters for the solution of y_t. It is this general interdependence that generates cross-equation restrictions (see Appendix 3C). Furthermore, time-series models could provide a statistical framework within which the cross-equation restrictions imposed by theoretical models could be tested. If the policy regime changed, the cross-equation restrictions, which linked the observable behavioral equations to policy variables, would require the coefficients to change in the behavioral equations. The advantages of this approach were that it was a safeguard against the Lucas critique and that it discovered or constructed a stable econometric system. The problem was that it was difficult to carry out successfully as a result of the highly nonlinear nature of the restrictions.

Hansen and Sargent (1996) argued that their goal had been "to create a class of models that makes contact with good dynamic economic theory and with good dynamic econometric theory" (p. 1).[62] This would allow Sargent to achieve conceptual integrity of theory and method and to serve his interests. What is good dynamic economic theory? What is good dynamic econometric theory? For Hansen and Sargent, this was determined when the forced moves further elaborated their free moves to vector autoregressions, general equilibrium theory, and rational expectations. I return to these in the next section, after outlining how Hansen and Sargent's approach also promised to remove the minor resistance regarding Sims's test.

Hansen and Sargent (1980) sought to get rid of the problem that Sims's test provided only sufficient and not necessary conditions for exogeneity: "So failure of n_t to Granger cause x_t is a necessary condition for x_t to be strictly exogenous. It is not a sufficient condition, however. . . . [Hansen and Sargent] develop a statistical test of a stronger sufficient condition" (p. 93). They also developed instrumental variables procedures for situations in which "disturbances are serially correlated and the instrumental variables are not exogenous" (Hansen and Sargent 1982, p. 263).[63]

Whereas Sims concluded that the difficulties encountered in estimating continuous time theoretical models with discrete data should be circumvented by abandoning models altogether, Hansen and Sargent accepted the challenge to defend the conceptual integrity of continuous time models and discrete data. Whereas Sims studied distributed lags, Hansen and Sargent studied the matching up of the moving-average representations.[64] They developed a "machinery [that] supplies an exact, asymptotically efficient procedure for estimating the parameters of the continuous time version of Cagan's model from discrete time data" (Hansen and Sargent 1983a, p. 2).[65] Subsequently, they used "these tools to study the effects of aggregation over time in substantially richer dynamic contexts" (p. 18).[66] The trouble was that predictability in this case required that the stochastic process was mean square differentiable. According to Hansen and Sargent (1991d), whereas "Sims argued that there is a class of economic variables that are best modeled as failing to be mean square differentiable" (p. 107), they asserted that "models typically lead to mean square differentiable endogenous variables, provided that the agent is posited to be facing mean square differentiable forcing processes" (p. 109). They somewhat misrepresented Sims's interests when they tried to enroll him in their project of linking theories and methods.[67] According to Hansen and Sargent (1990), Sims

originated and popularized the use of vector autoregressions especially among macroeconomists. An important use of linear rational expectations models and of recursive competitive equilibrium models has been as a bridge between "theory" and "evidence":

one asks what a particular theoretical structure implies about some or all aspects of a vector autoregression. (p. 3)

In a paper he wrote alone, Sargent (1984) also interpreted Sims's work by using theoretical arguments. Despite the fact that this was an "unauthorized interpretation of Sims" (p. 408n),[68] Sargent argued that dynamic rational expectations theory "can be used as forcefully to support Sims' style of more or less uninterpreted vector autoregressive empirical work as it can be to justify the 'fully interpreted' or structural vector autoregressive empirical work practices by rational expectations econometricians" (p. 408). According to Sargent, "Sims challenges rational expectations econometrics, and does so by appealing to the very same general body of dynamic economic theory that Lucas used" (p. 409). Furthermore, Sims's "forecasting exercises respect the principle of strategic interdependence underlying Lucas' critique, because they never involve hypothesizing an altered strategy for government outside of the sample period" (p. 412). Sargent criticized this view for leaving "no room for improving government policy in the future" (p. 413). Hence, Sargent's "own response to the tensions highlighted by Sims' arguments is to continue along the path of using rational expectations theory and econometrics" (p. 413). Unfortunately, Sargent encountered serious obstructions on this path.

3.5   Resistances to VAR with General Equilibrium Theory

In this section, we return to the question of what Hansen and Sargent meant by good dynamic economic theory and good dynamic econometric theory. They sought to find it through the use of deep parameters and the exploitation of the cross-equation restrictions that a rational expectations model imposes on those parameters. It should first be noted that this was one of two responses to Lucas's critique and Sargent's observational equivalence. The other line of work was to apply the method of moments estimators to estimating the parameters that appear in the Euler equations associated with dynamic optimum problems (see, e.g., Hall 1978; Hansen and Singleton 1982).[69] This approach held the promise of estimating some parameters without the need to estimate (or even to specify) a complete equilibrium model and had the advantage that it was easier to implement than Hansen and Sargent's approach. According to Hansen and Sargent (1991a), however, "[i]ts disadvantages are the restrictive assumptions on unobservables needed to validate the approach, and the fact that even when it is applicable, it does not attempt to estimate the full range of parameters that are typically required to analyze an interesting range of policy interventions" (p. 2). Hence, this approach would not fully satisfy Sargent's interest in conceptual integrity of theory and method. However, this line "caught on more than the first in applied work, undoubtedly mainly because of its ease" (p. 3).

Initially, Sargent could get away with adopting his search for deep parameters and exploitation of cross-equation restrictions by expressing optimism about the prospects of such an approach. In 1981, Lucas and Sargent argued (1981) that "theoretical and econometric methods for doing this are still in the stage of early development. However . . . these developments are proceeding rapidly, so that more and more sophisticated and faithful applications of the decision theory above can soon be expected" (p. xxv). Lucas and Sargent (1979) saw a bright future ahead:

So far, these new theoretical and econometric developments have not been fully integrated, although clearly they are very close, both conceptually and operationally. We consider the best currently existing equilibrium models as prototypes of better, future models which will, we hope, prove of practical use in the formulation of policy. (p. 10)

In his own writing, Sargent (1979b) raised a more cautious note:

While methods for implementing cross-equation restrictions delivered by dynamic theory are now being developed, they are not yet readily available and certainly have not yet proved to be successful in terms of delivering good estimates . . . for vector autoregressions of sizable dimension. Further, there remain many controversial points about what are the most appropriate assumptions for dynamic economic theories. (p. 11)

Unfortunately for Sargent, these controversial points just kept getting more nettlesome.

The trouble for Hansen and Sargent was that they saw *no neoclassical dynamics that commanded much consensus anywhere.* According to Sargent (1987b), "[A]t this moment there is no one widely accepted, all-purpose model" (p. 2; also see, e.g., Day and Eliasson 1986; Phelps et al. 1970). Furthermore, models "have typically been so simplified, and so much has been abstracted, that it is often difficult to take their predictions seriously" (p. 7). These difficulties have caused some critics of rational expectations economics to argue that "the theory becomes a straight jacket rather than a flexible framework for inquiry" (Pesaran and Smith 1992, p. 14).

What, then, did Hansen and Sargent mean by "good dynamic economic theory"? *Convenience* drove the further elaborations of the internal logic of Hansen and Sargent's (1980) free moves to vector autoregressions, general equilibrium theory, and rational expectations: "This paper describes methods for conveniently formulating and estimating dynamic linear econometric models under the hypothesis of rational expectations. An econometrically convenient formula for the cross-equation rational expectations restrictions is derived" (p. 91; also see Hansen and Sargent 1981a, p. 127; 1996, p. 7; Anderson et al. 1996, p. 173; Sargent 1996b, p. 15). Hence, although his agents were supposed to be rational, Sargent alluded to convenience to justify his own search for conceptual integrity. As discussed in more detail later, this convenience had its roots in engineering metaphors.

Having grounded "good dynamic econometric theory" in the engineering tools of vector autoregressions, Hansen and Sargent searched for "good dynamic economic theory" in the engineering theory of recursive dynamics (see, e.g., Hansen and Sargent 1990, p. 3; 1996, p. 1). These recursive competitive models were a special case of general equilibrium models. For Hansen and Sargent (1996), "the theory of recursive competitive equilibria holds out the promise of making much closer contact with econometric theory than did previous formulations of equilibrium theory" (p. 2).[70] General equilibrium models can be represented as choosing $u_0, u_1, \ldots, u_T, x_1, \ldots, x_{T+1}$ to maximize an objective function

$$\{x_{t+1}, x_t, u_t : x_{t+1} \leq g_t(x_t, u_t), u_t \in R^k\} \tag{3.6}$$

subject to

$$G(x_0, u_0, x_1, u_1, \ldots, x_T, u_T, x_{T+1}) \geq 0 \tag{3.7}$$

Recursive competitive equilibria, then, specialize the problem to prevent the need to compute all variables simultaneously. Assuming that $r_t(x_t, u_t)$ is a concave function and that the set $\{x_{t+1}, x_t, u_t : x_{t+1} \leq g_t(x_t, u_t), u_t \in R^k\}$ is convex and compact, we can replace (3.6) and (3.7) with the problem of maximizing by choice of $u_0, u_1, \ldots, u_T, x_1, \ldots, x_{T+1}$ the function

$$r_0(x_0, u_0) + r_1(x_1, u_1) + \cdots + r_T(x_T, u_T) + W_0(x_{T+1}) \tag{3.8}$$

subject to x_0 given and the "transition" equations

$$
\begin{aligned}
x_1 &= g_0(x_0, u_0) \\
x_2 &= g_1(x_1, u_1) \\
&\ \cdot \\
&\ \cdot \\
&\ \cdot \\
x_{T+1} &= g_T(x_T, u_T)
\end{aligned}
\tag{3.9}
$$

Unfortunately for Hansen and Sargent, computational difficulties remained and further restrictions had to be imposed.[71] This led them to restrict their attention to linear control models, a subset of recursive models (see Hansen and Sargent 1996, p. 161).

Using "classical" or "recursive" solution procedures, Hansen and Sargent could then establish

an intimate connection between two superficially different classes of problems: the class of linear-quadratic optimal control problems [on the theory side], and the class of linear least squares prediction and filtering problems [on the method side]. The classes of problems are connected in the sense that to solve each, essentially the same mathematics is used. (Sargent 1988, p. 1; also see Sargent 1983, p. vi)

"Classical" procedures solved the control problem via discrete time-variational methods and provided a solution to the prediction problem by the Wiener–Kolmogorov method (see Appendix 3D).[72] "Recursive" procedures solved the control problem by iterating on the matrix Riccati difference equation and provided a solution to the prediction problem via the Kalman filter (see Appendix 3E).[73] Convenience also drove Hansen and Sargent's (1991g) choice between these two procedures: "The second approach is valuable because it provides a convenient set of algorithms" (p. 55; also see Hansen and Sargent 1981a, p. 151; 1996, p. 161–81).[74] This point is discussed in more detail in the following section along with the fact that the mathematics used to unify economics in these solution procedures was engineering mathematics. Sargent (1987a) acknowledged as much in some instances: "The recursive relation is the foundation of Kalman filtering, a technique widely used by engineers" (p. 228; also see Sargent 1987b, pp. 7-8, 339).[75] How were these engineering techniques further elaborated in the form of *forced moves* when Hansen and Sargent applied them to economics?

On the theory side, the claim that theoretical restrictions in econometric modeling must be derived from individuals' optimizing behavior seriously restricted the range of possible models, mainly as a result of computational considerations and a lack of appropriate methods of statistical estimation. In particular, the optimizing models had to have *linear* constraints with *quadratic* objective functions to get a linear decision rule.[76] In addition, stability had to be assured in infinite-horizon problems through the assumption of *square summability or integrability* (see Anderson et al. 1996, pp. 181–3; Hansen and Sargent 1996, p. 45; Sargent 1987a, pp. 483–6). A further specialization was the assumption that the functions were *time-invariant,* so that the system yielded a set of time-invariant linear difference equations. The focus on conveniently achieving conceptual integrity of theory and method caused Hansen and Sargent (1980) to limit their attention to these equations: "Such setups are attractive because they are ones for which the dynamic stochastic optimization theory is tractable analytically, and because it is convenient for econometric reasons to remain within the well-developed domain of time invariant linear stochastic difference equations" (p. 92; also see Anderson et al. 1996, pp. 173–6; Hansen and Sargent 1996, pp. 54, 293). It is interesting to note that when using vector autoregressions without theory, as indicated in the previous section, Neftci and Sargent (1978) were driven to look for regime changes, that is, periods of noninvariance in the time domain, in their effort to make them work. Yet, when attempting to connect vector autoregressions and general equilibrium theory, Sargent had to posit time invariance in order to make the thing even appear to work. Although these models provided a good approximation in a variety of problems, in a range of important cases they did not.

Lucas and Sargent (1981) argued that "[i]f any success is to be possible, it will clearly involve some boldness in the use of economic theory" (p. xiv). Lack of statistical models was one reason for the adoption of these "bold" linear-quadratic problems, for they conveniently resulted in a linear reduced form (see Hansen and Sargent 1983b, p. 2). Computational limitation was another reason for not adopting a more general model, for there "are no theoretical reasons that most applied work has used linear models, only compelling technical reasons given today's computer technology" (Lucas and Sargent 1979, p. 13). Thus, linear-quadratic functions were not adopted for economic reasons at all.[77] In fact, the first to treat least square regulation along these lines seems to have been George Newton, who was writing about feedback control systems (Newton 1952a, 1952b; Newton, Gould, and Kaiser 1957). Very similar techniques were developed later by a research team of the electrical-engineer-turned-economist Charles Holt and other authors, including Herbert Simon (Holt et al. 1960).

Simon (1991) noted that the team had to make strong assumptions to get the project off the ground and attributed these to satisficing: "[W]e satisficed by finding the optimal policy for a gross approximation to the real world" (p. 167; also see Simon 1979, pp. 504–5; 1982c, p. 113). Simon's comment further illustrates the tightrope Sargent was walking in trying to link convenience and rationality. Simon (1956) also discussed the convenience of this satisficing strategy: "[O]nly a small number of special cases has been brought into the range of convenient, or even feasible, computation" (p. 74). Moreover, Simon (1956) pointed out that a special advantage of linear-quadratic models was that they exhibited certainty equivalence.[78] This is a special property of the linear control problem that follows from the quadratic nature of the objective function and the linear nature of the transition equation. However, it does not characterize stochastic control problems generally (see Sargent 1987b, p. 38).

Certainty equivalence permitted the separation of the maximum problem facing an agent into two parts, an optimization, or control, part and a forecasting part (see Lucas and Sargent 1981, p. xv; Sargent 1987a, p. 396). Furthermore, the optimal control law could be divided into a "feedback" part and a "feedforward" part. Note that this separation was another way of stating that temporal location did not matter in the process. It allowed the solving of the certainty equivalence problem in two steps (see Hansen and Sargent 1996, pp. 81–2). The first stage consisted of solving the deterministic version of the model, and the second step consisted of adding uncertainty (see Hansen and Sargent 1981a, pp. 139, 144–5; 1991a, pp. 8–9; Sargent 1996b, pp. 10–12).[79]

It is interesting to note that Sargent had earlier criticized pre–rational expectations economics for adding uncertainty, as discussed in the previous chapter (see, e.g., Klamer 1983, pp. 63–4). However, his rational expectations economics did not get much further, since it assumed that the decision maker knows the future with certainty even if her environment is in fact stochastic (see Lucas and

Sargent 1981, p. xv). Hence, Sargent's hopes for incorporating uncertainty in economic theory in an attempt to achieve conceptual integrity of theory and method were dashed and he ended up with a very tamed version of randomness, just as his opponents did (see Hansen and Sargent 1996, p. 161).

On the method side, Hansen and Sargent (1981a) initially wanted to combine the feedback–feedforward symmetry with the "classical" solution procedure based on the Wiener–Kolmogorov theory of linear least squares prediction, for "[t]here will be computational and other advantages from pursuing this strategy" (p. 139). This held out the promise of linking theory and method because it allowed the analytical characterization of the cross-equation restrictions necessary to combine rational expectations with vector autoregressions (see Sargent 1983, p. vii; Hansen and Sargent 1991c, p. 46). However, application of these formulas required further restrictions in the form of the assumption of *covariance stationary, linearly indeterministic processes* on the method side of conceptual integrity (see Hansen and Sargent 1981b, p. 256; 1980, pp. 96–7; Sargent 1987a, pp. 242–3; 1983, p. vii; Salemi and Sargent 1979, p. 741).[80]

The main step in linking covariance stationary, linearly indeterministic processes with the Wiener–Kolmogorov prediction theory was Wold's theorem (see Appendices 3D and 3F), which states that a covariance stationary, linearly indeterministic stochastic process has a Wold vector moving average representation (see Hansen and Sargent 1991a, p. 3; 1982, pp. 269–70). However, whereas every linearly indeterministic, covariance stationary process has a moving average representation, not all of them have the autoregressive representation needed to use the Wiener–Kolmogorov forecasting formula for expressing the feedfoward part in terms of information available at the decision date. Hence, the assumption that an *autoregressive representation* exists was the final restriction that had to be imposed (see Sargent 1987a, p. 291).

Kalman filtering provided Hansen and Sargent (1990, pp. 3, 14) with a convenient "recursive" procedure for linking theory and method (see Appendix 3E). In particular, the Kalman filter could be applied to a state-space form of the model to get the innovations representation, which can be directly transformed to yield a vector autoregression for the observables of the system (Hansen and Sargent 1996, p. 129).

After "a brief tour of our 'laboratory' for creating and studying recursive dynamic linear economies" (Hansen and Sargent 1990, p. 34), we are led to ask whether it is indeed "natural to represent the equilibrium of a dynamic rational expectations model in terms of its vector autoregression" (Hansen and Sargent 1991d, p. 77). From covariance stationary, linearly indeterministic processes to Wold's decomposition theorem to moving average representations to autoregressive representations to Wiener–Kolmogorov linear least squares prediction to feedback–feedforward symmetry to Kalman filtering to innovations representations – convenience drove Hansen and Sargent's contributions. While alluding to rationality of agents and optimality of outcomes, Hansen and Sargent were driven to reduce everything to the weak expedient of convenience to justify their own work. Faced with the disarray in economic dynamics, Hansen and Sargent sought to find unity in the use of engineering mathematics, and as a result their agents could have rational expectations only in a very restricted environment. Therefore, continued adherence to vector autoregressions, general equilibrium theory, and rational expectations ended up closing rather than opening doors for them.[81]

Hansen and Sargent (1996) used a market transaction metaphor to justify the large amount of restrictive assumptions they imposed: "This approach purchases the ability rapidly to compute equilibria together with a form of equilibrium that is automatically in the form of a vector autoregression. A cost of the approach is that it does not accommodate many specifications that we would like to be able to analyze" (p. 2; also see p. 280). Where do these costs come from? As we see in the discussion of the use of the cost metaphor by Roll and Sargent in the previous chapter, there is no universal interpretation of the notion of costs. Instead, a reasonable reading of Sargent's language of costs and benefits would be that it gains meaning through his motivation and moves.

Indications that their approach was not catching on were that Hansen and Sargent (1991a) themselves delayed the publication of many of their papers written between 1979 and 1982 and resorted to publishing them in an "underground classics" series in 1991. They started the book with the following disclaimer:

We doubt that the material in this book could be described as "classic," but so much of it has been "underground" for so long that we seized the opportunity to publish it in the "Underground Classics" series. . . . We delayed publishing these papers for one reason or another, mostly because we believed that some of the arguments could be improved or because we were too busy with other projects to put the finishing touches on these papers. (p. 1)

Furthermore, they are still keeping us waiting for the long-promised book that builds on this analysis (see Hansen and Sargent 1990, p. 36n).

3.6   Convenience in Engineering

Sargent was interested in establishing a connection between theory and method; however, he did not pick just any kind of method. Indeed, he chose to concentrate on stochastic processes, which were statistical models that described a system changing over time according to probabilistic laws (see, e.g., Bartlett 1966; Granger 1994; Gigerenzer et al. 1989; Yaglom 1962). In particular, he focused on wide-sense stationary, linear processes with a finite variance and a covariance independent of the point in time that was chosen. He usually added the condition that the mean was constant.[82] Stationarity was an extremely useful property for developing the statistical theory of a process. In a stationary process there was no distinction among past, present, and future; because of this its future statistical properties could in principle be predicted with absolute certainty if the statistical state at any time was known in all details. For stationary processes, time-domain estimation and the frequency-domain approach were not independent and in fact were Fourier transforms of one another.

I should note that this stationarity does not imply complete symmetry between the past and the future, as Hansen and Sargent had thought. In particular, Elliott Sober (1993) established that a system whose expected state changes with time cannot have both a forward-directed translationally invariant probabilistic law and a backward-directed translationally invariant law. For translationally invariant laws, the date at which a temporal interval begins or ends is irrelevant to calculating the probability of the system's state after some fixed amount of time has elapsed. The combination of the ideas of law and probability requires that temporal symmetry be broken when they are taken together. An asymmetry between cause and effect may help to explain why temporally oriented laws are usually forward-directed. The preference for forward-directed laws reflects the assumption that "same cause, same probability of effect" is true, but "same effect, same probability of law" is not. Though this is an important argument, it never filtered into economics, possibly because Sober is a philosopher of biology.

Despite these concerns, stationary stochastic processes are now a modeling tool for a wide variety of scientific disciplines, such as econometrics. The first attempts at a mathematical investigation of probabilistic models leading to the notion of a stochastic process appeared very early in this century. However, the formulation of the corresponding general theory lagged behind by a decade or two. Furthermore, most of the success was confined to the development of a theory of the two most important special cases of random functions, namely, Markov processes – by Kolmogorov – and stationary processes – by Khinchin. In subsequent years, both the theory of Markov processes and the theory of stationary stochastic processes underwent a remarkable development. Kolmogorov was the first to formulate the problem of extrapolating (predicting) and filtering stationary stochastic processes clearly and to give a general formula for the mean square error of the best linear extrapolation of an arbitrary stationary sequence. He showed the possibility of a spectral representation for any arbitrary stationary process. So where is the engineering alluded to so frequently in the previous section?

Many attempts at a practical investigation of stationary stochastic processes occurred in engineering. According to Peter Galison (1994), "it was the mass development and deployment of guided missiles, torpedoes, and antiaircraft fire that centralized the technology to scientists and engineers" (p. 263). Wiener, for example, considered problems similar to those of Kolmogorov and tried to use

them in the building of an antiaircraft predictor aimed at destroying enemy war-
planes during World War II (see Galison 1994). Though this device never
worked, Wiener (1964) did show the practical significance of prediction and filtering for the fields of radio and communications engineering: He wrote that
the operations involved in transmitting messages, "although carried out by electrical or mechanical or other such means, are in no way essentially different
from the operations carried out by the time-series statistician" (p. 2). For Sargent, they also were in no way essentially different from the operations carried
out in the economy. In using these engineering techniques to unify the dispar-
ity in economic dynamics, he ended up with the view of an economy as a trans-
mission of messages.

Some have criticized Wiener for simplifying and making Kolmogorov's general theory somewhat more concrete by diluting the content of Kolmogorov's
general investigations through a focus on a much narrower class of processes
(see, e.g., Bartlett 1966; Yaglom 1962). I should also note that Wiener (1956)
did not think his techniques were particularly useful in economics: "In economics, the so-called econometric science of economic dynamics suffers under
the radical difficulty that the numerical quantities which are put into the dynamics are not well-defined and must be treated as gross statistical estimates.
... Econometrics will never get very far until [certain] steps are taken" (p. 260).
Well, Sargent did take certain steps, but not the ones suggested by Wiener.

As discussed in the previous section, Sargent sought to connect Wiener–
Kolmogorov methods with variational methods through the use of "classical"
solution procedures. Variational methods started a new era in the development
of many branches of physics, most notably mechanics, both classical and quantum, and thermodynamics. Although these methods originated as a study of certain isolated maximum and minimum problems not treatable by the techniques
of elementary calculus, they are at present powerful techniques for the solution
of problems in dynamics. However, the development of these variational principles ironically never aroused much enthusiasm in scientific circles. Instead,
it was merely tolerated as an efficient tool in describing mechanical phenomena. Although the actual solution of differential equations through the use of
variational methods is possible only for a restricted class of problems, it so happens that many important problems of applied engineering belong precisely to
this class. As a result, variational methods have assumed an increasingly important role in the field of engineering.[83]

Wulwick (1990, 1995) criticizes the use of these formalisms by economists
on the grounds that they have not discussed the substantial negative analogies
between the conservation of energy that is central to variational methods and
the theory of economic dynamics (also see Mirowski 1989a). In particular,
economists have not addressed what the analog of energy conservation would
be in an economic system. Moreover, although the conservation of energy has

played an important theoretical role, the conservation of utility has had no theoretical significance. Furthermore, there is no influence of history in conservative systems.

The trouble for Sargent in his attempts to use "classical" procedures was their inability to furnish numerical answers, especially in the analysis of the multistage decision process. In the classical formulation, that entire process was treated as essentially one stage, at the expense of vastly increasing the dimension of the problem. According to Richard Bellman (1957), "The fundamental problem that confronts us is: How can we avoid this multiplication of dimension which stifles analysis and greatly impedes computation?" (p. ix). How can we get a more convenient formulation? Bellman found the answer in the state-space structure, which was to dominate the analysis of stochastic processes. This led him to the creation of the theory of dynamic programming (see Bellman and Dreyfus 1962, p. vii), which is part of "modern" control theory and referred to as "recursive" procedures by Sargent.[84] Optimal control gives equivalent results to variational methods, but it sometimes affords insights into a problem that might be less readily apparent through variational methods. It also applies to problems for which variational methods are not convenient, such as those involving constraints on the derivatives of functions sought. Instead of determining the optimal sequence of decisions from some fixed state of the system as in variational methods, Bellman proposed to determine the optimal decision to be made at any state of the system. Only if we know the latter, Bellman argued, do we understand the intrinsic structure of the solution. This reduced the dimension of the decision that confronts us at any particular stage and made "the problem analytically more tractable and computationally vastly simpler" (Bellman 1957, p. ix). It furnished Sargent with a convenient tool for unifying the disarray in neoclassical economic dynamics and a type of approximation that had the unique mathematical property of monotonicity of convergence.[85]

A systematic development of "classical" optimal control techniques began around 1930 in the United States, where the migration of German scientists in the interwar period, the military problems during the Second World War, and the missile race during the Cold War period gave a substantial boost to the research in this field (see Wulwick 1990, 1995). Control engineering was used to develop power-assisted gun turrets in bombers, guidance systems for acoustic and magnetic torpedoes, and the V weapons. Starting in the late 1950s and early 1960s, optimal control theorists such as Bellman developed the first methods for dynamic optimization based on the time-domain, state-space representation of dynamic systems, which now forms the core of the so-called modern control theory. It was also during this period that the most important applications of optimal control techniques in the American space program took place. In addition, Bellman was a research associate at the RAND Corporation and his research was funded by the U.S. Air Force as part of an investigation of the control of the trajectory of air weapons; his dynamic programming approach was used to analyze the optimal policy for missiles (see Wulwick 1990, 1995).[86]

Control theory is often regarded as a branch of the general subject of systems theory. Systems engineering has been successfully applied to the design of many large-scale engineering systems, including industrial process control systems, factory automation, resource allocation systems, and spacecraft guidance and control systems. Control theory is mostly concerned with the physical behavior of systems. Control may be achieved by means of mechanical, electrical, electromechanical, electronic, and other devices, which should function without direct human intervention or supervision. A classic example of optimal control is the servomechanism problem in which optimal missile trajectories are determined. An application in the field of minimum energy problems is the maximization of range for a given amount of fuel and payload in a rocket mission. Finally, optimal control techniques provided the tools needed to design guidance systems to send satellites into space and to assure a soft landing for a spacecraft. Therefore, in using these methods, Sargent effectively created the metaphor of an economy that can be guided, just as missiles, rockets, and spacecraft can (also see Miller 1994, p. xiii).

Wulwick (1990, 1995) summarizes the limitations of optimal control in economics. In contrast to economists, defense strategists recognized the gap between mathematical and physical models; economists concentrated increasingly on abstraction and formalism rather than the real world. In contrast to optimization in aeronautical engineering, the objective function in economics lacked an empirical counterpart; economists ignored the underpinning of the maximum principle and dynamic programming.

Interestingly enough, Bellman himself referred to economics. In particular, he considered dynamic processes involving two decision makers essentially opposed to each other in their interests. This led him to the discussion of multistage games (see Bellman 1957, p. 283). Hence, Bellman considered game theory more fundamental than general equilibrium theory.[87] How could Sargent hang on to general equilibrium theory while using these metaphors? He could not. In fact, in a review of a game theory book, Sargent (1992) referred to its practitioners as a "tribe" and added, "I write this review as a member of another 'tribe,' one that practices macroeconomics" (p. 665). As is discussed in the next chapter, the internal logic of the free moves to vector autoregressions, rational expectations, and general equilibrium theory eventually caused Sargent to change direction.

Engineering metaphors appeared again with Sargent's attempts to connect optimal control with Kalman filtering. It was not until the late 1950s and early 1960s that the Kalman filter theory was developed to deal with some of the problems associated with Wiener's approach. Whereas Wiener–Kolmogorov prediction theory assumes that the underlying signal and noise processes are stationary, the Kalman filter does not require this stationarity assumption. One reason is that the former approach was developed and thought of in frequency-domain terms, and the latter was developed in time-domain terms. As a result, Wiener filters were implementable with amplifiers and time-invariant network elements such as resistors and capacitors, whereas Kalman filters could be implemented with digital integrated circuit modules. Kalman's analysis of linear filtering was similar to Wiener's in the sense that he stressed engineering applications; like Wiener, he addressed theoretical and practical problems in communication and control engineering. For example, he applied his methods to the role of digital computers in the dynamic optimization of chemical reactors (see, e.g., Kalman and Koepcke 1959; Kalman 1960, p. 36), to the noise voltage produced in a resistor as a result of thermal agitation (see Kalman 1960, p. 39), and to discovery of the optimal estimate of the position and velocity of a particle at the time of the last measurement (see Kalman 1960, p. 43).

As we saw in the previous section, Sargent restricted his focus to linear decision rules and as discussed now, linear systems are particularly important in engineering. Such systems have been under study for a long time, and from several different points of view, in physics, mathematics, and engineering (see, e.g., Anderson and Moore 1979; Kailath 1980; Kwakernaak and Sivan 1972). Although linear systems have been extensively studied since the early 1930s, the frequency-domain techniques used during that time did not specifically exploit the underlying linearity of the systems involved. Moreover, these techniques were unable to analyze the kind of systems that became increasingly important in aerospace and process control in the late 1950s. This fact, plus the importance of time-variant systems and time-domain characteristics in aerospace problems, led to a resurgence of interest, sparked by the work of Bellman and Kalman, in the state-space description of linear systems. For a variety of reasons, the state-space approach has been largely developed in control theory, and not communication theory.

Linear system analysis is important primarily because of its utility, for even though physical systems are never completely linear, a linear model is often appropriate over certain ranges of application. Also, a large body of mathematical theory is available for engineers to use in the analysis of such systems. The range of processes in the "real world" for which linear systems serve as effective models encompasses elementary electrical networks, communications systems, signal processing systems, control systems, and complicated mechanical processes, most notably those that arise in aerospace applications. Input–output linear systems may also be used as models for processes associated with no well-defined concept of what constitutes an internal situation. A great number of the mathematical problems of engineering fit into this category, such as the functioning of an amplifier, a digital computer, and a quantum-mechanical system. When Sargent sought to fit rational expectations economics into this category, a very restricted environment resulted.

Aside from the state-structure representation, the "error-stationary" case has been seen as a useful special case. It applies to situations in which one has an observation history extending from the indefinite past and a horizon for action optimization in the indefinite future in which all those variables that may induce cost can be made jointly stationary. This hypothesis allows the use of Fourier or generating function methods and implies observability and controllability hypotheses. According to Whittle (1983), it "is particularly the economists who have faithfully maintained interest in the stationary approach" (p. xii). How did this come about?

In economics, theory played an ambiguous role in the development of stationary processes during the first few decades of this century (see Klein 1995). On the one hand, microeconomists, or value theorists, expected to find nonstationary processes of convergence and found stationary processes. On the other hand, macroeconomists, or business cycle theorists, expected to find stationary processes and found nonstationary processes. This discrepancy between theory and method spurred the development of methods of detrending and decomposing. Herman Wold showed that all stationary processes could be decomposed into a deterministic and an indeterministic, or stochastic, component. Furthermore, he determined that the indeterministic part could be modeled as autoregressions or moving averages of random disturbances. The beauty of this decomposition was that it secured the application of least squares regression to stationary processes. According to Klein (1995), "If you were a time series person who liked your distributions normal and your regressions ordinary, the stationary process was for you" (p. 1).

The trouble was that the mean value and covariance generating function did not specify the stochastic process uniquely. In response, the assumption of normality was piled on top of that of wide-sense stationarity, because a Gaussian stochastic process was completely defined by its mean value and covariance generating function. Furthermore, for normal random functions, the concepts of stationarity in the wide sense and of stationarity in the strict sense were exactly the same. Moreover, for Gaussian stochastic processes with stationary covariances, the covariance generating function is independent of time and it becomes simple to write down the spectral measure.

Does this explain why Sargent used stationary stochastic processes? We see how convenient they are, but what has not been discussed yet is the flurry of activity in nonstationary random processes (see, e.g., Granger 1994; Treviño 1992). During the 1950s to 1960s, the study of nonstationary processes was invariably regarded simply as a new development within the study of stationary processes, and perforce more or less dependent on traditional "stationary" ideas. During the 1970s to 1980s, however, much research progress was made – enough that this dependence is no longer necessary – and the subject now spans many disciplines. What characterizes these nonstationary processes is that their statistics are not independent of the choice of reference origin and the prevalence of transient behavior. In the time domain, a nonstationary process requires that its statistics be explicit functions of time.

The concept of a nonstationary process is not what would normally be considered an "idealized" type of random behavior, for it does not display a readily discerned "universal structure" or order. In nonstationary theory one can never speak about stochastic phenomena without simultaneously speaking about oneself. In particular, depending on how the phenomena are observed, they appear stationary in some respects and nonstationary in others. Furthermore, nonstationary processes cannot be decomposed easily into a deterministic and an indeterministic part. These considerations render such processes difficult to comprehend, for not all features can be taken into account uniformly. Hence, only a few significant characteristics have to be duly selected for analysis. Because of the more general character of nonstationary random processes, however, the results concerning it are likely to have a much wider field of immediate practical application. Consider the analysis of regime changes. Why would these be characterized by stationary stochastic processes? Many economic time series exhibit rather infrequent volatility bursts at all time scales and their structure can change over time, consistently with nonstationarity.

This recognition was the basis of an attack by Davidson (1982–3, 1988, 1991) on rational expectations economics. He claimed that Sargent's models relied on the assumption of ergodicity and argued that many meaningful economic phenomena were characterized by nonergodicity. Nonstationarity is a sufficient, but not a necessary, condition for nonergodicity. If a process is nonstationary, and if the rates of changes in the distribution functions are not independent of calendar time, then the world is nonergodic. If the economy is a process moving through historical time, then the relevant distributions are time-dependent and the economic process is nonergodic. In a nonergodic world, the future is uncertain in the sense that history and current events cannot provide a reliable statistical guide to future outcomes. Any estimated statistical average, which represents rational expectations, can be persistently and nonsystematically different from the future time averages actually occurring in the economy. If decision makers realize this, Davidson contends, then they will reject the rational expectations taken with respect to the objective distributions functions existing in the current period. He concludes that the possibility of nonergodic economic conditions demonstrates the lack of generality of Sargent's analysis as a general case.

Even the mainstream econometrician Granger (1994), one of Sargent's heroes, moved away from stationary processes: "An assumption of stationarity is often quite unreasonable" (p. 531). Granger is an interesting figure in many respects, for not only did he criticize the assumption of stationarity, he also argued that economists should move away from the linearity assumption, which was originally so central to the idea of Granger causality. Nonlinear models played an important role in modeling economic dynamics during the first part of this century. By the 1960s, however, the profession had largely switched to the linear approach, making use of Slutsky's observation that stable low-order linear stochastic difference equations could generate cyclical processes that mimicked actual business cycles. In this context, three reasons for the dominance of linear stochastic difference equations can be identified (see, e.g., Granger and Teräsvirta 1993): First, nonlinear systems seemed incapable of reproducing the statistical aspects of actual economic time series; second, linear stochastic difference equations had a lot of empirical success; finally, linear or log-linear models were much easier to solve and estimate.

Interest in highly nonlinear models has been stimulated by recent theoretical and experimental work on chaos in natural science. The vast progress in the mathematics of nonlinear systems and the large number of techniques and models available for investigating nonlinear relationships have had an impact on economics. On the theoretical side, how complicated economic dynamics can be even in the most benign environment has become clear. On the empirical side, new tools to detect dependence have been developed. It seems to be generally accepted that the economy is nonlinear, in that major economic variables have nonlinear relationships. This nonlinearity could result because the economy is continually being shocked by small innovations and unforecastable news items that affect decisions, as well as the occasional large unexpected shock. Granger (1994) concluded: "My personal beliefs, which I think are widely shared by other econometricians, are that . . . relationships should be nonlinear, and that the models should be truly stochastic rather than deterministic" (p. 532). Whereas Sargent thought that linear and stationary processes were convenient, Granger argued that nonlinear and truly stochastic processes were easy to use and would constitute an improvement (see Granger 1994, pp. 536, 538). Hence, convenience is in the eye of the beholder. It does not have a universal interpretation, but depends on interests and moves. Although Sargent did not immediately agree with Granger's observations, he eventually did take some steps in the direction of nonstationarity and nonlinearity, as discussed in Chapter 5. Before we get to those, we need to tackle a few more resistances.

3.7   Conclusion

Rational expectations held out the promise of solving the problem of reflexive predictions. Following Sargent's several interpretations of rational expectations, however, we have discovered that these hopes were dashed and that rational expectations closed doors rather than opening them. Two themes are central to the preceding narrative: First, as a result of Sargent's reliance on convenience, his rational expectations agents lived in a very restricted environment. Whereas Sargent claimed that his agents were searching for the rational "this" and the optimal "that," he was driven to reduce everything to the weak expedient of convenience to justify his own work, thereby effectively creating an asymmetry between his agents and him, as is considered in more detail in the following chapter. His own rational expectations were aimed at the lowest common denominator of economists. However, convenience is instrumental, the very opposite of an atemporal law-governed rationality. What would happen if a government ran its monetary policy according to the canons of convenience? Is this not the same as Simon's "satisficing"? The second theme is how Sargent's quest for a more scientific macroeconomics was dominated by engineering conceptions. Accepting the fact that no neoclassical dynamics commanded much consensus anywhere, Sargent sought to create a new common language for economics through the use of engineering metaphors. However, engineers are not theorists; they just want to get the job done in a convenient way. This links the two narratives of this chapter and reminds us of the old chestnut in philosophy that rationality, pushed to its extremes, turns into its opposite.

Inspired by Wallace, Sargent made the free move to IS-LM models that incorporate non-Keynesian assumptions. This setup resulted in the policy ineffectiveness proposition and caused Sargent to change his free moves on the theory side to general equilibrium theory. Inspired by Sims, he chose to focus on vector autoregressions on the method side and was led to accept an econometric interpretation of rational expectations and to attempt to use these econometric insights in the construction of his theoretical models. Several resistances, however, soon caused Sargent to supplement this approach. A minor problem was that Sims's test was a necessary but not a sufficient condition for establishing strict exogeneity. Furthermore, Sargent's analysis of observational equivalence implied that, within any policy regime, there were an infinite number of equally accurate representations of the data. Although these resistances led Sargent to change his free moves, they did not interfere with Sims's interests, for his work would suggest that he was not particularly concerned with conceptual integrity of theory and method. Sargent stuck with vector autoregressions through thick and thin because ultimately they were more convenient than structural estimation. Inspired by Lucas and Hansen, Sargent made the combined free moves to general equilibrium theory, vector autoregressions, and rational expectations. The trouble was that this trio was technically not terribly successful, difficult to implement, and based on controversial assumptions. In particular, it relied on the assumptions of linear-quadratic models, square summability or integrability, and time invariance on the theory side and covariance stationary, linearly indeterministic models on the method side. At first, Sargent considered such setups attractive because they were tractable analytically and because it was convenient for econometric reasons to remain within the well-developed domain of time-invariant linear stochastic different equations. However, the large amount of very stringent conditions did not sit well with Sargent.

In addition, Sargent's analysis relied on apparently outdated engineering techniques, for a new generation of technocrats argued that nonstationary behavior was an important aspect of the economy and that major economic variables have nonlinear relationships. Furthermore, techniques had been developed to analyze nonstationary and nonlinear systems. Moreover, even Granger started advocating these new techniques. Sargent had largely avoided questions about the way in which economic agents make choices when confronted by a perpetually novel and evolving world. This was so, despite the importance of the questions, because his tools and formal models were ill-suited for answering such questions. Forced to confront the limitations to prediction within the rational expectations framework, Sargent eventually moved to a complexity approach to prediction, using insights from the economics workshop he attended at the Santa Fe Institute. The complexity approach presented Sargent with another valid way to do economics, by providing the metaphors and the tools that were needed deal with adaptation and perpetual novelty rather than equilibrium, built-in dynamics rather than statics, open-ended evolution rather than steady states, diverse rather than representative agents, inductive learning rather than deductive logic.

Changes in his environment and the appearance of a few extra resistances were necessary, though, before Sargent took these steps. These developments are the topic of the next chapter.

Appendix 3A: Impulse Response Analysis and Innovation Accounting

Consider the process $\{x_t : t = 1, 2, \ldots\}$ represented by

$$x_{t+1} = Ax_t + Cw_{t+1}, \quad \text{for} \quad t = 0, 1, \ldots \tag{3A.1}$$

where A is an n by n matrix and C is an n by N matrix. Using this expression repeatedly, one can obtain the moving average representation

$$
\begin{aligned}
x_t &= Ax_{t-1} + Cw_t \\
&= A^2 x_{t-2} + ACw_{t-1} + Cw_t \\
&= \left[\sum_{\tau=0}^{t-1} A^\tau Cw_{t-\tau} \right] + A^t x_0
\end{aligned}
\tag{3A.2}
$$

The moving average component of this representation

$$\left[\sum_{\tau=0}^{t-1} A^{\tau} C w_{t-\tau}\right] \tag{3A.3}$$

depicts the response of current and future values of $\{x_t\}$ to an imposition of a random shock w_t and is called the impulse response function (also see Hansen and Sargent 1996, pp. 8–9, 129–60).

Shifting (3A.2) forward in time gives

$$x_{t+j} = \sum_{s=0}^{j-1} A^{S} C w_{t+j-s} + A^{j} x_{t} \tag{3A.4}$$

Projecting both sides of (3A.4) on the information set $\{x_0, w_t, w_{t-1}, \ldots, w_1\}$ results in the optimal j-step ahead prediction

$$E_{t} x_{t+j} = A^{j} x_{t} \tag{3A.5}$$

The j-step ahead prediction error is then represented by

$$x_{t+j} - E_{t} x_{t+j} = \sum_{s=0}^{j-1} A^{S} C w_{t+j-s} \tag{3A.6}$$

The covariance matrix of the j-step ahead prediction error is then given by

$$E(x_{t+j} - E_{t} x_{t+j})(x_{t+j} - E_{t} x_{t+j})' = \sum_{k=0}^{j-1} A^{k} C C' A^{k'} \equiv v_{j} \tag{3A.7}$$

This matrix can be decomposed by using

$$v_{j,\tau} = \sum_{k=0}^{j-1} A^{k} C i_{\tau} i_{\tau}' C' A^{k'} \tag{3A.8}$$

where i_τ is an N-dimensional column vector with a 1 in position τ and 0s elsewhere, and where

$$\sum_{\tau=1}^{N} v_{j,\tau} = v_{j} \tag{3A.9}$$

Innovation accounting, then, relies on the fact that the matrices $\{v_{j,\tau}, \tau = 1, \ldots, N\}$ give an orthogonal decomposition of the covariance matrix (3A.7) of j-step ahead prediction errors into the parts attributable to each of the components $\tau = 1, \ldots, N$ (see Hansen and Sargent 1996, pp. 9–10).

Appendix 3B: Observational Equivalence

In order to understand the possibility of observational equivalence, consider the following example:

$$y_t = \sum_{i=0}^{\infty} a_i m_{t-i} + \sum_{i=1}^{\infty} b_i y_{t-i} + \varepsilon_t \qquad (3B.1a)$$

$$m_t = \sum_{i=1}^{\infty} c_i m_{t-i} + \sum_{i=1}^{\infty} d_i y_{t-i} + u_t \qquad (3B.1b)$$

where the a_i, b_i, c_i, and d_i's are fixed numbers and ε_t and u_t are serially uncorrelated random variables. Substituting lagged y terms, incorporating linear least squares projections, and eliminating infinite errors yield

$$y_t = \sum_{i=0}^{\infty} a_i'(m_{t-i} - E_{t-i-1}m_{t-i}) + \sum_{i=1}^{\infty} b_i' y_{t-i} + \varepsilon_t \qquad (3B.2a)$$

$$m_t = \sum_{i=1}^{\infty} c_i m_{t-i} + \sum_{i=1}^{\infty} d_i y_{t-i} + u_t \qquad (3B.2b)$$

where $E_{t-1}m_t$ is the linear least squares projection of m_t on $m_{t-1}, m_{t-2}, \ldots, y_{t-1}$, $y_{t-2}, \ldots$; a_i', b_i' are fixed numbers; and the c_i, d_i, u_t, and ε_t are identical to those in (3B.1a) and (3B.1b). Since the ε_t, u_t processes are identical in (3B.1a)–(3B.1b) and (3B.2a)–(3B.2b), model (3B.1) is observationally equivalent to model (3B.2); that is, the models fit equally well. If model (3B.1) is invariant under changes in the policy regime, Keynesian policy conclusions follow. If model (3B.2) is invariant across policy regimes, we obtain the strong neutrality results of new classical economics. Hence, reduced forms estimated for a given sampling interval cannot settle the policy-rules controversy (also see Sargent 1976b).

Appendix 3C: Cross-Equation Restrictions

Consider the following difference equation

$$y_t = \lambda y_{t+1} + x_t, \qquad |\lambda| < 1 \qquad (3C.1)$$

where $\{x_t\}$ is a sequence of exponential order less than $1/\lambda$. The unique bounded solution of this equation is given by

$$y_t = \sum_{j=0}^{\infty} \lambda^j x_{t+j} \qquad (3C.2)$$

Representation (3C.2) can be converted to an alternative representation expressing y_t as a function of current and past x's only. Given (3C.2), such a representation in terms of current and past x's can be attained by positing a specific difference equation for $\{x_t\}$ itself, using this difference equation to express x_{t+j} for $j \geq 1$ as functions of $\{x_t, x_{t-1}, \ldots\}$, and then using this difference equation to eliminate x_{t+j} for $j \geq 1$ from (3C.2). For example, suppose that x_t and expectations of x_t, which are set equal in the rational expectations formulation, are governed by the difference equation

$$x_t = \sum_{j=0}^{\infty} a_j x_{t-j} \tag{3C.3}$$

which can be rewritten as

$$a(L)x_t = 0 \tag{3C.4}$$

where $a(L)x_t = (1 - a_1 L - a_2 L^2 - \cdots - a_r L^r)x_t = x_t - a_1 x_{t-1} - a_2 x_{t-2} - \cdots - a_r x_{t-r}$ and the 0s of $a(z)$ exceed $1/\lambda$ in absolute value. Hansen and Sargent (1980) show that the solution of (3C.2) can then be represented as (also see Sargent 1987a, chaps. IX, XI)

$$y_t = a(\lambda)^{-1} \left[1 + \sum_{j=1}^{r-1} \left(\sum_{k=j+1}^{r} \lambda^{k-j} a_k \right) L^j \right] x_t \tag{3C.5}$$

Equations (3C.4) and (3C.5) display the presence of cross-equation restrictions between, on the one hand, the parameters of the process $\{x_t\}$ and, on the other hand, the solution for y_t in terms of $\{x_t, x_{t-1}, \ldots\}$. These restrictions illustrate that models taking representations of a variable like y_t as a function of $\{x_t, x_{t-1}, \ldots\}$ cannot treat them as being invariant with respect to alterations in the difference equations generating the $\{x_t\}$. It is this general interdependence that generates cross-equation restrictions and the failure of invariance.

Appendix 3D: Classical Solution Procedures

Consider the discrete-time control problem, to maximize

$$\lim_{N \to \infty} \sum_{t=0}^{N} \beta^t \left\{ a_t y_t - \frac{1}{2} h y_t^2 - \frac{1}{2} [d(L)y_t]^2 \right\}, \quad h > 0, \quad 0 < \beta < 1 \tag{3D.1}$$

where $d(L) = d_0 + d_1 L + \cdots + d_m L^m$, L is the lag operator, $\{a_t, t = 0, 1, \ldots\}$ is a sequence of exponential order less than $\beta^{-1/2}$, and β is the discount factor. The maximization is subject to the initial conditions for $y_{-1}, y_{-2}, \ldots, y_{-m}$ (for simple examples of this problem, see Sargent 1987a, chap. IX).

Using discrete-time variational methods, the solution to this problem can be shown to be

$$(1 - \lambda_1 L) \cdots (1 - \lambda_m L) y_t = \sum_{k=0}^{m} (\beta \lambda_j)^k a_{t+k} \tag{3D.2}$$

where $\lambda_j = 1/z_j$, $j = 1, \ldots, m$, and z is defined by $[h + d(\beta z^{-1}) d(z)] = 0$, the characteristic equation for the Euler equation.

For prediction purposes, let us rewrite this solution for simplicity as a moving average, covariance stationary process

$$y_t = \sum_{j=0}^{\infty} d_j u_{t-j} \quad \text{or} \quad y_t = d(L) u_t, \qquad d(L) = \sum_{j=0}^{\infty} d_j L^j \tag{3D.3}$$

where $\{u_t\}$ is the sequence of one-step ahead linear least squares forecasting errors (innovations) in predicting y_t as a linear function of $\{y_{t-1}, y_{t-2}, \ldots\}$. Using the Wiener–Kolmogorov prediction formulas, we get the following expression for the k-step ahead linear least squares forecast

$$P_{t-k} y_t = \sum_{j=k}^{\infty} d_j u_{t-j} = \left(\frac{d(L)}{L^k} \right)_+ u_{t-k}$$

$$P_{t-k} y_t = \left(\frac{d(L)}{L^k} \right)_+ \frac{1}{d(L)} y_{t-k} \tag{3D.4}$$

where $(\ )_+$ means "ignore negative powers of L" (for the complete derivation, see Sargent 1987a, pp. 204–7, 290–4).

Appendix 3E: Recursive Solution Procedures

The linear-quadratic optimal control problem has the form

$$\max_{\{u_t\}} - E \sum_{t=0}^{\infty} \beta^t [x'_t R x_t + u'_t Q u_t + 2u'_t W x_t], \qquad 0 < \beta < 1 \tag{3E.1}$$

subject to

$$x_{t+1} = A x_t + B u_t + C w_{t+1}, \qquad t \geq 0 \tag{3E.2}$$

where $\{w_{t+1}\}$ is a vector white noise, x_t is a vector of state variables, and u_t is a vector of control variables; the matrices R, Q, and W are conformable with the objects they multiply. The maximization is subject to the requirement that u_t be chosen to be a function of information known at t, namely, $\{x_t, x_{t-1}, \ldots, x_0, u_{t-1}, \ldots, u_0\}$.

Iterating on the matrix Riccati difference equation and using the optimal control law given by $u_t = -Fx_t$, the equilibrium for this problem can be shown to have the so-called state-space representation[88]

$$x_{t+1} = A^0 x_t + C w_{t+1}$$
$$y_t = G x_t + v_t \tag{3E.3}$$

where $A^0 = A - BF$, v_t is a martingale difference sequence of measurement errors, some or all of the variables in x_t are not observable, and the y_t process is observable and representable as a vector autoregression of the form

$$y_t = E[y_t | y_{t-1}, y_{t-2}, \ldots] + a_t \tag{3E.4}$$

where $E[y_t | y_{t-1}, \ldots]$ is the linear least squares estimator of y_t based on the conditioning information $[y_t, y_{t-1}, \ldots]$ and a_t is a least squares residual that satisfies $E[a_t y'_{t-j}] = 0$ for all $j \geq 0$.

For prediction purposes, the state-space representation can be converted into the following innovations representation

$$\hat{x}_{t+1} = A^0 \hat{x}_t + K a_t$$
$$y_t = G \hat{x}_t + a_t \tag{3E.5}$$

where $\hat{x}_t = \hat{E}[x_t | y_{t-1}, y_{t-2}, \ldots, y_0, \hat{x}_0]$, K is a matrix to be determined, and $a_t = y_t - \hat{E}[y_t | y_{t-1}, y_{t-2}, \ldots, y_0, \hat{x}_0]$. Using the Kalman filter technique, K can be shown to satisfy

$$K = A^0 \Sigma G' (G \Sigma G' + E v_t v'_t)^{-1} \tag{3E.6}$$

where the so-called matrix Riccati difference equation for Σ satisfies

$$\Sigma = A \Sigma A' + CC' - A \Sigma G' (G \Sigma G' + E v_t v'_t)^{-1} G \Sigma A' \tag{3E.7}$$

under a set of assumptions that are typically met (for the complete derivation, see Hansen and Sargent 1990, pp. 13–15).

Appendix 3F: Covariance Stationary, Linearly Indeterministic Processes

The process $\{x_t\}$ is covariance stationary (in the wide sense) if Ex_t is independent of t and $E[(x_t - Ex_t)(x_s - Ex_s)]$ depends only on $t - s$. Assume for simplicity that $Ex_t = 0$. Following from Wold's decomposition theorem, the process can be written as

$$x_t = \sum_{j=0}^{\infty} d_j \varepsilon_{t-j} + \eta_t \tag{3F.1}$$

where $d_0 = 1$ and where $\sum_{j=0}^{\infty} d_j^2 < \infty$, $E\varepsilon_t^2 = \sigma^2 \geq 0$, $E\varepsilon_t \varepsilon_s = 0$ for $t \neq s$, $E\varepsilon_t = 0$, and $E\eta_t \varepsilon_s = 0$ for all t and s; and $\{\eta_t\}$ is a process that can be predicted arbitrarily well by a linear function of only past values of x_t: That is, η_t is linearly indeterministic.

When x_t is purely linearly indeterministic, η_t can be removed, and x_t has the moving average representation

$$x_t = \sum_{j=0}^{\infty} d_j \varepsilon_{t-j} \quad \text{or} \quad x_t = d(L)\varepsilon_t, \qquad d(L) = \sum_{j=0}^{\infty} d_j L^j \tag{3F.2}$$

Under further restrictions, x_t also has the autoregressive representation

$$a(L)x_t = \varepsilon_t, \qquad a(L) = a_0 - \sum_{j=1}^{\infty} a_j L^j \tag{3F.3}$$

required for the application of the Wiener–Kolmogorov prediction formulas (for the complete derivation, see Sargent 1987a, pp. 285–92).

CHAPTER 4

Accommodating Symmetry

Tyger Tyger, burning bright,
In the forests of the night;
What immortal hand or eye,
Could frame thy fearful symmetry?

William Blake, *The Tyger*

Symmetry is a deep epistemological problem for the social sciences. If social scientists are asymmetric with their objects of study, then how can they provide an intimate view? And on what is their privileged position based? If social scientists are symmetric with their objects of study, then how can they provide a cool assessment? And why would we take their word over that of the objects of study? This chapter discusses how in the early to mid-1980s Sargent was confronted by the paradoxical nature of symmetry as a result of his eventual interpretation of rational expectations as individual rationality and mutual consistency of perceptions. Section 4.1 gives a few examples of discussions of symmetry in some social sciences. Sargent's attempts at dealing with the symmetry that followed from his combined free moves of vector autoregressions, general equilibrium theory, and rational expectations are considered in section 4.2. Later sections shed some light on Sargent's moves: In particular, section 4.3 sets Sargent's saga in a bigger perspective by appealing to ideas from physics and philosophy. In section 4.4, the view is widened further in a discussion of findings from science studies, which are also used to provide an insight into my perspective.

4.1   Symmetry in Some Social Sciences

Symmetry is a vast topic and opens up fascinating horizons. Readings of sameness and difference are a major mode of scientific discourse, but knowing where extensions of symmetry must permanently halt is an impossible task. If everything were symmetric, there would be no difference or change, and nothing to explain. If nothing is symmetric, then there are no generalizations to be made at all.

Symmetry is particularly troubling for social scientists. If they and the agents

99

they study are truly distinct, then social scientists can only claim some kind of epistemic privilege in understanding the agents' quandaries more deeply than they do themselves by using some criteria of superiority. Where do these criteria come from? If, on the other hand, social scientists and the agents they study are not distinct, their interdependence suggests that the social scientists' research processes assume (at least part of) the answers they set out to find. And if the social scientists are able to reproduce the agents' reasoning in their own terms, then why should one take their word over the agents'? Thus, social scientists' voices either undermine their own assertions or become indistinguishable from the voices they wish to observe. If the agents are unintelligible, then how come social scientists can make sense out of them? If the agents are intelligible, then why would we listen to social scientists? We are all, sociologists, anthropologists, experimental psychologists, and economists alike, in the same boat on the stormy sea of symmetry. Understanding involves navigating perilously between the Scylla and Charybdis of sweeping sameness and irreducible difference.

The subversive nature of the symmetry postulate is indicative of tensions at the heart of social science over the relationships among observation, observer, and observed. Most reflexive attempts to assign sameness and difference through symmetries lead to infinite regress. The problem of establishing a symmetric or asymmetric relationship between the analyst and the actor is one of the hottest areas of controversy in sociology of scientific knowledge, as is discussed in section 4.4.[1] Similar explorations of symmetry can be found in anthropology, in particular the ethnographic approach (see Geertz 1988). Anthropologists try to be both symmetric and asymmetric with their objects of study in their negotiations between "being there" among subjects and "being here" among scholars. While "being there," anthropologists make themselves symmetric with their objects of study. In order to give an intimate view of their subjects, they must truly understand them; however, this provokes charges of impressionism. While "being here," anthropologists make themselves asymmetric with their objects of study. In order to create a scientific text from their experiences, they need to give a cool assessment; however, this raises charges of insensitivity. The challenge of being both symmetric and asymmetric at the same time has led to a loss of confidence in the achievements of anthropology.

The current crisis in anthropology is a result of the fact that both the world that anthropologists study and the one that they study it from have changed. The energies that created anthropology were connected with both the colonial expansion and the belief in the powers of science. However, these foundations were severely shaken by decolonization and a general loss of faith in scientism. One response has been a radically factualist approach involving extended descriptions or lengthy theoretical discussions; another has been a radically introversive approach in which anthropologists openly worry about these issues and introduce themselves into the text. Unfortunately, none of these responses escapes the paradoxes called forth by symmetry.

Next, the discipline of experimental psychology has been built on asymmetry between experimenters and subjects. Though it started with a symmetric relationship between them during the first half century of its existence, it moved to an asymmetric relationship toward the end of the nineteenth century (see Danziger 1985, 1987, 1988, 1990). This switch took place in the move from the "Leipzig model" to the "Paris model" to the "American model." In the so-called Leipzig model, which emerged in the context of collaborative research seminars to study aspects of normal cognition, experimenter and subject roles were interchangeable. In fact, the subject function had a higher status than the experimenter function. In the Paris model, which emerged in the context of medical research to study abnormal functioning through the use of experimental hypnosis, there was no reciprocity between experimenter and subject roles. Furthermore, the role of the lay subjects, who were generally female, was subordinate to the role of the mostly male scientists. The problem with both models is that they were unable to establish a kind of knowledge about human beings that would be ahistorical and universal. In the American model, which emerged in the context of educational and military administration around the turn of the century to study the distribution of psychological characteristics in populations, experimental subjects played an anonymous role and the experimenter was interested in the aggregate data to be obtained from many subjects.

With the switched structure of relationships from superior subjects to superior experimenters to anonymous subjects, experimental psychology changed its focus from individual minds to mass minds. At the same time, it became more focused on rationalizing administrative decisions than increasing psychological knowledge. A similar use of asymmetry to build professional recognition and provide practical applications can be found in elements of twentieth-century economics. Devastated by the Great Depression, econometricians started using standard statistical methods developed for the analysis of laboratory experiments in an attempt to build models of entire economies populated with anonymous agents. The goal was to rationalize and design effective policies for changing economic systems. In this endeavor, the government was imagined to behave precisely as an agent with rational expectations. It was not until the 1950s that expectations of the agents were taken into account in the form of the adaptive expectations hypothesis. For nearly two decades, agents were postulated to rely on mechanistic backward-looking extrapolative rules in which they used information on past forecasting errors to revise current expectations.

As indicated in the previous chapter, structural estimation came under severe attack during the 1970s. At the same time, the adaptive expectations hypothesis was being criticized for overlooking the capacity of people to learn from experience. It produced models that presumed to forecast better than agents, because it allowed individuals to make systematic forecasting errors period after period. Sargent (1996a) looked back at this work as a "memorial plaque to the Keynesian tradition in which we had been trained to work" (p. 539). Some rational expectations economists responded by developing models in which the agents were on an equal footing with economists and governments. Though Sargent welcomed this development, he was also aware of the paradoxical nature of symmetry: "There is a logical difficulty in using a rational expectations model to give advice, stemming from the self-referential aspect of the model that threatens to absorb the economic advisor into the model" (Sargent 1987c, p. 78). And: "The dynamic systems under study are full of self-referential aspects, which threaten to draw the analyst into the system" (Sargent 1987a, p. 436).[2] This leads us into a discussion of Sargent's symmetry saga.

4.2   Sargent's Symmetry Saga

In the early to mid-1980s, Sargent was surrounded by economists using the concept of rational expectations, taking as their point of departure the idea that individuals should not make systematic errors. Rational expectations contributed the insight that agents were not stupid: that they learned from their mistakes and drew intelligent inferences about the future from what was happening around them. The interpretation of the concept of rational expectations differed among its proponents, and even some individual economists changed their renditions. Whereas the first advocates of the hypothesis of rational expectations in econometrics were seeking methods for restricting distributed lags, in the late 1970s the focus of attention shifted to restricting vector autoregressions.

What did Sargent make of all this? On the econometric side, he initially chose to take time-series econometrics as given in his attempt to find conceptual integrity between theory and method. As discussed in Chapter 2, he focused on restricting the parameters of lag distributions by using an econometrically motivated interpretation of rational expectations according to which agents use the same statistical models as econometricians. As we saw in the previous chapter, Sargent subsequently focused his attention on restricting *vector autoregressions*. As far as economic theory was concerned, he signed on to Lucas's *general equilibrium theory* approach. To satisfy his interest in linking vector autoregressions and general equilibrium theory, he availed himself of the concept of *rational expectations*. The previous chapter elaborates on the engineering roots of these free moves; this chapter focuses on further forced moves and resistances that followed from these free moves.

Before doing so, I would like to make two brief remarks about Sargent's justification of his free moves. First, as we have seen in the previous chapter, Sargent argued that the conceptual integrity of theory and method following from his free moves would ultimately allow prediction. Second, the free moves can be seen as related to each other; for example, Sargent identified a link between general equilibrium theory and rational expectations. When "rationally" reconstructing his own history in an interview, Sargent said: "The force of rational expectations is that it imposes a general equilibrium discipline. In order to figure out people's expectations you had to assume consistency" (Klamer 1983, p. 66).[3] When "rationally" reconstructing the history of rational expectations theory in a textbook, Sargent (1987a) inverted the direction of causation by arguing that the general equilibrium discipline, or more specifically intertemporal optimization, led to rational expectations:

From the viewpoint of this long line of research, exploring the implications of rational expectations was an inevitable step. The very same reasons that convinced economists that it is a good idea to analyze investment, consumption, and portfolio decisions by assuming expected utility maximizing agents who solve rich intertemporal problems, also commended the idea that agents would form their expectations optimally, i.e., "rationally." (p. xxi)[4]

Furthermore, Sargent (1996a) asserted that large-scale econometric models gave rise to both general equilibrium models and rational expectations macroeconomics.[5] Regarding general equilibrium models, he wrote, "The stage had been set for general equilibrium models by the triumph of simultaneous equations" (p. 536); of rational expectations economics, he said: "I could construct an argument that rational expectations macroeconomics is the logical, continuous consequence of what people like Koopmans and Hurwicz and other people, who founded the econometric techniques underlying Keynesian models, had in mind" (Klamer 1983, p. 64).[6] Interestingly enough, the downfall of these econometric models led to the rise of vector autoregressions, as already discussed in the previous chapter. In addition, Sargent has argued that Keynesian macroeconometric models were "overturned by the application of rational expectations" (Sargent in Jordan et al. 1993, p. 210). I return to these stories of the relationship between vector autoregressions, general equilibrium theory, and rational expectations in section 4.4.[7]

In his symmetry saga, Sargent really wanted economists and econometricians to be "alike" in many ways, which can be identified with being symmetric. According to Sargent (1993), in "constructing our models of economic agents, economists often describe their beliefs about the dynamics of the environment in terms of a vector autoregression. We use vector autoregressions to formulate our own forecasting problems, and often model economic actors as doing the same" (p. 39). What does symmetry between economists and econometricians signify? And what does it mean for rational agents not to make systematic errors? This section argues that there is *symmetry among agents, economists, and econometricians* according to the rendition of rational expectations that follows as a *forced move*.

4.2.1   *Subplot of Symmetry in General Equilibrium Theory*

Since general equilibrium theory needs symmetric actors, Sargent's free move to general equilibrium theory involved an a priori bias toward this species of symmetry. Sargent could make use of this notion in his extension of symmetry between economists and econometricians. There are three pieces of evidence in making the case that neoclassical theory has always had trouble with distinctly differentiated actors. First, consider *Edgeworth's cloning argument.* Edgeworth (1881) made his most fundamental and original contribution in the analysis of exchange. He introduced as a fundamental concept the contract curve, defined as the set of all those allocations of goods to individuals that cannot be improved for any individual without making it worse for at least one other individual. He pointed out that a free bargaining process will always lead to some point on the contract curve, which must be at least as good as the no-trade point. This restricts the final outcome to what Edgeworth called the "available portion" and what became known as the "core" in the era of game theory.

The question is at which point in the core the negotiating process will eventually settle. Edgeworth started with the idea that exchange between single traders is, to some extent, indeterminate, whereas exchange among numerous buyers and sellers in a competitive market is determinate.[8] Generally, there will be other points in the core than just the market equilibrium. However, if we allow the economy to grow by increasing the number of agents, we will have more possible coalitions and hence more possibilities for improvement. Edgeworth, following Cournot's lead, proposed to begin with bilateral monopoly and work his way toward perfect competition.[9] This was his famous "recontracting" process, which is based on the suspicion that the core might shrink as the economy grows. However, this process cannot handle distinctly differentiated agents. The core is a subset of the allocations space, and thus as the economy grows the core keeps changing dimension. This led Edgeworth to limit himself to a particularly simple type of growth in which the number of types of agents stays constant. Thus, large economies just have more agents of each type.

Next, consider the *Sonnenschein–Debreu–Mantel result.*[10] In 1972, Sonnenschein (1972) considered the restrictions imposed on the structure of aggregate demand functions; in 1974, Debreu (1974) continued this line of work. Under standard assumptions on the individual consumers, like strict convexity and monotonicity of preferences, so that each agent is characterized by textbook indifference curves and a positive bundle of endowments of all goods, we can derive an excess demand curve for each individual. Summing over all individuals, of whom it is assumed that there are only a finite number, gives the excess demand curve for society as a whole. Under certain not-very-restrictive conditions, three properties will carry over from the individual's excess demand curve to the aggregate demand curve: continuity, a value of total excess demand that must equal 0 at all prices, and excess demand that is homogeneous of degree 0.

However, Sonnenschein and Debreu found that these three properties are the only properties that carry over from the individual to the aggregate demand function. In particular, the weak axiom of revealed preference (WARP) may not be satisfied at the aggregate level. Yet, if we are to obtain uniqueness and stability of equilibria, some such restrictions must be imposed. Hence, if WARP is imposed on aggregate excess demands, the economy is presumed to act as if it were just one big consumer. This line of work did not remain isolated, and research by Mantel (1976) showed that the same situation obtains even if the class of admissible preferences is restricted even further. Now if the behavior of the economy could be represented as that of a representative agent or a number of identical agents, the situation might be saved, since textbook individual excess demand functions do have unique and stable equilibria.

I close my case by considering the fact that general equilibrium theory does not successfully apply to an economy that is fully *specialized* and in which the possibility of self-sufficiency is the exception rather than the rule.[11] Again we witness a move away from distinctly differentiated actors. When not every individual in the economy is endowed with sufficient quantities of all commodities required for subsistence, exchange is a necessity for participants' survival. Since the magnitude of equilibrium prices cannot be prejudged, subsistence might not be possible for all agents. The approach taken in existence proofs of general equilibrium before 1975 was basically to remove those agents who are specialized and who need the market to trade into their consumption sets from further consideration, which means that the economy is not specialized. Nevertheless, even for an economy of self-subsistent individuals, existence could not be shown without further assumptions because the possibility of 0 prices precluded a successful demonstration of continuous demand. The continuity problem was remedied by one of two assumptions that further reduce the differences among agents: The interiority assumption increases the endowments of all goods to levels exceeding even those minimally required for self-subsistence; the irreducibility assumption is aimed at securing the use of more realistic, but still self-subsistent, endowments.

Some work after 1975 gave existence proofs for economies that are to a certain extent specialized (see Rizvi 1991). However, rather than supposing self-subsistence, this line of research assumed that goods produced by firms were included in what agents may supply, thus forcing a symmetry between an individual's sources of income and the physical goods or services he or she is able to supply. This is clearly not legitimate, because rights to receive a share in the profits of a firm are not the same as the right to dispose of the same share of the firm's physical plant and inventory. Furthermore, the existence proof now requires a stronger irreducibility assumption, as the links among individuals must not only be present, but also be strong enough to allow for high enough prices.

It seems fair to conclude that there

is a symmetry to the general equilibrium model, in the way that all agents enter the model individually motivated by self-interest (not as members of distinct classes motivated by class interests), and simultaneously, so that no agent acts prior to any other on a given market (e.g., by setting prices). If workers' subsistence were not assumed, for example, that would break the symmetry; workers [sic] income would have to be guaranteed first, otherwise demand would (discontinuously) collapse. (Geanakoplos 1989, p. 50)

Now, if there is no distinct difference among agents in general equilibrium theory, how could economists and econometricians be different in knowing more than the agents?

4.2.2   Picking up the Plot of Sargent's Saga Again

This is where Sargent enters the stage again, for he attempted to satisfy his interest in conceptual integrity, implying symmetry between economists and econometricians, with the free move toward general equilibrium theory. The intricate interplay of his interest and the a priori bias toward symmetry among the agents in general equilibrium theory led him to complete the picture of symmetry among agents, economists, and econometricians. Janssen (1993), for instance, argues: "[I]ndividual rational price expectations coincide [with the rational expectations hypothesis] price expectation only if all individual agents expect the average price expectation to conform [with the rational expectations hypothesis]" (p. 140). This is a forced move in our framework because it followed from the complex interaction of Sargent's interest in conceptual integrity and the free move toward general equilibrium theory. Correspondingly, expectations are rational when they depend, in the proper way, on the same things that economic theory says actually determine that variable. A collection of agents is solving the same optimum problems by using the relevant economic theory and the solution of each agent is consistent with the solution of other agents. Econometric methods can then be used to estimate the vector autoregressions that result from this economic model.

According to this rendition of rational expectations, agents do not make any systematic errors because they are symmetric with economists and econometricians. Sargent was quite happy with this forced move, because he really wanted everyone to be alike. According to Sargent (1993):

The idea of rational expectations is . . . sometimes said to embody the idea that economists and the agents they are modeling should be placed on an equal footing: the agents in the model should be able to forecast and profit-maximize and utility-maximize as well as the economist – or should we say econometrician – who constructed the model. (p. 21)[12]

Or: "The concept of a rational expectations competitive equilibrium . . . has the attractive property that . . . [the agents] in the model forecast . . . as well as the economist who is modeling them" (Sargent 1987a, p. 411).

The story continues as symmetry among agents, economists, and econometricians calls forth other *forced moves,* which highlight the emergence of *resistances.* These moves are forced because Sargent did not make them in a direct attempt to serve his interest in conceptual integrity. Even though he wanted to treat the individuals as interchangeable, they had to differ in the complex setting of his free moves. Sargent explicitly acknowledged the emergence of three resistances in the form of forced moves: First, if there is symmetry among the agents, then there is no reason for them to trade with each other, even if they possess different information. Second, agents and econometricians have to be different in order to justify the error term. Furthermore, as we saw in the previous chapter, while Sargent depended heavily on convenience, his agents were supposed to be fully rational. Third, asymmetric actors are necessary for the concept of policy recommendations to make sense. A fourth resistance, which is not mentioned by Sargent, deals with the problem of conceptualizing learning if agents are thought to be symmetric with econometricians. This one is closely linked to the no-trade theorems and error term justification, as we witness shortly. Finally, Sargent's changed stance in the debate on seasonal adjustment illustrates how eventually the resistances jointly transformed his entire program.[13] I discuss these five further consequences one at a time.

If there is no distinct difference among the agents, then how can there be trade among them? Could it be, following a line of research started by Lucas (1972a), that equilibrium probability beliefs differ and that agents actually trade on the basis of this different information? Unfortunately, this will not work, since a series of *no-trade* theorems overrule this commonsense intuition (see Hakansson, Kunkel, and Ohlson 1982; Milgrom and Stokey 1982; Rubinstein 1975; Tirole 1982; Varian 1987). Hence, the symmetry picture does not allow trade. Instead of there being a hive of activity and exchange, Tirole (1982) proved that a sharp no-trade theorem characterizes rational expectations equilibria. Consider a purely speculative market, meaning that the aggregate monetary gain is 0 and that insurance plays no role. When it is common knowledge that traders are risk-averse, are rational, and have the same prior and that the market clears, then it is also common knowledge that a trader's expected monetary gain given her information must be positive in order for her to be willing to trade. In other words, if one agent has information that induces her to want to trade at the current asset price, then other rational agents would be unwilling to trade with her, because they realize that she must have superior information. The equilibrium market price fully reveals everybody's private information at zero trades for all traders. Eventually, Sargent (1993) acknowledged this resistance: "The remarkable no-trade outcome works the rational expectations hypothesis very

hard. This is revealed clearly in Tirole's proof, which exploits elementary properties of the (commonly believed) probability distribution function determined
by a rational expectations equilibrium" (p. 113; also see p. 25).[14]

Hence, in order to examine models with different equilibrium beliefs and
nonzero trading volume, the only solution is to consider models that lack one of
the necessary hypotheses for these no-trade theorems. For Sargent (1993), this
would involve dropping some of his free moves or ignoring the forced move in
the direction of symmetry: "To explain volume data from financial markets, one
needs a model for which the no-trade theorem fails to hold. For rational expectations models, it has proved very difficult to produce a compelling rational expectations model that breaks the no-trade theorem" (p. 25). First, there may be
some risk-loving or irrational traders; the problem with pursuing this approach
lies in deciding what kinds of irrational behavior are plausible. Second, insurance and diversification considerations may play a significant role. However,
after a single round of trading based on hedging and insurance considerations,
there is no further reason to trade when new information arrives for exactly the
same reasons described by Tirole: In a market of rational individuals there
would be no one with whom to trade. Third, agents may have different prior beliefs. Now, if differences in prior beliefs can generate trade, then these differences in belief cannot be due to information as such, but rather can only be pure
differences in opinion. Allowing for differences of opinion in this sense can be
viewed as allowing for a certain kind of irrational agents.

Even if Lucas's commonsense intuition that differences in information are
the source of trading volume were correct, other resistances in the form of
forced moves would arise on Sargent's path to satisfying his interests. The reason is that economists and econometricians are continually searching for data,
theories, techniques, models, and methods. Now, when agents are symmetric
with econometricians, they use econometric tools that are not equipped to incorporate *information gathering* and do not allow Sargent to maintain his symmetry structure. These methods are in fact a hybrid of theories that theoretical
statisticians regard as distinct and even incompatible: Fisher's theory of null
hypothesis testing, supplemented by concepts from Neyman and Pearson and
sometimes by Bayesian interpretations. Driven by the hope of mechanizing inference and testing, some of the controversies within statistics proper have been
disregarded by some econometricians.

Econometric metaphors of reasoning possess a blind spot for the process of
information search and errors made in information collecting. First, econometric theories of inference and hypothesis testing are applied after the data have
been collected and do not start until the variables and numbers needed for the
formulas are available. Second, they are not concerned with the preceding
measurement process or with the search processes to determine what the relevant information is and how to look for it. In the framework of econometric

problems, thinking means mental work on suitably prepackaged information.[15] If econometrics is not a theory of learning or inductive inference, then how can it be a theory of the economic actor? Are there any tools that allow the agents to search for information "like scientists"? As we see in the next chapter, Sargent eventually tried to remove this resistance by appealing to some techniques developed by artificial intelligence experts. Instead of getting wrapped up in another story of free and forced moves, I now comment on the problem of aggregation over time before moving on to other hurdles on Sargent's track.

Hansen and Sargent, in addition, acknowledged an asymmetry between econometricians and agents in their papers on the so-called aliasing problem (see Hansen and Sargent 1983b, 1991f, 1995b). This problem occurs because the actions by the agents result in a continuous time process that is observed with discrete time data.[16] In other words, there is only a discrete time record of agents acting in continuous time. According to Hansen and Sargent (1983b): "It is a well known result . . . that the continuous time spectral density function cannot, in general, be inferred from equispaced discrete time observations" (p. 377). This identification problem bears some resemblance to the observational equivalence problem discussed in the previous chapter, where the problem is associated with linking vector autoregressions to underlying reduced forms. The problem here is connected with linking discrete time observations to an underlying continuous time process. Hansen and Sargent sought to solve the aliasing problem by specifying a particular type of density matrix and using cross-equation restrictions. They concluded, "The assumption of rational expectations often provides enough identifying information to infer a unique continuous time model from discrete time data" (Hansen and Sargent 1995b, p. 4). It is interesting to note the paradox that under the interpretation of rational expectations in this chapter, there is symmetry between agents and econometricians, implying that the aliasing problem would not occur.

Next, consider how *error term justification* obstructed Sargent's path. He thought that the combined free moves would deliver a tightened link between the determinism of economic theory and the randomness of econometrics, because subsumed within them are "explicit models of the various sources of 'disturbances' or errors in economic relations, aspects of econometric models that drive estimation and inference, but about which pre-rational expectations (mostly non-stochastic) macroeconomic theories had typically been silent" (Hansen and Sargent 1991a, p. 2). The reason is that this

modeling strategy virtually forces the researcher to think about the sources and interpretations of the error terms in the stochastic equations that he fits. The explicitly stochastic nature of the theorizing makes it difficult to "tack on" error terms after the theorizing is done, a usual procedure in the past. (Sargent 1981a, p. 217)[17]

However, Sargent was unable to establish this link because close scrutiny of the justification of error terms revealed the forced move that identification and estimation of the models require the econometrician to know less than the agents (see Appendix 4A). Since this clashed with the forced move to symmetry among agents, economists, and econometricians, Sargent encountered yet another resistance. Recalling that rational expectations economists and econometricians challenged adaptive expectations advocates for fitting models that forecast better than agents, we now observe a reversal of the contested asymmetry. When implemented numerically or econometrically, rational expectations models impute more knowledge to the agents within the model (who use the equilibrium probability distributions in evaluating their Euler equations) than is possessed by an econometrician, who faces estimation and inference problems that the agents in the model have somehow solved.

I now consider Sargent's rendition of the revelation of this resistance. After he embarked on the expedition for error terms, he found that within the framework of rational expectations several interpretations of the error processes are possible: "Errors in the estimated equation crop up perhaps because the econometrician has less information than the agents, in some sense, or else because the model is misspecified in some way" (Lucas and Sargent 1981, p. xxii).[18] Initially reluctant to relinquish the free moves of vector autoregressions, general equilibrium theory, and rational expectations, Sargent did not explore the misspecification route. Instead, he removed econometricians from the symmetry picture, thereby compromising his interest in conceptual integrity and ignoring the further elaboration of his tentative choices, by using "versions of the assumption that private agents observe and respond to more data than the econometrician possesses" (Hansen and Sargent 1980, p. 93).[19] Under this interpretation, error terms can have a variety of sources. There could be shocks observed by agents but not by the econometrician, there could be interactions with hidden decision variables simultaneously chosen by agents but unobserved by the econometrician, agents could be using larger information sets than the econometrician as a result of data limitations à la Shiller,[20] or the econometrician could have data sampled at a coarser interval than the agents (see Hansen and Sargent 1983a, 1990, 1991a, 1991d, 1991f).[21] At first, Sargent (1981a) saw this as the "only tractable way that has so far been discussed of introducing random errors" (p. 237)[22] and restricted "the econometrician's information set relative to that of private agents in a way both that is plausible and that leads to a tractable statistical model of the error term" (p. 237).[23]

Later, Sargent explored the errors-in-variables justification of error terms. The problem with this interpretation is that error is not confined to the single dependent variable, making it hard to settle on the correct method to model these equations.[24] Furthermore, Sargent (1989) acknowledged that this approach ran into the same resistance of a crumbling symmetry structure. It "require[s] a model of the data reporting agency" (pp. 251–2) that introduces asymmetry because the "economist (though not an agent within the model) is dependent for data on a reporting agency that observes only error-ridden versions of the data" (p. 253), whereas the "economic agents in the model are not dependent on the data reported by the measurement agency" (p. 253).[25] Sargent avoided the problem of whether actors should rationally model the practices of data-reporting agencies.

In terms that appear very close to the framework used in this analysis, Sargent acknowledged that the interplay of his interests and free moves resulted in forced moves: "The rational expectations or equilibrium modeling strategy virtually forces the econometrician to interpret the error terms in behavior equations in one of these ways" (Hansen and Sargent 1980, p. 93); and, the "theory summarized above virtually forces the econometrician to think of the error terms along lines like those developed by Hansen and Sargent" (Lucas and Sargent 1981, p. xxii). Furthermore, Sargent also identified the emergence and causes of resistances:

[T]he dynamic theory implies that agents' decision rules are exact (nonstochastic) functions of the information they possess about the relevant state variables governing the dynamic process they wish to control. The econometrician must resort to some device to convert the exact equations delivered by economic theory into inexact (stochastic) equations susceptible to econometric analysis. (Hansen and Sargent 1980, p. 93)

Because, "[d]espite its explicit recognition of uncertainty in modeling behavior, [rational expectations] theory actually generates behavioral equations without residuals. As with most macroeconomic theory then, we must tack on residuals to obtain empirically usable models and the theory is silent about the nature of the residuals" (Sargent and Sims 1977, p. 54).

Sargent even admitted the severe shaking of the grounds on which the concept of rational expectations was built: "The idea of rational expectations is . . . sometimes said to embody the idea that economists and the agents they are modeling should be placed on an equal footing. . . . These ways of explaining things are suggestive, but misleading" (Sargent 1993, p. 21). The reason is that the "private agents in this model typically forecast far better than the economist studying them. This situation reverses the asymmetry in forecasting abilities of the economist and the private agents which Muth challenged in the beginning" (Sargent 1987c, p. 79).[26] This elaboration on errors eventually led Sargent to explore the misspecification route, thereby relinquishing some of his initial free moves, while maintaining a "taste for symmetry between the econometrician and the agents in the economy" (Evans, Honkapohja, and Sargent 1993, p. 706). However, he faced more obstacles before changing his initial combination of free moves.

Moving on to another forced move that encountered resistance, *policy recommendations* cannot be part of Sargent's symmetry picture. Rational expectations models can be used either as a vehicle for making policy recommendations for improving policy decisions or as a positive model of history, which implies that the historical data were not generated by a process that can readily be improved by choosing a different government strategy.[27] There is a big gap between these views in terms of the scope for and the nature of the advice that economists give the government:

The former view analyzes the historical data by imposing an asymmetry between the performance of private agents (which is purposeful and optimizing) and that of government agents (which is arbitrary). That asymmetry leaves scope for suggesting improvements. The latter view imposes symmetry of purposes between private and government agents, in modeling the historical time series, thereby eliminating the scope for recommending improvements of government policy strategy. (Sargent 1987a, pp. 435–6)[28]

How did Sargent run into a resistance here? When policy recommendations are possible, the combined free moves and their resulting implications about symmetry are impossible.[29] Making recommendations for improving policy amounts to assuming that in the historical period the system was not really in a rational expectations equilibrium, having attributed to agents expectations about government policy that did not properly take into account the policy advice.[30] Because, a "rational expectations model during the estimation period ought to reflect the procedure by which policy is thought later to be influenced, for agents are posited to be speculating about government decisions into the indefinite future" (Sargent 1984, p. 413). When the combined free moves and their resulting implications about symmetry are possible, policy recommendations are impossible. Making the assumption that in the historical period the system was in a rational expectations equilibrium raises a question of why we study a system that we cannot influence, for "if this procedure is not thought likely to be a source of persuasive policy recommendations, most of its appeal vanishes" (Sargent 1984, p. 413). Sargent (1987c) identified the source of this resistance: "There is a logical difficulty in using a rational expectations model to give advice, stemming from the self-referential aspect of the model that threatens to absorb the economic advisor into the model. . . . That simultaneity is the source of logical difficulties in using rational expectations models to give advice about government policy" (p. 78).[31] It is interesting to note that the hypothesis of rational expectations was initially adopted to deal with the problem of self-referentiality of economic systems, as discussed in the previous chapter (see Marcet and Sargent 1992, p. 139).

Sargent's (1984) initial response to these resistances was to "continue along the path of using rational expectations theory and econometrics. . . . Dynamic rational expectations models provide the main tool that we have. . . . I believe that economists will learn interesting and useful things by using these tools" (p. 414).[32] Furthermore, in 1984, he was "unaware of an alternative approach . . . that avoids these contradictions and tensions" (p. 414n). Initially, Sargent accepted the posited rational expectations symmetry and saw no way out. What about bounded rationality? Could policy recommendations be made if agents, economists, econometricians, and governments were all in some sense bound-edly rational? Eventually, as we see in the next chapter, Sargent did see this as a way out and dropped the posited rational expectations symmetry.

Why is this resistance important for Sargent? As discussed in the previous chapter, one of the characteristics that attracted Sargent to economics was its concern with policy issues. Hence, Sargent (1987b) claimed that the "tasks of macroeconomics are to interpret observations on economic aggregates in terms of the motivations and constraints of economic agents and to predict the consequences of alternative hypothetical ways of administering government economic policy" (p. 1).[33] Sargent (1987a) even went so far as to claim that the treatment of policy "in the Keynesian tradition . . . led inevitably toward rational expectations" (p. xxii).[34] According to Sargent, the line of work in the Keynesian tradition, extending back to Tinbergen, pursued the idea of applying optimal control theory to macroeconometric models in order to make precise quantitative statements about optimal monetary and fiscal policies. Therefore, he argued, "[i]t was inevitable that macroeconomists would eventually apply these ideas to private agents' decision rules as well as those of the government. This would instill symmetry into these policy experiments by assuming that private agents, as well as the government agents, have 'rational expectations'" (p. xxii).[35]

This kind of revisionist history is dangerous, because it does not present knowledge contemporaneously with historical actors and actions. For revisionist historians, currently received theory is taken to be superior to earlier theories. Consequently, these earlier theories are studied and evaluated in the light of contemporary theory. Distortions inevitably result because, for these historians, the value of earlier theories lies solely in their contributions to contemporary theoretical problems and questions. Furthermore, Sargent was not a true believer in the rational expectations of policymakers. He departed from his student days at Berkeley and Harvard believing strongly in government intervention. During the Vietnam War, he served for a time in the Pentagon, where his tour of duty left him broadly doubtful about the effectiveness of government policymakers. "I came to understand more clearly the limitations of government actions. . . . We didn't do a very good job. There was an incredible volume of inefficient and bad decisions, which one must take into account when devising institutions for making policy" (Klamer 1983, p. 62). Now, if "[t]he people in Washington aren't all that much smarter than anybody else" (Sargent quoted by Guzzardi 1978, p. 74), then why did Sargent not pursue the path of making government agents just as boundedly rational as the agents in pre–rational expectations models? While we see in the following chapter that he did take this direction eventually I first digress a bit on the changing signals Sargent has sent concerning his position on the issue of seasonal adjustment of data.

The debate over the *seasonal adjustment* of data resulted in the final forced move I want to discuss. Sargent's shifting stance on seasonal adjustment nicely illustrates his change of heart about the posited rational expectations symmetry. Initially, Sargent (1978b, 1978c, 1987a) stuck to the combined free moves and their resulting implications about symmetry and argued that because the agents being modeled are themselves assumed to be using seasonally unadjusted data, economists and econometricians should follow the same practice. Even though he maintained that adjusted data should be used,[36] Sargent argued for applying the unadulterated seasonally unadjusted data – provided there is stationarity,[37] the model is true,[38] and there are no measurement errors[39] – because the model "misspecifies the relationship . . . if agents are responding to forecasts of the seasonally unadjusted series while the economist attributes to agents their responding to forecasts of the seasonally adjusted series. Alternatively . . . deducing the cross-equation restrictions on the basis of the seasonally adjusted data misspecifies the relationship" (Sargent 1987a, p. 338). Sargent was unconvinced by the arguments of opponents appealing to uncertainty of the adequacy of the model's specification as it pertains to seasonal variation.[40]

More recently, Sargent moved away from the spirited defense of his initial free moves by appealing to two points of view that seem to bolster a recommendation for using seasonally adjusted data.

First . . . when the mechanism generating seasonality is misspecified, superior estimates of economic parameters are made with seasonally adjusted data. . . . Second . . . in situations where the model is correctly specified, using seasonally adjusted data induces no asymptotic bias even when some of the key parameters are those governing behavior primarily at the seasonal frequencies. (Hansen and Sargent 1993, p. 22)

Letting econometric considerations take precedence over his initial free moves, Sargent eventually stressed that empirical examples

tend to suggest an asymmetry that favors [this] recommendation [for using seasonally adjusted data]: when the model is correctly specified, there is no loss of statistical consistency in estimating it with seasonally adjusted data; but when the model is misspecified, large reductions in asymptotic bias can emerge from using seasonally adjusted data. (Hansen and Sargent 1993, p. 48; also see Hansen and Sargent 1996, pp. 299–325)

What are we to make of Sargent's shift on seasonality? When the combination of rational expectations and general equilibrium theory makes specification mistakes, then modelers should use seasonally adjusted data, thereby relinquishing symmetry among agents, economists, and econometricians. When the combination of rational expectations and general equilibrium theory specifies correctly, then dropping symmetry is no big loss. In either case, Sargent is ignoring the forced move to symmetry when accounting for seasonality. Where does the misspecification path take us next?

Sargent's encounters with resistances set in motion a *process of accommodation*. As discussed in Chapter 5, Sargent tried to reimpose symmetry among the agents, economists, and econometricians. Before discussing these new moves, I link Sargent's discussion of symmetry with general symmetry considerations.

4.3   Symmetry Considerations

As Sargent's perspective on his symmetry saga sheds light on the involved interaction of his interests and moves, a general analysis of symmetry considerations provides further insight. Why is Sargent's symmetry among economists, econometricians, and agents so important? This may be answered by starting with a more basic question: What do we mean by symmetry? The prevalent image of symmetry at its most fundamental level is the possibility of making a change that leaves some aspect of the situation unchanged. Therefore, symmetry is immunity to possible change. This is the conceptual or qualitative formulation, which can be contrasted to the group-theoretical or quantitative interpretation, expressed in terms of transformations and transformation groups. In this version, symmetry is invariance under one or more (possible) transformations, known as "symmetry" or "invariance" transformations. Furthermore, it turns out that conservations (called "conservation laws" in the past) that hold for isolated systems are intimately and fundamentally related to a group of symmetry transformations.[41]

What allows Sargent to maintain symmetry among agents, economists, and econometricians? What is the source of his desire to find identity and invariance rather than diversity and change? Three general justifications of symmetry come to mind. The reader must decide which is most compelling, since this evaluation depends largely on one's stance in the unresolved debates on realism and relativism. The first defense of the symmetry concept sees it as a quality inherent *in things*. This has an ontic interpretation, meaning that it entails an intrinsic invariance among economists, econometricians, and agents.

According to the second justification, symmetry follows from a power of recognition inherent *in the mind*. This interpretation is partly ontic and partly epistemic and can be clarified by an appeal to Kantian regulative principles, implying that symmetry among economists, econometricians, and agents is an ideal of reason (see Falkenburg 1988). Kant held that the concept of a systematic unity of nature was an ideal of reason directed toward a completeness of empirical knowledge unattainable through concepts of understanding. Ideals of reason in Kant's sense bring about a generalization or totalization of concepts of the understanding. They do not possess objective reality, since the completeness of empirical knowledge of particulars can never be the object of objective knowledge. However, they lead to regulative principles that can guide our acquisition of knowledge to the establishment of systematic unity. Since symmetry principles enable us to discover parts of this specific systematic structure, they have a regulative character in Kant's sense.

According to the third justification of symmetry, it depends crucially on *metaphoric reasoning* (see Mirowski 1989a). The recognition underpinning this epistemic interpretation is that we live in a world of broken symmetries and partial invariance. Foundational conservation principles are factually false and no posited invariance holds without exceptions or qualifications. However imperfect the world, human reason operates by means of assigning sameness and differences through symmetries in an attempt to force a reconciliation of constancy to change.[42] Our very livelihoods, in the broadest possible sense, are predicated upon invariants whose existence cannot be proved but whose instrumentality renders our actions coherent.[43] According to this justification, Sargent served his interests by creating symmetry between economists and econometricians and projected his practice onto economic actors, thereby effectively creating a metaphor of the agent as an economist and econometrician.

Regardless of its justification, why was Sargent able to build an entire crusade around models populated by economists and econometricians? The unifying principles of symmetries help classify objects and are heuristics in theory building. The steps of this argument are, first, that symmetries allow an ordering of unexplained phenomena – the *phenomenological classification of objects* of an as-yet unformulated theory. With their help objects and findings can be provisionally systematized before a comprehensive theory of the phenomena in question exists. For Sargent's saga, this would involve classifying agents, economists, and econometricians as the elements of one system. Second, the phenomenological classification leads to the explanation of the symmetry structure in fundamental theories – the *building of theories* in the form of symmetry principles – thereby enabling us to define the heuristic potential of symmetries as unifying principles. In Sargent's case, this means theorizing about the nature of the symmetry in his group. These symmetries point out the invariants of the theoretical description of nature and facilitate a systematic search for phenomena that are part of these structures. Third, symmetries allow the testing of predictions based on these claims and discovery of fundamental theoretical structures – the *disclosure of properties of the resulting theories*. When Sargent's symmetry structure was further elaborated by the forced moves of no-trade theorems, information gathering, error term justification, policy recommendations, and seasonal adjustment, it started to crumble. Eventually Sargent was led to build up another symmetry structure by making everyone boundedly rational, as we see in the next chapter. Fourth, if symmetries are considered to be metaphors, they engender innovations at the level of *notions of scientific behavior.* Extensions in the application of the idea of symmetry allow one to draw on tools and methods to revisit taken-for-granted assumptions that underpin particular phases or research perspectives. At a deeper level, they free up the activity of theoretical speculation vis-à-vis the dictates of nature and allow a blending of relativist and determinist theorizing. I postpone a further clarification of this use of symmetry until the next section.

Now that we have a sense of why symmetry is so important, we could then ask, Why this one and not another? Can you imagine what it would be like to live in a world with only economists and econometricians? Indeed, the attraction of Sargent's particular symmetry follows from something else, namely, his interests and tentative choices. He was motivated by conceptual integrity, implying symmetry among economists and econometricians, and made free moves to vector autoregressions, general equilibrium theory, and rational expectations to satisfy this interest. Along with his free move to general equilibrium theory came the forced move that he could not distinctly differentiate agents, because there is an a priori bias toward symmetry among the agents in general equilibrium theory. If this is the case, then how can one justify that economists and econometricians get to be different? For Sargent, turning agents into economists and econometricians just follows as a not unwelcome forced move from his interests and free moves. This notion of symmetry then suggests others. Indeed, if we were to endorse an ontological account, a quick look at symmetry in physics would teach us that symmetry's essential nature has five fundamental manifestations: reproducibility, predictability, evolution of isolated physical systems, symmetry of states of physical systems, and gauge symmetry (see Rosen 1990). Now, for example, reproducibility and predictability would mean that agents, economists, and econometricians all react in the same way to a certain change. As we know, this is where things started falling apart in Sargent's symmetry saga.

4.4   Symmetry in Science Studies

As mentioned in section 4.1, there is a lot of controversy over the problem of according privilege or no privilege of the analyst over the actor in science studies (see, e.g., McMullin 1992; Mulkay 1979; Pickering 1992). Different symmetry postulates distinguish distinct phases in the history of social studies of science and give rise to distinct notions of scientific behavior. For example, Mertonian approaches to science effectively proposed a symmetry between science and other social institutions. According to this symmetry postulate, scientific achievements are as socially influenced, and as sociologically problematic, as other institutions. However, the validity of scientific knowledge was considered to be exempt from sociological analysis (see Bloor 1991, pp. 164, 175–9). Accordingly, social scientists drew on existing tools and methods for studying social institutions to reveal the nature of social relationships among scientists, while remaining silent about the content of scientific knowledge. This chapter of the symmetry saga was closed in the 1970s, but the story continued.

After many years in which it seemed to have been conclusively settled that the content of scientific knowledge was exempt from sociological analysis, philosophers, sociologists, and historians asserted persuasively that the orthodox philosophical view of science was beset by grave difficulties. According to this account of science, the scientist is different since her conclusions are uniquely determined by the natural world and because she judges knowledge claims by using universal and ahistorical criteria.

How can one justify that the natural world occupies a privileged position? Instead, the principle of the stability of nature is best seen as a part of scientists' resources for constructing their accounts of that world. Fact and theory, observation and presupposition, are interrelated in a complex manner. Since the physical world does not uniquely determine scientists' conclusions, the factual content of science should not be treated as a culturally unmediated reflection of a stable external world. Where can one find universal and ahistorical criteria? Instead, scientists' criteria for assessing knowledge claims are always open to varied interpretations. The formation and acceptance of interpretative constructions of the world by scientists are based on their own specific intellectual commitments, presuppositions, and objectives and the social negotiation of knowledge in various kinds of scientific research contexts. Since general criteria for assessing scientific knowledge claims cannot be applied universally or independently of social context, as orthodox philosophy of science had previously assumed, the cognitive/technical resources of scientists are open to continual change of meaning.

I continue the symmetry story by putting some people in the picture. Bloor's articulation of symmetry as a methodological principle focused on the question of what is so special about scientific analysis. According to Bloor, knowledge is to be construed, in science as elsewhere, as accepted (and not true) belief.[44] Hence, he extended symmetry to the content of scientific knowledge itself, arguing that the symmetry postulate enjoins us to seek the same kinds of causes for both true and false, rational and irrational, successful and failed beliefs, thus eliminating methodological asymmetry (see Bloor 1991). The form of study used by the analysts of science ought not to depend, then, on the truth status of the scientific claim being investigated. Thus, Bloor argued for an explanation that would be symmetric in its style, because the same types of causes would explain both sides of the dichotomies. Even though the natural world exerts some constraint on scientific theory, it is the various commitments that scientists bring to their theorizing that are decisive in explaining the outcome. Bloor argued that these commitments themselves can best be understood in social terms, thereby granting that the social occupies a privileged position.[45] Rather than conceding that the natural world is different, as in traditional philosophical analysis, Bloor privileged the social by using it to find an understanding of how rules and practices are joined.

Bloor's methodological symmetry seems to fly in the face of common sense, since our everyday attitudes are evaluative and judgments are by their nature asymmetrical. However, according to Bloor (1991, p. 176), the fact that these evaluations are socially structured is the very reason they need to be overcome. Two residual forms of asymmetry will be left intact: First is what we can call psychological asymmetry. Classifying beliefs as false or true, rational or irrational, successful or failed, requires psychological asymmetry. However, because the explanation of these beliefs is independent of the classification, methodological symmetry is saved. The second is known as logical asymmetry, which follows from the realization that endorsing and rejecting are not symmetrical. Again there will be methodological symmetry, because choosing the true, rational, or successful option is no less problematic than choosing the false, irrational, or failed one.

By the late 1980s, a variety of approaches in the tradition of sociology of scientific knowledge were staying afloat on the stormy sea of social studies of science. They were united by a shared rejection of philosophical apriorism coupled with a sensitivity to the social dimensions of science but differed at the same time along many axes (see, e.g., Pickering 1992, pp. 16–22). Our symmetry story continues with Callon and Latour (1992), the progenitors of the so-called actor–network approach, and the explorations of reflexivity by Ashmore (1989) and Woolgar (1988a, 1992). These analysts questioned the justification for making science studies scholars different from other scientists and thereby reintroducing asymmetry. How can science studies advocates claim to give an objective account of science if they deny a similar ability to natural scientists in their pursuit of natural knowledge? The two approaches give different but similar twists to the answer to this question.

Callon and Latour claimed to see in their predecessors certain taken-for-granted conceptual dichotomies that in fact guarantee the very hegemony of the natural sciences. They asserted that traditional thought on science and society had situated itself on a spectrum between nature at one end and society at the other. In particular, scientists and their academic spokespersons in history, philosophy, and sociology had situated their accounts of science at the "nature" end of the spectrum – scientific knowledge is dictated by nature – whereas the radical move of sociology of scientific knowledge had been to situate itself at the other extreme, that scientific knowledge is dictated by society. They wished to disprivilege the prevailing asymmetry by proposing a radical symmetry with regard to agency. The actor–network approach extends symmetry in admitting agency to the realm of nonhuman actors and attacks the dichotomy between nature and society.

Callon and Latour questioned the privileged position of the social and argued for allowing symmetry between humans and nonhumans. Their actor–network approach seeks to capture the nature of scientific practice in the metaphor of the making and breaking of alliances among actors, human and nonhuman, while seeking to avoid imputing different properties to either category. It assigns capacities for action, thought, and intention to nonhuman elements; human and nonhuman actors are thus in effect treated as somehow on a par with one another. This is a step away from the society end of the spectrum and toward nature. Furthermore, the actor–network approach rejects the very concept of the nature–society spectrum, by arguing that nature and society are intimately entangled in scientific and technological practice. According to Callon and Latour, practice is where nature and society and the space between them are continually made, unmade, and remade. Inasmuch, then, as we can confidently attribute properties to nature and society, it is as a consequence of practice, and those properties cannot count as the explanation of practice. In appealing to the social as the explanatory principle, the dichotomy between nature and society, on which the authority of natural scientists rests, would be granted.

Not everybody went along with the extension of symmetry in the actor–network approach, because there is no limit to the application of the extension of symmetry (see, e.g., Pickering 1992, pp. 16–22; Collins and Yearly 1992a, 1992b). After achieving symmetry of the natural and the social by grounding them in network building, we could go on defining some hypersymmetry principle that achieves symmetry of, on the one hand, the natural and the social, and, on the other hand, networkism, by grounding them in another activity, which could be called hyperactivity.[46] There is nothing to stop this philosophically progressive regress, which has led some science studies scholars to argue that we should all appreciate the potential endlessness of this regress, while resting content with recognizing the problem and dealing with it pragmatically.

The symmetry postulate in Ashmore and Woolgar's explorations of reflexivity challenges the assumption that the science studies scholar enjoys a privileged position vis-à-vis the subjects and objects that come under the authorial gaze. If the analyst of science and the scientist were truly distinct, the inquirer would have no way of knowing the characteristics of the latter in advance of studying it. If, on the other hand, the means of study and the object of study are not distinct, their interdependence suggests that our research process assumes (at least part of) the answer it sets out to find. The researcher is required to participate, in the course of her research, in activities that are also the object of that research. She produces knowledge claims about the production of knowledge claims; she aims to explain how explanation is done, to understand how understanding is produced, and so on. Ashmore and Woolgar see their quest for consistency through symmetry, which leads them to question the privileged position of social scientific knowledge, as the next natural development of social studies of science. After the growing confidence with which scholars have argued that natural scientific knowledge is a social construct, the next step is a growing interest in the consequences of applying this same argument to knowledge generated by the social sciences.

Reactions to this investigation of reflexivity are varied. According to its advocates, reflexivity may provide an occasion for exploring new ways of addressing long-standing questions of knowledge and epistemology. The reflexivity approach self-consciously seeks to capitalize on the strains and tensions associated with all research practice that can be construed as part of its own phenomenon. The idea is to take such tensions as the starting point for exploration of the questions and issues that arise, to use them to direct our attention to, say, the particular form of subject–object relationship that our research conventions reify and reaffirm. This gives us the capacity to revisit taken-for-granted assumptions that underpin particular phases or research perspectives. One source of antipathy to the reflexive project is the assumption that such work is incompatible with good research practice because of its self-regarding quality or because of its quality of leading to a regress of metastudies (see Pickering 1992, pp. 16–22; Collins and Yearly 1992a, 1992b). Critics claim that the serious reflexivist just leaps into the skeptical regress of deconstruction. Since it has no message about anything apart from itself, it is left with nothing constructive or positive to say.

Interestingly enough, the fate of Sargent was little different from that of the postmodern science studies advocate, for, as section 4.1 indicates, Sargent also explicitly acknowledged the problem of self-reflexivity. Now, is my fate different from that of Sargent? If Sent and Sargent are truly distinct, then Sent can only claim some kind of epistemic privilege in understanding Sargent's quandary more deeply than he does himself by availing herself of criteria whose existence she denies. And if she is so superior, then why does she not just do better macrotheory than he? If, on the other hand, Sent and Sargent are not distinct, their interdependence suggests that her research process assumes (at least part of) the answer it sets out to find. And if she is able to reproduce his reasoning in his own terms, then why should you take her word over his? Thus, my voice either undermines its own assertion or becomes indistinguishable from the voice about which it wishes to make an observation. However, one point in my favor is Sargent's own rewriting of history. Recall the earlier discussion of the link between his free moves. When "rationally" reconstructing his own history, Sargent argued that rational expectations led to general equilibrium theory. When "rationally" reconstructing the history of rational expectations theory, Sargent inverted the direction of causation from general equilibrium theory, or more specifically intertemporal optimization, to rational expectations. In addition, Sargent has argued that both rational expectations and general equilibrium theory followed from large-scale econometric models. If Sargent is allowed to rewrite his own history, then what prevents me from (re)writing his history? In addition, as discussed in Chapter 1, I am trying to track the temporal emergence of different interpretations of rational expectations by Sargent rather than bowing to after-the-fact retrospective accounts given by him.

Now, there is no reason for you as the reader to sit back and relax. For what is your fate? Is it different from that of Sent? You as the reader are not free to choose as you will, since you are caught up in the same web of distinct difference and sameness. If you want to assert your difference, you must claim some privileged knowledge of Sargent and economics unavailable to Sent. If you want claim symmetry, you run into all the paradoxes already identified for Sargent and Sent. The point is that there are always analytical options in any program that are never developed for reasons too complex to be summarized by their being "wrong" or "not fruitful." I have shown that some lines of inquiry simply become unfathomable or impossible to prosecute, given the prior context of the project. Sargent chose to relinquish certain ideas, but this had little to do with "falsification" or any rigid "scientific method."

4.5   Conclusion

Although symmetry promises to solve certain problems, it also leads to epistemological paradoxes. Under the more qualitative definition, symmetry is immunity to possible change. A quantification of this notion characterizes symmetry as invariance under one or more (possible) transformations. The justifications of symmetry regard it as either a quality inherent in things or a power of recognition inherent in the mind or the result of metaphoric reasoning. No matter how it is justified, symmetry fulfills many functions in science. It allows a phenomenological classification of objects, it facilitates the building of theories and the analysis of the properties of the resulting theories, and it leads to innovations in notions of scientific behavior.

Whenever symmetry comes up in the social sciences, it leads to paradoxes. If sociologists of scientific knowledge are symmetric with scientists, then why should we take their word over that of the scientists? If sociologists of scientific knowledge are asymmetric with scientists, then what kinds of standards can they employ to establish their privileged position? Anthropologists try to negotiate between being symmetric with their objects of study while "being there" and being asymmetric with their objects of study while "being here." Symmetry allows them to provide an intimate view, whereas asymmetry allows them to supply a cool assessment. Now, how can they have it both ways? Experimental psychology has built professional recognition and provided practical applications by increasing the asymmetry between experimenters and subjects up to the point where subjects became anonymous. The symmetry that was part of the first psychological experiments did not allow for the production of the kind of universal and ahistorical knowledge that psychologists were looking for.

Sargent is one economist who has openly worried about symmetry. He wanted to get rid of the asymmetry between economists and agents that existed in the large-scale macromodels with adaptive expectations of the 1950s and 1960s. Resistances loomed large on Sargent's horizon when he employed symmetry to satisfy his interest in conceptual integrity of economic theory and econometrics. His combined free moves of vector autoregressions, general equilibrium theory, and rational expectations were unable to tackle the hurdles of symmetry among analysts and actors, no-trade theorems, information gathering, error term justification, policy recommendations, and seasonal adjustment, which were erected by forced moves. Sargent eventually attempted to accommodate these resistances by relinquishing his prior choice of rational expectations in favor of bounded rationality. With his new combination of tentative choices, achieving conceptual integrity implied changing the practice of both econometrics and economic theory. This is yet another story illustrating how the involved interaction of interests and moves shapes Sargent's analysis, which takes us to the next chapter.

Appendix 4A: Error Term Interpretation

Suppose the closed form expression for an agent's decision rule has the form

$$n_t = \rho_1 n_{t-1} - \frac{\rho_1}{\delta} U \zeta(\lambda)^{-1} \left[I + \sum_{j=1}^{r-1} \left(\sum_{k=j+1}^{r} \lambda^{k-j} \zeta_k \right) L^j \right] x_t$$
$$+ \frac{\rho_1}{\delta} \alpha(\lambda)^{-1} \left[1 + \sum_{j=1}^{q-1} \left(\sum_{k=j+1}^{q} \lambda^{k-j} \alpha_k \right) L^j \right] a_t + \frac{\rho_1 \gamma_0}{\delta} \left(\frac{1}{1-\lambda} \right) \tag{4A.1}$$

where n_t is the decision variable and $a_t = \alpha(L)^{-1} v_t^a$ is a random shock.[47] In order to justify the presence of an error term, it is assumed that the random shock is seen by the decision maker but unobserved by the econometrician. This imposes the structure on the error process needed for identification and estimation of the model. The disturbance in the decision rule is then given by

$$e_t = \frac{\rho_1}{\delta} \alpha(\lambda)^{-1} \left[1 + \sum_{j=1}^{q-1} \left(\sum_{k=j+1}^{q} \lambda^{k-j} \alpha_k \right) L^j \right] \alpha(L)^{-1} v_t^a \tag{4A.2}$$

where v_t^a is the serially uncorrelated random process of innovations in a_t (also see Hansen and Sargent 1980, pp. 101–4).

CHAPTER 5

Accommodating Learning

Why wait for Science to supply the how
When any amateur can tell it now?
The way to go away should be the same
As fifty million years ago we came –
If anyone remembers how that was.
I have a theory, but it hardly does.

Robert Frost, *Why Wait for Science*

This chapter contains a case study of Sargent's changing attitude toward learning. Rather than looking at his accomplishments from the perspective of orthodox philosophy of economics or conventional history of economic thought, I am searching for the story Sargent is likely to have told about how he arrived at the idea of learning with artificial intelligence and what resistances he had to overcome to put his interpretation of this concept to use. Whereas this type of analysis has been used in the previous three chapters in the discussion of Sargent's different interpretations of rational expectations, it is employed here to analyze how Sargent moved away from rational expectations. In fact, Sargent (1993) finally made a "call to retreat from . . . rational expectations . . . by expelling rational agents from our model environments" (p. 3) and "to create theories with behavioral foundations by eliminating the asymmetry that rational expectations builds in between the agents in the model and the econometrician who is estimating it" (pp. 21–2). Before discussing this move, I illustrate in section 5.1 how Sargent's social environment in the late 1980s was shaped by his involvement with the Santa Fe Institute.[1] Section 5.2 analyzes the role of learning when expectations are rational; section 5.3 discusses the moves made by Sargent in an effort to incorporate learning in the context of adaptive expectations. Section 5.4 analyzes Sargent's embracement of learning with artificial intelligence. The narrative shifts in the following sections to provide a wider perspective on Sargent's endeavors: The next section of the chapter contrasts his and Simon's interpretations of bounded rationality and artificial intelligence; section 5.6 examines how Sargent's adaptive computing relates to several interpretations of artificial intelligence, and section 5.7 analyzes the relationship between Sargent and science studies scholars.

124

5.1   Complexity and the Santa Fe Institute

What counted as cutting-edge science was changing in the early 1980s (see, e.g., Anderson, Arrow, and Pines 1988; Lane 1993a, 1993b; Mirowski 1996b; Pool 1989; Waldrop 1992). Scientists started realizing that messiness is inherent in the systems they analyze. Indeed, the exemplar of ideal science itself was shifting away from physics and toward biology. According to Resnick (1994), "a new set of models and metaphors has begun to spread through the scientific community, and gradually into the culture at large. Many of these new ideas come not from physics but from biology" (p. 229). Physicists were notorious for sneering at engineering and "soft" sciences like sociology and psychology. Rather than trying to grapple with real-world complexity, the physical sciences had traditionally attempted to make virtues of conceptual elegance and analytical simplicity. Then there arose the field of molecular biology, which described incredibly complicated living systems that were nonetheless governed by deep principles. In addition, many physicists started incorporating complexity into their analyses. Once elegance and simplicity were given up, it also became easier to start rethinking scientificity in economics and other social sciences.

At the same time, scientists were also beginning to analyze complex systems simply because the advance of computer power enabled them to do so. Furthermore, new techniques in mathematics had greatly increased the capacity to deal simultaneously with many variables, nonlinear dynamics, and adaptive paths in evolutionary systems. In part because of their computer simulations and in part because of these new mathematical insights, scientists had begun to realize by the early 1980s that with nonlinear dynamics and positive feedback even some very simple systems could produce amazingly rich patterns of behavior. Nonlinear equations are notoriously difficult to solve by hand, and that is why scientists had avoided them for so long. Yet, as intriguing as molecular biology, computer simulation, and nonlinear science were, they were only the beginning. The idea was that there is an underlying unity that ultimately would encompass not just biology, but physics, chemistry, information processing, economics, political science, and every other aspect of human affairs. This brings us to the complexity movement fueled by the Santa Fe Institute.

Researchers at the Santa Fe Institute took up themes such as complexity, intractable unpredictability, spontaneous self-organization, adaptation, nonlinear dynamics, computational theory, upheavals at the edge of chaos, inductive strategies, and new developments in computer and cognitive science. They all shared the conviction that disorder can flow from order, and order can flow from disorder. The complexity movement was held together by the vision of an underlying unity, a common theoretical framework for complexity that would illuminate not only "the natural" and but also "the social." If it could illustrate that the patterns of the world are a historical accident following on sensitive dependence on initial conditions, then prediction would have to make room for comprehension and explanation, for analysis of the fundamental mechanisms of nature. Researchers at the institute believed that they had the mathematical tools available to create such a framework by drawing from the past twenty years of intellectual developments in such fields as neural networks, evolutionary ecology, cognitive science, and chaos theory.

Researchers at Santa Fe studied systems composed of many "agents." These agents might be molecules or neurons or species or consumers or even corporations. Whatever their nature, they were shown to form self-reinforcing dynamic systems, or systems with local positive feedbacks, that tended to possess a multiplicity of asymptotic states or possible emergent structures. Complexity researchers found that the initial starting state, combined with early random events or fluctuations, acted to push the dynamics into the domain of one of these asymptotic states and thus to select the structure into which the system eventually locked. However, they also discovered that the agents were constantly organizing and reorganizing themselves into larger structures through the clash of mutual accommodation and mutual rivalry. These local interactions were found to give rise to emergent patterns and structures on stratified levels that the agents were able to exploit. Thus, the challenge for the complexity approach was to find the fundamental laws of emergence through a hierarchical, building-block structure. Once a set of building blocks had been adjusted and refined and thoroughly debugged through experience, then it could generally be adapted and recombined to build a great many new concepts. To complexity researchers, that seemed to be a much more efficient way to create something new than starting all over from scratch.

Begun by a number of distinguished physicists at the Los Alamos National Laboratories, the Santa Fe Institute originally had nothing to do with economics. This changed with the workshop "Evolutionary Paths of the Global Economy" held September 8–18, 1987, at the institute campus in Santa Fe (see Anderson et al. 1988; Pool 1989). The workshop was convened by David Pines, cochair of the Santa Fe Institute Science Board, who served as moderator, and chaired by the physicist Philip Anderson and the economist Kenneth Arrow, who both selected the participants and arranged the program. To trade tools and techniques, the workshop divided up into three subgroups, of which one covered cycles, which are predictive theories of dynamic behavior, such as nonlinear deterministic systems; a second discussed webs, which are theories of large numbers of interacting units with evolution as the paradigm; and a third analyzed patterns, which are theories of inhomogeneity and of self-maintaining differences. The gathering was successful enough to continue the economics program at the institute, which has anywhere from eight to fifteen researchers in residence at any given time, evenly divided between economists and physical scientists. Brian Arthur, who served as the director of the institute's economics program, sees a "Santa Fe approach" emerging that views the economy as a complex, constantly evolving system in which learning and adaptation play a major role. Eventually . . . this could expand the current view, much influenced by classical physics, that depicts the world as relatively simple, predictable, and tending to equilibrium solutions. (Pool 1989, p. 703)

The Santa Fe scientists believed they had something to offer because they analyzed complex systems whose many parts interact nonlinearly and thought economists were doing the same. Though economists were somewhat hesitant, they were still interested in finding out what the scientists had to offer. As might have been expected, the two counterparts discovered that the collision of such different cultures led to some interesting insights. Both groups went to the meeting with skepticism and preconceived ideas. Once their languages were translated, they found that they approached their subjects in quite different ways.[2] The economists were astonished at the physicists' apparent lack of rigor. Since they could not believe that back-of-the-envelope calculations or computer simulations without theorems and proofs constituted research, they felt the physical scientists could not possibly help with their problems. However, the economists were taken aback when it turned out that a computer shortcut reached the same solution to a problem as an exact rigorous method using pencil and paper. The physical scientists thought that economics was a mess and that there was not much one could do with it but were surprised to discover how mathematically rigorous theoretical economists were. Modern economics had physics beat by using much more "fancy mathematics" and hard-to-understand notation.

The noneconomists who attended the workshop saw complex economic systems as an entire new playground for their ideas. They believed they could improve economic forecasting by taking some of the classical problems in economics and trying to solve them through the application of a hybrid theory that uses some of the tools and techniques developed in such fields as physics and biology. The scientists and economists discussed the possible use of new approaches to nonlinear forecasting in economics and found that in some instances their results were roughly fifty times better than those of standard linear models. These results led the workshop participants to believe that the quest for low-dimensional chaotic behavior may be appropriate in economics (see Farmer and Sidorowich 1988).

The scientists and economists at the Santa Fe workshop gave a great deal of attention to the more general theme of how to model a system as complicated as a nation's economy, which generated several different efforts. One was an attempt to see whether the tools developed to analyze spin glasses, a concept in condensed matter physics, had any applications in economics. A second grew out of the idea of "rugged landscapes," as analyzed in evolutionary biology. Many parallels between ecology and economics were found, suggesting that ecological models may capture many aspects of an economy (see, e.g., Depew and Weber 1995, pp. 429–57). Both physicists and economists had used hill-climbing analogies in their own work, but the direction in which an economy should go in order to improve had typically been analyzed in models with only one hill.

Since economic agents have foresight, however, the ecological models could not be applied directly. For the workshop participants, this raised the question of how economic agents take the future into account when making decisions. Given their awareness of the difficulties inherent in predicting the future, the physical scientists felt that the axiom of "rational expectations" was clearly untrue. The problem in developing a more realistic model was that if economic agents were assumed to be able to anticipate the future, but not perfectly, then determining how imperfect rationality should be is difficult. One suggestion was to work with probability distributions for each possible future, instead of with expected values. Another was to investigate the consequences of laying down axioms or assumptions that supposed limits to economic agents' computational ability or memory. However, adding such a modicum of irrationality had the drawback of being arbitrary. A different approach was to develop theoretical economic agents that learned in the way actual economic agents did. These adaptive learning models could then either replace or supplement orthodox theory. Imagining an economy consisting of machines that learn in more or less the same way as biological entities do, one could analyze whether an economic system itself learns by its mistakes in a cumulative way. Instead of adding learning as an afterthought, these techniques built it into the cognitive network from the beginning.

Anderson, who invited ten physical scientists, remarked, "one of the economists in the program can't open his mouth without talking in terms of theorem–lemma–corollary." On the basis of some supporting evidence, I believe that he was referring to Sargent,[3] who was one of the ten economists invited by Arrow. Sargent said in an interview: "I interact with physical and biological scientists on a regular basis at the Santa Fe Institute in New Mexico. . . . During the meetings, we exchange ideas about how to better understand the economy as a complex, evolving structure and how biological ideas about adaptation and evolution can be put to work in economics" (Parkin 1996, p. 650). Sargent participated in the working group studying webs, which focused on two broad themes in its analysis of adaptation and evolution in economics (Anderson et al. 1988, pp. 245–6). The first topic centered on the two-nation overlapping generations model in economic theory. The participants in the subgroup identified several ways of modifying the model that would allow comparisons of the standard equilibrium solutions (which require agents with perfect one-step foresight) and the solutions that would arise if adaptive rule-based agents were to replace the agents with foresight. The second theme was more weblike, and more abstract. It began with considerations of coevolution of technologies and continued with discussions of walks over rugged adaptive landscapes.

The suggestions for incorporating learning were music to Sargent's ears, because his engineering metaphors had turned out to be less convenient than he had thought, as discussed in Chapter 3, and he had developed an interest in including learning in the context of rational expectations models to restore symmetry among agents, economists, and econometricians, as we see in the following sections. If Sargent could rely on convenient techniques to facilitate prediction, why could the agents not do likewise? As we will see, Sargent had already replaced the hypothesis that individuals knew the value of probability distributions by the assumption that these distributions were learned by repeated exposure. However, the problem he ran into was that the environment in which the learning took place was influenced by the fact that other agents were also learning. Before jumping ahead of the story, I now use the concepts of interests and free and forced moves to analyze Sargent's research leading up to his visit to the Santa Fe Institute.

5.2 Learning with Rational Expectations

When Sargent tried to meet his interests with the combined *free moves* toward *vector autoregressions, general equilibrium theory,* and *rational expectations* in the early to mid-1980s, as analyzed in the previous two chapters, he resisted incorporating learning. As discussed in the previous chapter, Sargent really wanted everyone to be alike and had previously thought that one of the attractive properties of the concept of rational expectations was that it established symmetry among agents, economists, and econometricians. However, he subsequently discovered that *asymmetry between agents and econometricians* followed as one of the *resistances* in terms of *forced moves* from his tentative choices. In particular, identification and estimation of the econometric models required that the econometricians were learning things that the agents in the model already knew. Now, could symmetry not be restored by making the agents learn as well?

Initially reluctant to give up the rendition of rational expectations following from his free moves, Sargent argued that analytical convenience and limitations of existing research on learning prevented him from incorporating the learning assumption: "But it has been only a matter of analytical convenience and not of necessity that equilibrium models have used . . . the assumption that agents have already learned the probability distributions they face" (Lucas and Sargent 1979, p. 13). And although models incorporating "learning . . . are both technically feasible and consistent with the equilibrium modeling strategy, we know of almost no successful applied work along these lines" (p. 14). When asked in an interview in 1982 how he dealt with learning, Sargent responded:

It's an important issue, but I don't think anyone's going to get very far. There are some really hard technical problems. My prediction is that in terms of models for explaining time series, the models of learning aren't going to be a big help because of the technical problems in the structure of learning. (Klamer 1983, p. 73; also see p. 69)

In fact, Sargent identified three *resistances* that would appear if agents were to learn as he himself did.

First, as discussed in Chapter 3, Sargent saw making predictions as the ultimate goal in achieving conceptual integrity of theory and method. He thought that from "this viewpoint, the suggestion that one ought to build a learning mechanism into rational expectations models is not useful" (Sargent 1981a, p. 235). The reason is that the Wiener–Kolmogorov prediction formula and the chain rule of forecasting were known to be correct for the case in which there is no learning. If there is learning, then there is in general *no known closed-form prediction formula,* and that implies that it is impossible to derive closed-form versions of decision rules and hence equilibria. At the same time, Sargent felt that for the kind of empirical work he was advocating "it is important to have a closed form" (p. 235). This resistance is related to the problem of self-referentiality discussed in Chapter 3: "Because the agents are learning about a system that is being influenced by the learning processes of people like themselves, these systems are sometimes called 'self-referential'" (Sargent 1993, p. 127); this "means that standard econometric proofs of convergence of estimators . . . cannot usually be applied" (p. 127).

Even if the decision rules could be calculated in closed form under the learning assumption, then the resulting time-series models would have time-varying coefficients and so be *nonstationary:* "Equilibrium theorizing in this context thus readily leads to a model of how . . . learning applied by agents to the exogenous variables leads to time-dependent coefficients in agents' decision rules" (Lucas and Sargent 1979, p. 14; also see Bray 1983).[4] Furthermore, Lucas and Sargent (1979) believed that "non-stationary time series models are cumbersome and come in so many varieties" (p. 14). Using some form of a market metaphor, Sargent argued that the "loss of stationarity . . . may well be a price that the applied economist would not be prepared to pay even in exchange for the 'greater realism' of the learning assumption" (Sargent 1981a, p. 235n). This price may be avoided by assuming a stationary environment in which the learning mechanisms would eventually settle on time-invariant decision rules, for in "such settings, even if the researcher erroneously assumes that the [parameters] are known with certainty when in reality agents are learning about them in an optimal way, the researcher continues to obtain consistent estimators of the underlying parameters" (p. 236).[5]

Sargent's final objection to incorporating learning dealt with the question of where, between perfect rationality and its complete absence, to set the *dial of rationality* and whether this dial setting could be built into the theoretical models. Introducing the learning assumption would have added a number of parameters, because it had to be decided how the decision-making processes were represented and how they were updated. Sargent (1981a) discussed this problem in the context of Bayesian learning: "Another drawback with incorporating learning is that . . . the issue would arise of how to determine the prior used to initiate the learning model" (p. 235). Furthermore, "[d]etermining a prior distribution from the data would involve estimating initial conditions and would proliferate nuisance parameters in a very unpleasant way" (Lucas and Sargent 1979, p. 14).[6] Lucas and Sargent conjectured that the dial of rationality could be built into a theoretical model, "albeit at a cost in terms of simplicity of the model" (p. 13). Again, notice the use of some form of a market metaphor.

Why did Sargent identify these three arguments as resistances with respect to incorporating learning? By considering them, he illuminated further refinements of his interest in conceptual integrity of theory and method. He saw making predictions as the ultimate goal in achieving conceptual integrity of theory and method and thought this process would be facilitated by simple models, which do not have many cumbersome variates and do not contain nuisance parameters. Considering the three resistances that would arise if he were to incorporate learning as more important than the resistance with respect to asymmetry among agents, economists, and econometricians, Sargent (1981a) drew "the conclusion that incorporating optimal . . . learning . . . on the part of agents is not a research avenue that soon promises appreciable dividends for the economist interested in applying . . . models of the sort described here" (p. 236). Notice Sargent's use of the term *dividends* here and the appeal to *prices* and *costs* earlier. As argued in Chapters 2 and 3, the interpretation of these terms is not universal. As the follow section indicates, their definition follows from Sargent's interests and free moves.

5.3   Learning with Adaptive Expectations

Sargent's encounters with these conflicting resistances eventually set in motion a *process of accommodation*. The asymmetry of agents, econometricians, and economists did not sit well with Sargent and he searched for ways to deal with this hurdle without encountering the resistances that he identified with respect to incorporating learning. In the mid-1980s, he was led to revise some of the prior free moves in an attempt to satisfy his interest in conceptual integrity of theory and method. Instead of starting with rational expectations, he made the *free move* toward agents with *adaptive expectations* in a series of papers mostly coauthored with Albert Marcet, who was a graduate student at the University of Minnesota during Sargent's tenure. Marcet also spent a semester at Stanford University while Sargent was there and subsequently followed in Sargent's footsteps by accepting an assistant professor position at Carnegie Mellon University.

The models they developed were adaptive in the sense in which that term is used in the engineering control literature rather than the macroeconomics literature (see Appendix 5A). According to Sargent, "[I]n this new literature, what's being revised is not your expectation about a particular variable, but your expectation about a function that you are going to use for forecasting that variable" (Sargent in Jordan et al. 1993, p. 211). In particular, the agents were posited to behave as if they know with certainty that the true law of motion is time-invariant. Because the agents operate under the continually falsified assumption that the law of motion is time-invariant and known for sure, the models do not incorporate fully optimal behavior or rational expectations (see Marcet and Sargent 1989a, p. 338).

Accordingly, Sargent (1996a) acknowledged that "adaptive expectations has made a comeback . . . in the guise of non-Bayesian theories of learning" (p. 542). Somewhat surprisingly, he also indicated that "the power of rational expectations . . . has virtually inoculated us against the recurrence of adaptive expectations" (p. 542). The only explanation I can think of for the incongruity between his work with Marcet and this statement is that it was written in a paper celebrating the achievements of rational expectations economics. This again warns us against bowing to post hoc rationalizations.

Unwilling to relinquish the free move to rational expectations entirely, Sargent saw learning as a way of strengthening rational expectations and dealing with some of its problems.[7] He thought the rational expectations concept would be strengthened if agents could be modeled as groping their way toward the rational expectations equilibrium even when they were not perfectly rational: "Rational expectations is an equilibrium concept that at best describes how such a system might eventually behave if the system will ever settle down to a situation in which all of the agents have solved their 'scientific problems'" (Sargent 1993, p. 23). Since Marcet and Sargent felt that the rational expectations equilibrium would be more attractive if learning would drive the system toward this equilibrium (Marcet and Sargent 1992, p. 140), they were led to focus on convergence to the rational expectations fixed point (see Marcet and Sargent 1988, p. 168; 1989a, p. 360; 1989b, p. 1306; 1992, p. 140; Sargent 1993, p. 133). In addition, Sargent hoped that incorporating learning with adaptive expectations would allow him to deal with some of the problems associated with rational expectations: First, rational expectations models sometimes have too many equilibria (see Sargent 1993, p. 25); at the same time, a system with learning agents could be used to select an equilibrium path (see Sargent 1993, p. 134; Marcet and Sargent 1988, p. 168; 1992, p. 140).[8] Second, in certain instances such as those covered by the no-trade theorems, the outcomes predicted by rational expectations are difficult to reconcile with observations (see Sargent 1993, p. 25). At the same time, as indicated in the previous chapter, some kind of bounded rationality such as learning would allow Sargent to modify the sharp predictions that arise in some rational expectations models (see Sargent 1993, p. 134).[9] Third, rational expectations models were incapable of dealing with regime changes (see Sargent 1993, p. 27). Sargent believed that such regime changes could be analyzed through the incorporation of learning. Finally, rational expectations equilibria might be difficult to compute, whereas incorporating learning could assist in the computation of equilibria by suggesting algorithms for performing this task (see Marcet and Sargent 1988, p. 171; 1989b, p. 1320; 1992, p. 161; Sargent 1993, pp. 106, 152).

Once he moved to restore symmetry between agents, economists, and econometricians by incorporating learning, Sargent had to figure out what version of the learning assumption to use: "We are only just beginning to learn how models of learning influence macroeconomic performance" (Parkin 1996, p. 652). It is interesting to note the symmetry here in that both economists and agents are learning. Since Sargent was after conceptual integrity of theory and method with the free moves toward adaptive agents on the theory side of the coin and vector autoregressions on the method side, he could only satisfy his interest if the adaptive agents were to use vector autoregressions:

We model the agents in the economy as forming beliefs by fitting vector autoregressions. Each period, the agents add the latest observations and update their vector autoregressions. They use these updated vector autoregressions to form forecasts that influence decisions that they make, which in turn influence the motion of variables in the economy. (Marcet and Sargent 1992, p. 140; also see Marcet and Sargent 1988, p. 168; 1989b, p. 1307)

Hence, in his effort to restore symmetry among agents, economists, and econometricians, Sargent ended up with an *econometrically motivated interpretation of adaptive expectations* as a *forced move.* Under this rendition, agents used the same vector autoregressions and least squares estimation techniques as econometricians. In particular, his agents were modeled as learning through the sequential application of least squares (see Marcet and Sargent 1988, p. 169; 1989a, p. 337; 1989b, p. 1306; 1989c, p. 119; 1992, p. 142). This move is forced because it followed from the interplay of his interest in conceptual integrity and his free moves to adaptive expectations and vector autoregressions.

Before discussing why Sargent eventually did move toward incorporating learning despite the resistances he had earlier identified, I would like to make two brief remarks: First, Sargent's econometrically motivated interpretation of adaptive expectations resonates with his first moves in his career toward an econometrically motivated interpretation of rational expectations, as discussed in Chapter 2. In addition, his appeal to adaptive control theory echoes the free moves discussed in Chapter 3. Second, least squares learning might appear to be an oxymoron. As discussed in the previous chapter, econometric metaphors of reasoning do not confront the process of information search and errors made in information collecting; therefore, learning in a least squares framework is necessarily very limited.

Why did Sargent change his mind about incorporating the learning assumption? For one, his economic environment had changed, as "the problem of 'transition dynamics' forced itself on economists and statesmen" (Sargent 1993, p. 1). Rational expectations dynamics had its best chance of being applied when people were in recurrent situations, but the transition in Eastern Europe was not such a situation. Rational expectations economists could use their theories to describe how to expect a system to operate after it had fully adjusted to a new and coherent set of rules and expectations but had "virtually no theories about the transition itself" (p. 1).[10] Furthermore, regime changes, though widely applied, were inconsistent with rational expectations modeling. Under rational expectations, if the government were to have had the option of changing its behavior at future points in time, the agents in the model should have been given the opportunity to take this possibility into account. However, "[d]espite the fact that they are inconsistent with rational expectations, these types of regime change experiments have been a principal use of rational expectations models in macroeconomics" (p. 27).[11] Interestingly enough, Sargent (1996a) indicated that preference for these types of experiments had indirectly led to the adoption of rational expectations models: "The a priori insistence on best responses, inherited from the types of cross-regime policy question we prefer to study, is what pushed adaptive expectations to the sidelines in macroeconomics" (p. 542). By making the *free move* to analyzing *historical changes,* to involve these stories of government mess-ups and literal regime changes that could not be anticipated, Sargent (1993) was led to repudiate the idea of full prospective rationality as a *forced move* and let *learning* loose on "unprecedented opportunities, new and ill-defined rules, and a daily struggle to determine the 'mechanism' that will eventually govern trade and production" (p. 1).

In addition, Sargent's changed research environment encouraged him to deal with transition dynamics and to incorporate learning: "Recently, a number of researchers have begun studying this 'learning' problem" (Marcet and Sargent 1992, p. 140).[12] Furthermore, he received grants through the University of Minnesota from the National Science Foundation to research the subject of learning (see Sargent 1993, p. vi; Marcet and Sargent 1988, p. 168n; 1989a, p. 337n; 1989b, p. 1306n; 1989c, p. 119n; 1992, p. 139) and started his collaboration on adaptive expectations with his graduate student at Minnesota Albert Marcet and continued it during Marcet's visits to the Federal Reserve Bank of Minneapolis (see Marcet and Sargent 1989a, p. 337n). Also, certain techniques for adaptive systems, developed in the control literature by Ljung in the late 1970s to early 1980s, allowed Sargent to prove convergence of the learning scheme to rational expectations: "By applying theorems of Ljung, we extend some of our earlier results to characterize conditions under which a system governed by least-squares learning will eventually converge to a rational expectations equilibrium" (Marcet and Sargent 1989b, p. 1306; also see Marcet and Sargent 1988, p. 168n; 1989a, pp. 338n, 339n, 360; 1989b, pp. 1306–7; 1992, p. 141).

You may wonder how these moves relate to the three *resistances* connected with incorporating learning that Sargent had identified earlier. Two of the three disappeared thanks to the free move to adaptive expectations and the techniques developed for these models. First, under this interpretation of learning, a closed-form prediction formula could be established through the use of stochastic approximation methods based on the theorems of Ljung. In particular, "it can be shown that the limiting behavior . . . is described by a much simpler ordinary differential equation. The differential equation involves the operator mapping perceived laws of motion into actual laws of motion" (Marcet and Sargent 1992, p. 141; see Appendix 5A). Second, this ordinary differential equation made the problem of time invariance manageable, because despite nonstationarity, "agents erroneously believe that they live in an environment governed by a constant coefficient linear difference equation" (Marcet and Sargent 1989a, p. 341n). Moreover, since Sargent focused on convergence to rational expectations, time invariance was only temporary: "We know how the perceived law of motion and the actual one may converge to one another, depending on the behavior of a particular ordinary differential equation" (p. 337; see Sargent 1993, p. 132; also see Appendix 5A). The final problem, where to set the *dial of rationality*, remained: "These uses of least squares learning . . . are not entirely robust with respect to alternative specifications of the learning scheme. . . . Moreover . . . least squares learning specifications are irrational. . . . It is open and problematic whether the learning system . . . can ever be expected to yield econometric models that can be applied" (Marcet and Sargent 1988, p. 171).

Recall that Sargent had earlier used the language of prices, costs, and dividends to argue against incorporating the learning assumption. If there had been no problems with rational expectations, incorporating a learning mechanism would not have generated many dividends, because it would have had nonstationarity on its price tag and would have led to costs in terms of a proliferation of nuisance parameters. What happened to this language when Sargent started advocating the learning assumption? If there is such a thing as a free marketplace of ideas, then should not the interpretation of prices, costs, and dividends by Sargent have stayed the same? As discussed in Chapters 2 and 3, the interpretation of prices, costs, and dividends is not universal, but gains meaning through interests and free moves. With the free move to rational expectations, the dividends of incorporating the learning assumption were low and the price and costs were high. With the free move to adaptive expectations, the reverse was the case. These different interpretations of prices, costs, and dividends complicate the use of these metaphors as a serious analytical device.

Going back to Sargent's saga, we find another *forced move* following from his free moves: He obtained a *very limited interpretation of learning.* With the setting of the dial of rationality under adaptive expectations, agents still have to be quite smart, because

although sequential application of linear least squares to vector autoregression is not rational for these environments, it is still a pretty sophisticated method. Further, in the setups that appear in this literature, the agents are typically supposed to be quite smart about all aspects of their decision making except their forecasting decisions. (Marcet and Sargent 1992, pp. 161–2)

When his free moves were further elaborated, Sargent found that the only things the adaptive expectations agents did not know about the system within which they operate were particular parameters.[13] Whereas the agents were now posited as using the same kinds of control techniques that Sargent was applying, as discussed in Chapter 3, the behavior of these agents continued to be asymmetric with his own mixing of technical tools and economic models in his journey of discovery (see Marcet and Sargent 1992, p. 162; Marimon, McGrattan, and Sargent 1990, p. 330n). The only learning that the agents did consisted of updating their estimates for particular parameters. In addition, it is questionable how the agents can be almost fully rational and knowledgeable about the system when there are regime changes, one of the reasons Sargent started focusing on incorporating learning.

Furthermore, Sargent's ultimate goal of prediction, as identified in Chapter 3, was compromised by the *forced move* that when agents extract signals from endogenous variables by fitting first-order vector autoregressions, the *prediction errors* from these vector autoregressions will *not* be *orthogonal* to information lagged two or more periods, and "it can be shown that there is no finite-order vector autoregression that is long enough to make the prediction errors orthogonal to the Hilbert space generated by the infinite past history of agents' information" (Marcet and Sargent 1989b, p. 1320n; also see Marcet and Sargent 1989a, pp. 360–1). This problem eventually led Sargent to model agents as forecasting by fitting vector ARMA models for whatever information they have available:

In order to recover an equilibrium in which agents are conditioning on the entire history of their data record (as they have an incentive to do in this signal-extraction setting), we ought to model agents as fitting infinite-order autoregressions. . . . It is natural to conjecture that this problem can be neatly circumvented within the Marcet–Sargent framework by modeling the agents as fitting vector ARMA processes rather than pure autoregressions. (Sargent 1991, p. 249)[14]

However, Sargent was still left with a rather weak attempt at restoring symmetry among agents, economists, and econometricians. In fact, Marcet and Sargent (1992) suggested that the "next frontier . . . is to study the consequences of withdrawing from agents some of the knowledge that has been attributed to them in the least-squares learning literature" (p. 162).[15] As the following section discusses, this led Sargent to find different ways of satisfying his interests.

5.4   Learning with Artificial Intelligence

Unhappy with the arbitrary setting of the dial of rationality and the restricted interpretation of learning under adaptive expectations, Sargent continued his *process of accommodation*. The learning models he developed with Marcet assumed that agents had already formed a more or less correct model of the situation they were in, and that learning was just a matter of sharpening up the model a bit by adjusting a few knobs. What he wanted was something much more realistic, closer to the way economists and econometricians learn. He thought this might be achieved "by combing the recent literature on artificial intelligence as a source of methods and insights" (Sargent 1993, pp. 23–4). Hence, he made the *free move* toward learning agents with the help of *artificial intelligence* and referred to this as his bounded rationality program. Sargent thought he could restore symmetry "by expelling rational agents . . . and replacing them with 'artificially intelligent' agents who behave like econometricians. These 'econometricians' theorize, estimate, and adapt in attempting to learn about probability distributions which, under rational expectations, they already know" (p. 3). This move was partly inspired by Sargent's participation in the first economics workshop in Santa Fe: "My interest in studying economies with 'artificially intelligent' agents was spurred by attending a meeting . . . at the Santa Fe Institute in September 1987" (p. vi). Moreover, he left his subgroup on webs with some suggestions for how to deal with some of the classical problems in economics by replacing agents that have perfect foresight with adaptive rule-based agents who learn. As a result, Sargent was "optimistic about neural networks as devices in terms of which we shall eventually be able to formulate theories of learning" (Cho and Sargent 1996, p. 444).

Out of the several approaches to artificial intelligence, such as symbol processing in digital computers, adaptive computing systems, and expert systems, Sargent chose classifier systems and genetic algorithms after learning about them from John Holland at Santa Fe: "Our agents are artificially intelligent and are modeled as using classifier systems to make decisions" (Marimon et al. 1990, p. 329). In addition, Marcet and Sargent (1992) saw the "literature on genetic algorithms [as] a good source of ideas on how to proceed" (p. 162). John Holland had suggested applying classifiers to economics by finding an established model that "should be easily extendible in several dimensions so that even more realistic situations can be studied. In [Holland's] opinion, the two-nation overlapping generations model (see the discussion in Sargent) goes a long way toward meeting these criteria" (Anderson et al. 1988, p. 123).[16] This model could be modified by using classifier systems and subsequently compared with the standard rational expectations equilibrium solutions.[17]

Classifier systems were part of what could be called the adaptive computing approach to artificial intelligence, along with neural networks and other connectionist systems (see Anderson et al. 1988; Holland 1995; Holland and Miller 1991; Koza 1992; Lane 1993a, 1993b; Waldrop 1992).[18] They were parallel, message-passing, rule-based systems that modeled their environments by activating appropriate clusters of rules.[19] This structure allowed them to model complicated, changing environments; to interpret the internal states of agents in the theory so that the agents seemed to "model" their world progressively; to make agents able to build up behavioral repertoires that included chains of actions that were initiated long before the agents obtained the reward; and to make agents able to develop the capacity to plan future actions on the basis of their expectations of what the consequences of those actions would be. In addition, classifier systems had two particularly desirable efficiency properties: They did not impose heavy memory requirements on the system, and they allowed much of the information processing to be carried out in parallel.

In classifier systems, the agent was modeled as a collection of basic cognitive units, called "classifiers." In contrast to standard economic theory, there were no consistency requirements on the classifiers of which an agent was composed. In fact, there were some advantages to the notion of an agent as a bundle of possibly inconsistent behavioral propensities: First, requiring consistency imposed great computational costs on the system, as it entailed a lot of internal structure and frequent consistency checking among different structural components. Second, since the world was always more complicated than our personal experience, maintaining consistency in an agent's behavioral or conceptual system almost necessarily required a reduction in the agent's range of possible action, in particular in response to novel situations. Finally, evidence seemed to suggest that we humans do in fact maintain overlapping and inconsistent conceptual systems and associated behavioral propensities.

An agent that maintained inconsistent behavioral propensities had to have some mechanism that determined on which of these propensities it would actually act. This is where competition entered the stage. In Sargent's (1993) words: "The classifier system incorporates elements of the genetic algorithm with other aspects in a way that represents a brain in terms that Holland describes as a competitive economy" (p. 77). There might be more than one winner of the competition at any given time, and as a result a cluster of rules could react to external situations. The competition mechanism in classifier systems depended on a number that was associated with each of the agent's classifiers, its strength, which registered the "memory" of how well the classifier had served in the past in the agent's quest for reward. A classifier's strength was modified over time by one of the system's learning algorithms.

A classifier system adapted or learned through the application of two well-defined machine learning algorithms.[20] The first, the bucket brigade algorithm, changed classifier strengths by identifying actions that led to rewards – not just those that produced a reward directly, but also those that "set the stage." It changed the strength associated with each classifier with experience in two ways: First, any classifiers whose action was implemented passed some of their strength to their immediate predecessors. Second, the strength of classifiers whose action was implemented when the agent received an externally specified reward was increased as a function of the reward received. The system could be started off with a set of totally random classifiers. And then, as the environment reinforced certain behaviors and as the bucket brigade did its work, the classifiers would organize themselves into coherent sequences that produced at least a semblance of the desired behavior.

Even if the bucket brigade credit assignment algorithm worked perfectly, it could only rank the rules already present. By itself, it could only lead the system into highly optimized mediocrity. Two mechanisms were required to carry out the operation of replacing old classifiers with new ones. The first determined when replacements took place; it had to recognize situations in which the agent "needed" new classifiers. The second mechanism constructed new classifiers, which would probably improve the prospect that the agent would obtain a reward. This was a job for the genetic algorithm, which explored the immense space of possible new classifiers (see Holland and Miller 1991; Koza 1992; Lane 1993a, 1993b; Waldrop 1992). Genetic algorithms carried out a subtle search for tested, above-average "building blocks" and built new classifiers by combining parts of existing high-strength classifiers. The idea was that useful classifiers worked because they were composed of good building blocks, either in the features of the world that triggered them or in the actions they recommended. Trying out new combinations of these building blocks was more likely to produce useful new classifiers than was any kind of random search through the space of possible classifiers.

The genetic algorithm solved the problem of how to set the dial of rationality. The needle was set at 0 initially and then the genetic algorithm decided through mutation and recombination how far up the dial it went. By adding the genetic algorithm as a third layer on top of the bucket brigade and the basic rule-based system, an adaptive agent not only learned from experience but could also be spontaneous and creative. Sargent (1993) pointed out that, using the genetic algorithm,

[t]he "individuals" . . . do not "learn." (Each of them dies after one period.) Only the "society" of the sequence of populations . . . can be regarded as learning. This feature makes it difficult to accept the genetic algorithm as a model of an individual "brain." It is much easier to relate to John Holland's classifier system as a model of an individual's brain or thought process. (p. 76)

How could these classifier systems be applied to economics? Instead of being assumed to be perfectly rational, agents could be modeled with classifier systems and learn from experience as real economic agents do. Instead of modeling the economy as a general equilibrium, societies of classifier systems could organize a set of interacting economic agents into an economy. According to Sargent, "Economic systems . . . have some special features that physical and biological systems don't. An economic system is composed of individuals who are trying to figure out how the system works and to profit from this knowledge" (Parkin 1996, p. 651). Reluctant to give up ideas like representative agents or completed arbitrage and to renounce general equilibrium analysis, Sargent explored only one of these possibilities. Rather than using classifier systems to think about populations, he saw them as models of an individual's brain. Rather than relinquishing the neoclassical notion of an equilibrium, he focused on convergence to equilibrium.

One of the suggestions made during the economics workshop at Santa Fe in 1987 was to try to model the stock market Santa Fe style. The artificial stock market provided an environment for studying the behavior of many artificially intelligent agents who were trying to forecast the future of a traded asset that pays a random dividend. The idea was to go in with a scalpel, remove the perfectly rational agents from the standard neoclassical models, and substitute for them artificially intelligent agents that could learn and adapt as humans do.[21] The question was which phenomena would result from the interactions of different learning algorithms working in a simple trading environment and which kinds of real-world phenomena would be replicated in this computer-generated market. Would the agents just calmly settle down and start trading stock at the standard neoclassical price? Or would they enter a more realistic pattern of constant upheaval?

Sargent argued that the prices bid by the adaptive agents would very quickly settle down to the stock's "fundamental value," which is the price predicted by neoclassical theory for traders who share common beliefs about the world around them. The market might show a few random fluctuations up or down but would be drawn to the gravitational field of the fundamental value. Sargent appealed to a voluminous body of literature dealing with experimental economics to support his contention. In a number of laboratory simulations, with students playing the role of traders in simple stock markets, researchers had shown that the experimental subjects converged on the fundamental price very quickly (see, e.g., Day and Smith 1993; Friedman and Rust 1991; Grether, Isaac, and Plott 1989; Smith 1990). Moreover, Sargent collaborated with Marimon and McGrattan in the development of a Santa Fe–style computer model of his own (see Marimon, McGrattan, and Sargent 1990). Ramon Marimon, a graduate of Northwestern University, had become Sargent's colleague at the University of Minnesota. He and Sargent were also both Hoover Institute fellows at Stanford University for a year. Ellen McGrattan, one of Sargent's advisees and research assistants at Stanford, subsequently went to Duke University and then to the Federal Reserve Bank of Minneapolis.[22] "Their hope was that models with classifier system agents could support and even extend standard neoclassical theory, by providing a mechanism for arriving at equilibria, a tool for finding equilibria when direct calculation is intractable, and a way of distinguishing between multiple equilibria" (Lane 1993b, p. 184).[23] Marimon, McGrattan, and Sargent (1990) intended to continue their project: "The work described above is presented as the first steps of our project to use classifier systems of Holland to model learning in multi-agent environments. . . . [It] will facilitate formal analyses of systems of multi-agent classifier systems, which we intend to pursue" (pp. 369, 372). Two related characteristics of Marimon, McGrattan, and Sargent's classifier systems leap out: Their classifiers were of the representative agent type and converged on the rational expectations equilibrium.

First, compared to learning with adaptive expectations, the interpretation of learning with artificial intelligence was less restricted but still had limitations, because the

classifier systems that live in Marimon, McGrattan, and Sargent's version . . . receive much less prompting. . . . Still, they are prompted. They are told when to choose and what information to use. The size and the structure of their classifier systems, including the details of the accounting system, and the generalization and specialization operators, are chosen. (Sargent 1993, pp. 166–7)

A peculiar feature of Marimon, McGrattan, and Sargent's (1990) dynamics was that they imposed the same classifier systems on every agent of a given type: "We make this specification in order to economize on computer time and space" (p. 341n; also see Cho and Sargent 1996, pp. 448–50). This meant that when strengths were modified as a result of an interaction between any two agents, changes were made to all agents of the same types as the two interactors. They justified this imposition of "representative agents" in terms of savings in computer time and space, but it meant that they could not probe the extent to which (path-dependent) heterogeneity between initially homogeneous agents could arise in their economic environment. The "representative agent" constraint made it impossible to explore variant within-type agent behavior. By using classifier systems as models of populations rather than "representative agents," with within-type agent heterogeneity and some provision for differential replications rates for agents with different behaviors, more interesting behaviors might arise.[24]

Second, since Sargent was still unwilling to abandon rational expectations entirely, he resisted having a truly "evolutionary" model.[25] Focusing on convergence to equilibrium, he found that the classifier system agents did develop coherent economic identities and that the economy they formed was characterized by structured patterns of trade: "Marimon, McGrattan, and Sargent put collections of Holland classifier systems inside . . . economic environments and watched them converge to an equilibrium" (Sargent 1993, p. 153).[26] Marimon, McGrattan, and Sargent (1990) did acknowledge that this convergence property might be linked to their representative agent assumption: "[T]his specification speeds convergence relative to a setting in which each agent . . . uses his own classifier system" (p. 341n). They further suggested to adjust the system to speed up convergence:

[E]xisting algorithms can be improved. These improvements . . . will have the effect of improving the capacity of the classifier systems to settle upon optimal results more rapidly, and to avoid becoming locked in to suboptimal patterns of interaction. The improved algorithms will also help . . . to develop analytical results on the convergence of classifier systems. (p. 372)

Some have argued that this focus on convergence is not strictly compatible with the evolutionary principles governing classifier systems (see, e.g., Goldberg 1989, pp. 6–7; Weagle 1995, pp. 27–8).

In his collaboration with Marimon and McGrattan, Sargent continued to rely on convenient representations, as in the case study discussed in Chapter 3. Besides the two characteristics mentioned, he imposed further restrictions on standard genetic algorithms (see Weagle 1995 for a detailed discussion). In fact, Marimon, McGrattan, and Sargent (1990) acknowledged that "[m]ore standard Holland algorithms were first tried without much success, prompting us to produce the modified algorithm" (p. 358n). Rather than using the standard one-point crossover reproduction mechanism, they included a two-point method of recombination. Rather than adopting classifiers to model markets, they simulated single agents by the interaction of two autonomous classifier systems. According to Weagle (1995), Sargent's "[a]gents make virtual bids (to themselves?) and transactions (with themselves?) to gain control of their own actions" (p. 37). Rather than using genetic algorithms to provide the environmental flexibility that traditional artificial intelligence techniques lacked, they diminished their role.

Sargent's attempts to use his free move to artificial intelligence to support or even extend standard neoclassical economic theory led him to move away from standard interpretations of classifier systems. If he had adopted those more traditional versions, he would have found that they would have implied a *forced move* away from methodological individualism and neoclassical equilibrium (see De Vaney 1996). First, for standard genetic algorithms, the structures undergoing adaptation were a population of individual points from the search space, rather than a single point (see Koza 1992, pp. 18, 79). These genetic algorithms functioned as a highly parallel mathematical algorithm that transformed a set (population) of individual mathematical objects, each with an associated fitness value, into a new population using operations patterned after the Darwinian principles of reproduction and survival of the fittest and after naturally occurring genetic operations. These methods differed from methodological individualism in that they simultaneously involved a parallel search involving hundreds or thousands of points in the search space. Second, the population may converge (i.e., become identical) or fail to converge; in fact, premature convergence (i.e., convergence to a globally suboptimal result) was a major concern with genetic algorithms (see Booker 1987; Koza 1992, pp. 104, 191, 616–18, 701–2). Furthermore, Sargent found that the stable trade structures that emerged did not necessarily correspond to a Markovian Nash equilibrium. In particular, classifier system agents were reluctant to speculate even when it was "rational" for them to do so.[27] In this "survival of the mediocre," the genetic algorithm failed to find the global optimum. According to Lane (1993b), "As a result, the idea to use classifier system agents in a mere supporting role in equilibrium theory seems a dead end" (p. 186).

A model of an artificial stock market designed by Palmer, Arthur, Holland, LeBaron, and Tayler (1994) started from different motivations than those of Marimon, McGrattan, and Sargent. Like Sargent, Brian Arthur and John Holland had both participated in the economics workshop at Santa Fe. Unlike Sargent, they both had a strong instinct that the stock market had so much potential to self-organize its own behavior and to become complex that rich new behavior could emerge. They argued very strongly that realistic adaptive behavior would only lead to rational expectations if the problem were simple enough or if the conditions were repeated again and again. However, in an on–off situation that was never going to happen again or a situation that was very complicated, so that the agents had to do an awful lot of computing, then, Arthur and Holland conjectured, establishing convergence to rational expectations required loading almost impossible conditions onto these agents. They had to have knowledge of their own expectations, of the dynamics of the market, of other people's expectations, of other people's expectations about other people's expectations, ad infinitum. Under those circumstances, Arthur and Holland argued, the agents were so far from equilibrium that the "gravitational pull" of the rational expectations outcome would become very weak, and dynamics and surprise would be the driving forces.[28] Furthermore, if convergence did not occur, rational expectations would be ill-defined, because an individual trader's simple forecasting rule might outperform complete information forecasts when other traders were also using similar simple rules to determine behavior.

To gain insight into the reasons why real-world traders perceived their markets as they did, Palmer et al. (1994) designed an artificial stock market peopled by computer automata. Since their motivations were different from those of Marimon, McGrattan, and Sargent, they consequently had different results. Rather than trying to strengthen rational expectations economics, they rejected it:

In complex problems, R[ational] E[xpectations] theory runs into a number of difficulties. . . . These difficulties lead in turn to predictions that do not always fit observed outcomes. And even when final outcomes are correctly predicted by RE theory, the theory is silent about the dynamical process (typically involving trial and error, and learning) that agents actually take to reach that solution. (p. 265)

Palmer et al. hoped to design a system in which real-world features arose as the result of interactions among heterogeneous agents, each capable of learning about the world created by their joint actions but exploiting a different frame of reference that generated different "local" opportunities for successful actions. Initially, the automata were provided with simple rules for buying and selling, but as they went along, genetic algorithms learned by periodically generating new predictors for each agent.[29] Winning classifiers were rewarded on the basis of the (one-period) profits that resulted from the transaction they initiated. The stock price each period was determined by the actions of all agents, which in turn reflected complicated interactions among their constituent predictors. How well any given predictor functioned depended in turn on the market's overall price dynamics. As a result of this complexity of interaction and feedback between levels, the behavior that emerged in this system, both at the level of individual agents and at the level of the market's price dynamics, was very rich.

Palmer et al. (1994) contrasted their "approach to modeling a market . . . with conventional rational expectations approaches" and found that their "model does not necessarily converge to an equilibrium, and can show bubbles, crashes, and continued high trading volume" (p. 264).[30] In Arthur's summary account of the experiments, the price began by fluctuating around fundamental value, just as in the experiments by Marimon, McGrattan, and Sargent.[31] Subsequently, "mutually reinforcing trend-following or technical-analysis-like rules" established themselves in the predictor populations. Later, other phenomena, such as speculative bubbles and crashes, were observed to occur. Moreover, the market did not seem to settle down to any stationary state, as in the model of Marimon, McGrattan, and Sargent. When he cloned and "froze" successful agents and then reintroduced them much later into the system, Arthur found that they turned out to perform poorly, since they were no longer adapted to the behavior of other agents in the market. Although these results seem to call Sargent's "representative agents" and convergence to equilibrium into question, I do not want to suggest that Sargent was wrong and Palmer et al. were right; rather, I have contrasted the two approaches to illustrate how different motivations might lead to different interpretations of free moves.

I end this discussion by returning to Sargent's embrace of artificial intelligence in his effort to restore symmetry among agents, economists, and econometricians. Sargent's attempts to make the three types of actor equally boundedly rational through artificial intelligence were inspired by his visit to the Santa Fe Institute. Recall that his "research program [was] to build models populated by agents who behave like working economists or econometricians" (Sargent 1993, p. 22).[32] Or, "the agents in the model [are] more like the econometrician" (p. 22) and "the economist will assume that he is modeling sets of people whose behavior is determined by the same principles that he is using to model them" (p. 24). The extension of symmetry with the free move to artificial intelligence led Sargent to reexamine the connection he was trying to establish between traditional econometrics and neoclassical economics. As a result, this free move subsequently called forth some *forced moves* and *resistances.*

What happened on the *econometrics* side of the coin? Sargent (1993) saw statistics and econometrics as a "starting place because we propose to make our agents even more like statisticians or econometricians than they are in rational expectations models" (p. 35). He thought that his move to artificial intelligence would satisfy his interest in conceptual integrity and that he could restore symmetry by pointing out the parallels between artificial intelligence and econometrics in terms of the problems to be solved and methods to be used: "There are evidently many fascinating connections between research lines being pursued within the 'connectionist' literatures . . . and the econometrics and statistics literatures" (p. 81), and the "connections between the literatures on neural networks and econometrics provide additional perspective on our characterization of bounded rationality as a program to populate models with devices that mimic econometricians" (p. 54). He even went as far as claiming that "artificial intelligence . . . just implements recursive least squares in various ingenious contexts" (p. 35; also see Cho and Sargent 1996, pp. 444–6).[33]

Unfortunately for Sargent, he ran into the *resistance* that he was unable to fully establish parallels between the techniques of traditional econometrics and those of artificial intelligence. Handing over recursive least squares algorithms to agents (Sargent 1993, p. 81) was certainly not the same as giving them the use of classifier systems to make decisions (Marimon et al. 1990, p. 329). Recall that the genetic algorithm searched, generated, and tested new classifiers. These replaced weak rules and served in turn as plausible hypotheses to be tested under competition. This approach differed distinctly from econometric theories of inference and hypothesis testing, since these were applied after the data had been collected and possessed a blind spot for the search for information. Although "exploratory data analysis" or "data mining" had become standard practice, traditional econometrics was not concerned with the search processes involved in determining the relevant information and looking for ways to find this information. Furthermore, Sargent (1993) even acknowledged that the "genetic algorithm of John Holland was devised to find maxima of 'rugged landscapes' that lack the smoothness that Newton's method [that is used in recursive least squares] exploits" (p. 74).[34] Though Holland's algorithms also searched for tops of hills, their landscape might change as a result of their actions. Furthermore, premature convergence (i.e., convergence to a globally suboptimal result) was a major concern with classifier systems: There was no guarantee that they would uniformly cluster at the peak of the highest hill.

This brings us to a discussion of the *neoclassical theory* component of conceptual integrity. Once Sargent adopted artificial intelligence as a symmetry principle, extending this concept to economists led him to revisit his assumptions about economic theory. The problem was that "we do not really have a tight enough theory or description of how economists or other scientists learn about the world. And within economics and other sciences, there are important differences in how different practitioners go about the process of discovery" (p. 23).[35] So how could Sargent make agents act as scientists act if there is no clear picture of what scientists do? Sargent thought that "[s]ome of [the artificial intelligence] methods embody sensible versions of at least aspects of what we might mean by 'behave like a scientist' " (pp. 23–4). He felt that including economists and other scientists in the symmetry picture through the use of artificial intelligence would lead us to rethink their work, because "literatures on artificial intelligence and neural networks are full of ideas that are potentially applicable to our problems as researchers. . . . [W]e expect that in searching these literatures . . . we shall find ways to improve ourselves" (p. 33). Therefore, "adaptive agents are 'teaching' the economist in the same sense that any numerical algorithm for solving nonlinear equations 'teaches' a mathematician" (p. 155). This extension of symmetry to economic theory still left Sargent with a distorted picture of what economists do, because "when these agents can 'teach' us something, it is because we designed them to do so" (p. 155). I return to this point in section 5.7 by comparing Sargent's analysis with that of science studies scholars.

Interestingly enough, the free move to artificial intelligence left Sargent with an *asymmetry between him and the agents* in his models, because "[e]conometricians are now using genetic algorithms and stochastic Gauss–Newton procedures, even if the agents in the models that they are estimating are not" (p. 170). And when Sargent made the agents more bounded in their rationality, he had to be smarter because his models became larger and more demanding econometrically. For, "an econometric consequence of replacing rational agents with boundedly rational ones is to add a number of parameters" (p. 168) because there "are many choices to be made in endowing our artificial agents with adaptive algorithms" (p. 134) and we "face innumerable decisions about how to represent decision making processes and the way that they are updated" (p. 165).[36] Furthermore, this free move did not allow him to satisfy his interest in conceptual integrity of theory and method, because the proliferation of free parameters in his artificial intelligence approach also left him with an *asymmetry between economists and econometricians*:[37] Whereas some economists embraced bounded rationality through artificial intelligence, most econometricians were reluctant to do so:

Bounded rationality is a movement to make model agents behave more like econometricians. Despite the compliment thereby made to their kind, macroeconometricians have shown very little interest in applying models of bounded rationality to data. Within the economics profession, the impulse to build models populated by econometricians has come primarily from theorists with different things on their minds than most econometricians. (Sargent 1993, pp. 167–8)[38]

Sargent's saga ends in the present and we are left with the question of what is ahead. Will Sargent ever be able to satisfy his interest in conceptual integrity of theory and method? Will he ignore the forced moves and resistances? Will he make new free moves? Will he change his motivation? We will have to wait and see. For now, I shift the narrative by providing a perspective on Sargent's work through the glasses of Herbert Simon and the artificial intelligence community.

5.5   Sargent versus Simon

Sargent (1993) titled his most recent book *Bounded Rationality in Macroeconomics* and tried to link it to Simon's program of bounded rationality and artificial intelligence: "Herbert Simon and other advocates of 'bounded rationality' propose to create theories with behavioral foundations by eliminating the asymmetry that rational expectations builds in between the agents in the model and the econometrician who is estimating it" (pp. 21–2).[39] It is interesting to note that rational expectations theory was born at the same time in the same nest as bounded rationality, namely, in the late 1960s at Carnegie Mellon University. Muth, Lucas, Sargent, and Simon were all present at its inception and engaged in long arguments over the relevance of neoclassical theory. The irony continues when rational expectations theory, born from the same mother as bounded rationality, after trying to kill her big sister, now apparently came around to embracing her in the person of Sargent. However, was Simon's bounded rationality program really concerned about asymmetry in neoclassical economics and econometrics? And did Simon really advocate parallel processing and adaptive computing systems (see Crevier 1993; Egedi et al. 1992; Mirowski 1993a, 1994; Simon 1987, 1991, 1993)?

Simon (1991) was at the Graduate School of Industrial Administration of Carnegie Mellon University and mentioned that "Tom Sargent . . . was also with us for a short time" (p. 250). Simon was dismayed that the new faculty that had been recruited had little taste or talent for empirical research that did not start (and sometimes end) with formal model building. Although he had never thought he lacked sympathy with mathematical approaches to social sciences, he soon found himself frequently in a minority position when he took stands against what he regarded as "excessive formalism and shallow mathematical pyrotechnics. The situation became worse as a strict neoclassical orthodoxy began to gain ascendancy among the economists. It began, oddly enough, with Jack Muth" (p. 249). And it continued when "[b]eginning in 1971, Lucas and Tom Sargent . . . brought the theory of rational expectations into national and international prominence" (p. 250).

Simon noted, "It is not without irony that bounded rationality and rational expectations . . . though entirely antithetical to each other, were engendered in and flourished in the same small business school at almost the same time"

(p. 250). In what sense were the two programs opposed to each other? According to Simon (1987), "The term 'bounded rationality' is used to designate rational choice that takes into account the cognitive limitations of the decision-maker – limitations of both knowledge and computational capacity" (p. 266). And "[t]he theory of rational expectations offered a direct challenge to theories of bounded rationality, for it assumed a rationality in economic actors beyond any limits that had previously been considered even in neoclassical theory" (Simon 1991, p. 250). Controversies between economists advocating the opposing programs eventually led Simon to retreat from the Graduate School of Industrial Administration and to move his office to the Psychology Department around 1970 (p. 251).

Did the two opposing poles of Simon's bounded rationality and Sargent's rational expectations finally join hands again in Sargent's most recent venture? Not quite, for instead of using bounded rationality as Sargent did to try to strengthen the concept of rational expectations, Simon pointed out in his theory of bounded rationality why the basic assumptions of neoclassical economics did not always work in practice.[40] First, instead of assuming a fixed set of alternatives among which the decision maker chose, Simon's theory of bounded rationality postulated a process for generating alternatives. Appealing to studies in modern cognitive psychology on the processes that human subjects used to choose among given alternatives and find possible courses of action, Simon argued that under most circumstances it was not reasonable to talk about finding "all the alternatives." Generation and evaluation of alternatives was a lengthy and costly process, one in which, in real-world situations, even minimal completeness could seldom be guaranteed. Second, Simon detected another weakness associated with the basic assumptions of neoclassical economics in that individuals had difficulty generating original solutions to problems. Cognitive limits – a lack of knowledge and limited ability to forecast the future – played a central role in the evaluation of alternatives; these were not simply limits on specific information, but also limits on the adequacy of scientific theories that could be used to predict the relevant phenomena.[41] Such observations led Simon to speculate that the mind mostly functions by applying approximate or cookbook solutions to problems. Finally, instead of assuming the maximization of a utility function, Simon's bounded rationality theory postulated a satisficing strategy, which sought to identify, in theory and in actual behavior, procedures for choosing that were computationally simpler, and argued that individuals picked the first choice that met a preset acceptance criterion.

Simon's interpretation of bounded rationality was different from Sargent's, since it was shaped by different interests and moves. Simon (1991) wrote in his biography: "Actually, to say that I retreated from the Graduate School of Industrial Administration is only partly correct; I was also drawn to the Psychology Department and the burgeoning new activity around the computer by the shift in my own research interests" (p. 251). For Simon, the "Psychology Department provided the platform for launching the cognitive revolution in psychology. A sequence of organizations, culminating in the Computer Science Department, provided the corresponding platform for artificial intelligence" (p. 252). Simon was interested in finding out how people make decisions and was driven by the conviction that neoclassical economists were not all that serious about describing the formal foundations of rationality, whereas he was. His conclusions, though contrary to conventional economic theory, offered an open window into the workings of the human mind.

Furthermore, Simon's motivations and moves shaped an interpretation of artificial intelligence that was distinctly different from that of Sargent. The same ideas of "heuristic" or "rule-bound" search, "satisficing" behavior, and "goal, subgoal" strategy that shaped Simon's theory of bounded rationality also became key concepts in his problem-space approach to reproducing human-style reasoning. According to Simon's physical symbol system hypothesis, the necessary and sufficient condition for a system to be capable of thinking – doing those things that, if they were done by a human being, we would call thinking – was that it be able to perform symbolic processes. The two main processes predominant in this theory of thinking were problem solving by heuristic search and problem solving by recognition. This involved (1) putting symbols in; (2) putting symbols out; (3) storing symbols and relational structures of symbols; (4) constructing, modifying, and erasing such symbol structures; (5) comparing two symbol structures; and (6) following one course of action or another, depending on the outcome of such a comparison. The result was a step-by-step mental search through a vast "problem space" of possibilities, with each step guided by a heuristic rule of thumb: "If this is the situation, then that step is worth taking." If the hypothesis was true, several consequences followed: First, computers, appropriately programmed, were capable of thinking. Second, the human brain, since it was capable of thinking, was (at least) a physical symbol system.

Simon argued for constructing a theory of the architecture of the mind and the characteristics of that architecture at the symbolic level, even in the absence of any but a very incomplete and primitive theory of how these symbolic processes were implemented by neuronal structures:

Those efforts that undertake to introduce "neurons" possessing relatively realistic biological properties have been limited largely to simple, low-level structures containing few neurons, hence cannot yet be linked in any clear way to models or phenomena at the symbolic level. On the other hand the "neurons" of connectionist models are more numerous, but they have few of the properties of real neurons, and provide a foundation for only very abstract models of thought processes. Moreover, it has not yet been demonstrated that they can account for any wide range of complex cognitive performances in the domains of problem solving, use of language, or reasoning. (Simon 1991, p. 645)

Simon concluded, "it is improbable that [connectionist nets or neural networks] will supersede models of the more traditional serial kind as explanations of behavior at the symbolic level" (pp. 645–6).

Rather than treating individuals as a population of classifiers as Sargent had, Simon analyzed the architecture of the mind at the symbolic level without a theory of how these symbolic processes were implemented by neuronal structures. Simon (1993) wanted "to characterize most of the higher-level and complex cognitive phenomena at the symbol level, rather than attempting to describe it all solely in neurological terms" (p. 644). Rather than analyzing the brain as a predominantly parallel device as Sargent did, Simon settled on a serial system. Simon dismissed the conclusion that the brain was predominantly a parallel device and that for this reason a serial computer could not simulate a brain process, by arguing that this conclusion did not take into account that the details of neuronal implementation were largely independent of the theory of the mind's symbol structures and symbol processes: "Even extensive parallel processing at the neural level would not imply parallelism at the symbolic level" (p. 644).

Whereas Sargent's motivations and moves led him to focus on parallel adaptive computing systems and neoclassical choice theory, Simon's revealed the structural similarities of his serial symbol-processing program and the "bounded" alternative to neoclassical choice theory. Searching, rule-bound decisions, goal-oriented behavior – most of the basic ideas of Simon's bounded rationality theory – were carried over to his interpretation of artificial intelligence.

5.6   Artificial Intelligence

How well did artificial intelligence serve Sargent's and Simon's interests? It allowed them to make machines do things that would require intelligence if done by human beings (see Barrow 1992; Collins 1990; Crevier 1993; Forsythe 1993; Hodges 1983; Hofstadter 1979; Koza 1992; Penrose 1989; Simon 1991). Starting with the view that mental activity could be seen as simply the carrying out of some well-defined sequence of operations, frequently referred to as an "algorithm," proponents of artificial intelligence had the objectives of imitating by means of machines, usually digital computers, as much of human mental activity as possible, and perhaps even eventually improving on human abilities in these respects. Supposing it was simply the logical structure of the algorithms that was significant, and the particular physical embodiment being entirely irrelevant, machines could be made to simulate mental activity by programming them in a certain way, since programs relied on the correct functioning of their underlying hardware as much as brains relied on the correct functioning of their neurons. Some proponents of these computer programs argued that our minds were simply "computers made of meat," and some observers thought computers would eventually surpass humans in mathematical ability. Others argued that mathematics is an art, a creative act, that cannot be reduced to logic.

As briefly mentioned, there were at least three alternative approaches to artificial intelligence: symbol processing in digital computers, adaptive computing through neural networks and classifiers, and expert systems. Simon's interest in human decision making and the foundations of rationality made him move to the *symbol-processing* approach. The basic ideas here were that intelligence was nothing but the ability to process symbols and that thought consisted of expanding symbol structures in a rule-based manner, breaking them up and re-forming them, destroying some and creating new ones. Starting from these principles, Simon introduced a general-purpose computer model of human cognition, which did seem to capture much of what actually went on in our heads, since these computers behaved efficiently as search engines and could be trained to associate preset responses with appropriate stimulus patterns. Indeed, if you took this view literally, this kind of symbol processing was thinking and these machines could imitate boundedly rational mental activity.

Yet, the use of symbols to represent concepts was controversial. A symbol was simply a pattern, made of any substance whatsoever, that was used to denote, or point to, some other symbol, or some object or relation among objects. Where did the symbolic concepts originate? And how did they evolve and grow? Or how were they molded by feedback from the environment? By themselves, symbols were far too rigid and omitted far too much, because the interconnections between neurons in the brain were not in fact fixed, as they would be in a computer model, but were changing all the time. This difference between brain action and symbol-processing action was related to a phenomenon known as "brain plasticity," which gave rise to some form of learning. If machines could learn, it would be possible to counter the objection that a machine would be doing only what a person had explicitly designed it to do. However, symbol-processing computers could not generate useful ideas of their own to make sense of new situations. Learning implied relating newly acquired knowledge to previously known facts in a manner permitting its efficient use. In order to make computers learn in a manner approximating the human norm, it was thus necessary to solve an underlying problem beforehand: that is, to find out how to represent, within the memory of a computer, such different pieces of knowledge as these, as well as the links relating them. Hence, researchers in symbol processing put learning on a back burner and concentrated on the problem of knowledge representation instead.

Since Sargent wanted to restore symmetry among agents, economists, and econometricians by incorporating learning, the symbol-processing approach was not an attractive alternative for him. Visiting the Santa Fe Institute sparked his interest in simulations of intelligence that employed neural networks or other highly parallel architectures like classifiers, instead of a serial symbolic system; this approach, based on the phenomenon of brain plasticity, was also referred to as "connectionist." *Adaptive computing systems* were webs of interconnected specially designed processors that could be trained (through the application of varying degrees of voltage) to respond independently to external stimuli. Such models' capacity for some kind of rudimentary learning would seem to argue that brains and computers were essentially equivalent. However, they were a long way from being realistic models of the brain, because various differences between brain action and computer action remained. When a neuron fired, it was the frequency of successive pulses that increased enormously. There was also a probabilistic aspect of neuron firing, in that the same stimulus did not always produce the same outcome. Moreover, brain action did not have the exact speed that was needed for electronic computer currents; the action of neurons was very much slower than that of the fastest electronic circuits. Also, there seemed to be a great deal of randomness and redundancy in the detailed way in which neurons were actually connected (see Penrose 1989, pp. 374–404).

For Sargent, adaptive computing held out the promise of simulating learning by boundedly rational agents and parallel processing presented the prospect of aiding the calculation of rational expectations equilibria. Computer scientists called parallel processing the simultaneous application to a single task of many processors, be they neurons or computers. Applying parallel processing, as opposed to serial processing, to computers offered the advantage of tremendously increasing their power, since a very great number of separate calculations were carried out independently, and the results of these largely autonomous operations were only intermittently combined to contribute to the overall calculation.

Finally, *expert systems* were computer programs based on the idea that one could create systems that captured the decision-making processes of human experts (see, e.g., Crevier 1993; Forsythe 1993). They automated decision-making processes normally undertaken by a given human expert and assisted people in performing a variety of tasks, including diagnosis, planning, scheduling, and design. Many modern expert systems involved thousands of rules. It would be extremely tedious to find the rules pertinent to a given problem (or to follow the corresponding search tree) on paper. User-friendly program interfaces made the search itself transparent and turned the consultation into a question-answering session. At the design stage, the analyst could correct errors by asking the system how it reached a faulty conclusion. Since the rules were usually self-explanatory, end users could also follow the reasoning involved and thus satisfy themselves of the validity of the system's conclusion. To perform all these tasks, expert systems allowed the automatic chaining of rules: that is, entering the rules in an order different from the one in which they would appear in the reasoning. Problem solutions did not usually follow from a single string of rules or from a single branch of the tree. Several paths were usually open in the search down the tree. Since they were easy to change or improve, expert systems differed from printed rule books, or even from conventional computer programs, through their flexibility and modularity. Yet another difference of expert systems was their openness, or self-explanatory character, and they were much more resilient than conventional computer programs. One could usually remove any single rule without grossly affecting the program performance.

Visionaries in the artificial intelligence community believed that computers would increasingly be able to duplicate human expertise. However, expert systems were limited to specialized fields of application and inferior to the best human experts. First, they had a tendency to break down when the user reached the edge of their knowledge. A given program could not know the limits of its knowledge and knew even less where missing information might be. Even more basic weaknesses of expert systems involved their problems with time and causality, and their inability to learn, since learning involved the establishment of correspondences and analogies between objects and classes of objects. Since expert systems had problems with these types of activities, they were not helpful to Sargent's project of incorporating learning. Furthermore, to true human experts, these systems amounted to little more than sophisticated reminder lists. When, however, know-how was locally unavailable or too expensive, expert systems operating in a restricted field could make better decisions than untrained human beings.

With this understanding of why Sargent adopted adaptive computing as opposed to other approaches to artificial intelligence, we can move on by asking how well his approach suited his purpose. Could he restore symmetry among agents, economists, and econometricians by replacing perfectly rational agents with boundedly rational ones, or was he led to face some resistances? His adoption of adaptive computing systems amounted to arguing that an algorithm could have the same information-processing capability as the human mind (see Binmore 1985, 1987, 1988; Penrose 1989; Simon 1976, 1991).[42] The terms "algorithm" and "algorithmic" referred to anything that could be simulated on a general-purpose computer, which included "parallel action," "neural networks" (or "connection machines"), "heuristics," "learning," and interaction with the environment. Now, Gödel's incompleteness theorem and Turing's discovery of noncomputable mathematical functions constituted a challenge to artificial intelligence by casting doubt on the extent to which algorithms could replace human intelligence.

What Gödel showed was that any formal mathematical system of axioms and rules of procedure, provided that it was broad enough to contain descriptions of simple arithmetical propositions and provided that it was free of contradiction, must contain some statements that are neither provable nor disprovable by the means allowed within the system. The truth of such statements thus could not be determined by the approved procedures. It followed from Gödel's argument that the concept of mathematical truth could not be encapsulated in any formalistic scheme and that the validity of an algorithmic system must be established by external means, for lack of means allowed within the system. Turing established the insolubility of the halting problem after studying the work of Gödel. When a machine has access to all relevant information and can compute for an arbitrarily long period, it is necessarily the case that the machine will sometimes make erroneous predictions. The reason is essentially that the machine would sometimes calculate forever if this were permitted. To prevent this, a "stopping rule" must be built in. If such a stopping rule guillotines an exact calculation, then the machine will be forced to employ an alternative "guessing algorithm." There is necessarily an arbitrary element in the choice of stopping-rule-cum-algorithm, if only because it will always be better to stop later and hence guess less frequently.

Some concluded from the previous argument that no formal system could capture all the judgments and processes of the human mind and that the human brain conducted its operations by the employment of noncomputable operations (see, e.g., Penrose 1989).[43] If algorithms did not, in themselves, decide mathematical truth and if the mere carrying out of a successful algorithm did not in itself imply that any understanding had taken place, imitating mental activity with artificial intelligence was best thought of as an unattainable ideal. This argument would constitute a problem for Sargent, since it implied that he could not replace the brains of the boundedly rational agents by some computer algorithm. However, two alternative moves could be made in response to the preceding reasoning, other than that human mathematical understanding was not algorithmic (see, e.g., Barrow 1992; Hofstadter 1979).

First, some proponents of artificial intelligence suggested that the argument against algorithmic mental activity presented an oversimplified characterization of the artificial intelligence project; the idea of mathematical computability was neither necessary nor sufficient to produce a mind. There was no reason to believe that the mental processes of simple living creatures possessed all of the processing powers of a computer. Nor would we expect a single program to be able to simulate the behavior of a complex system linked to its chaotically unpredictable environment in all sorts of complicated (or even random) ways that produced noncomputable responses. Nor need this system do anything that we would characterize as intelligence. Most workers in the field of artificial intelligence were well aware of these issues and did not contend that the mere execution of an algorithm would evoke consciousness. They did not take it for granted that pleasure and pain, the appreciation of beauty and humor, consciousness and free will were capacities that would emerge naturally when electronic robots became sufficiently complex in their algorithmic behavior. Under this redefined interpretation of the artificial intelligence project, Sargent was still faced with the resistance that he could not imitate boundedly rational agents with artificially intelligent machines and, therefore, could not restore symmetry. So this move would not satisfy Sargent's interests.

Second, it could be argued that human beings simply made use of a fallible algorithm. For the most part, the algorithm that humans employed to judge mathematical truths was reliable just as they would expect it to be. After all, it had evolved through a process of natural selection that would have penalized defective algorithms if they resulted in misjudgments about everyday events whose correct appraisal was essential for survival. Similarly, as the intelligence of machines evolved, its underlying mechanisms would gradually converge to those underlying human intelligence. To create true intelligence, artificial intelligence workers would just have to keep pushing to ever lower levels, closer and closer to brain processes, if they wished their machines to attain the capabilities of human beings. This answer posed fewer problems in Sargent's attempt to satisfy his interest in conceptual integrity.

Another debate in the artificial intelligence community concerned the link between adaptive computing mechanisms, or connectionist networks, and commonsense psychology. Ramsey, Stich, and Garon (1991), for example, trained several connectionist networks, in which the encoding of information is widely distributed and subsymbolic, to report truth values. They found that because such networks do not contain functionally discrete, interpretable states, they cannot display distinct causal roles. In connectionist networks, no distinct state or part of the network represents any particular proposition. Since the information encoded is stored holistically and distributed throughout the network, it is impossible to ask whether a particular proposition played a central role in the network's computation. Because all units and connections are always involved in connectionist networks, they cannot be used to analyze why a person did something for one reason and not another. This runs counter to commonsense psychology, which seems to presuppose that there is generally some answer to the question of whether a particular belief or memory played a causal role in a specific cognitive episode. Ramsey et al. concluded that if connectionism is true, commonsense psychology must be false. Though not everyone has concurred with this evaluation (see, e.g., Bechtel and Abrahamsen 1991; Dennett 1978; Lycan 1991), it does illustrate that certain forms of epistemology are incompatible with connectionism. Since Sargent adopted this type of framework, he was not able to analyze the internal representation of a proposition and the justificatory argument for its truth. He could only study the capacity to produce a proposition and, if required, identify evidence for it. Though this limitation might lead epistemologists to abandon the framework, it is unlikely to lead Sargent, interested in conceptual integrity of theory and method, to relinquish it. If conceptual integrity does not require the analysis of internal representations of and justificatory arguments for propositions, the severed link between connectionism and commonsense psychology would not be a resistance for Sargent.

The discussion that follows provides a perspective on the relationship between Sargent and science studies scholars to shed further light on the symmetry paradoxes identified in the previous chapter.

5.7   Sargent as a Science Studies Scholar

How do economists relate to the agents in their models? What is the connection between science studies scholars and scientists? Is Sent different from Sargent or are their voices not distinct? Who is learning from whom? Sargent, science studies scholars, and Sent had similar choices between assigning sameness and difference, as analyzed in the previous chapter. While Sargent set out to assert difference through rational expectations in the 1960s to 1970s, science studies scholars focused on assigning sameness. However, their paths finally met in the 1980s to 1990s, when Sargent moved toward assigning some sameness through bounded rationality and science studies scholars made some steps toward assigning difference, even to the point of entertaining certain economistic images of science.

In the 1960s to 1970s, Sargent claimed a superiority of agents over scientists, a difference, by making them use mechanical optimization systems in the form of rational expectations models. While scientists were struggling with scientific problems, rational expectations represented an equilibrium situation in which all of the agents have solved their "scientific problems" (see Sargent 1993, p. 23). At the same time, science studies scholars started asserting sameness between them and their subjects of study, by moving toward a historically and sociologically informed picture of scientific activity. They urged rapprochement between history and philosophy of science, suggesting that "history is philosophy teaching by examples" (Laudan 1979, p. 40; also see Kuhn 1962; Lakatos 1976). Callebaut (1993) commented on the divergent paths of science studies and economics at this time:

It has always struck me that in a social science like economics, the practitioners of the discipline have showed a marked preference for the philosophy they produced themselves, to the almost complete neglect of what was going on "outside." I guess something similar is happening in physics, which has always been the paradigmatic science for economics. (pp. 193–4)

Whereas Sargent had his back turned to the historically and sociologically motivated interpretations, Simon (1967) went along with the sameness advocated by science studies scholars, claiming that the purpose of science studies "was to have examples formidable enough to demonstrate adequacy to handle real-world complexity, and not simple adequacy to handle toy situations" (p. 33).[44]

However, driven by the imperatives of certain forced moves, as outlined in the previous sections, Sargent had to acknowledge sameness between him and his agents in the form of mutual learning more directly, because he expected that searching for ways to improve his agents would lead him to find ways to improve his own work (see Sargent 1993, p. 33). And just as Sargent saw rational expectations equilibrium as the final outcome of the process of learning with bounded rationality, science studies scholars like Tweney adopted sameness in a way that did not threaten their commitment to the idea that science differed from other enterprises: "Science is not entirely irrational. Many irrational factors enter, to be sure. But ultimately there is a cultural mechanism that produces good models of the real world. And we somehow must understand how science reaches such models, using partially irrational means" (Callebaut 1993, p. 25).[45] Furthermore, philosophers of science met Sargent halfway by using certain economic metaphors for the final attainment of rationality (see, e.g., Bartley 1990; Goldman and Shaked 1991; Kitcher 1993; Laudan 1984, 1987; Radnitzky and Bartley 1987; Radnitzky and Bernholz 1987). According to Latour, philosophers "have the equivalent of rationality, which is the best allocation of resources – a typically American myth. It's a completely American myth of economists: the optimization of resources, and now of disputes" (Callebaut 1993, p. 315).

While Sent was learning about Sargent's rationality, Sargent was learning about the rationality of scientists and agents. Where does this process stop? As discussed in the previous chapter, most attempts to assign sameness and difference in this regard lead to infinite regress. It is not so clear by what process rationality was ultimately reached, because it is unclear how scientists learn about the world (see Sargent 1993, pp. 22n, 23). Whereas Sargent went searching for answers in artificial intelligence, science studies scholars were very wary of this approach (see Sargent 1993, pp. 23–4). Thus, their paths diverged again.

Historians and sociologists of scientific knowledge argued that the artificial intelligence experiment was not just a problem of engineering or psychology but an experimental test of deep theses in the philosophy of social sciences (see Collins 1990; Forsythe 1993). The history and sociology of scientific knowledge had shown that scientific activity was social in a number of ways. Learning scientific knowledge, changing scientific knowledge, establishing scientific knowledge, and maintaining scientific knowledge were all irremediably shot through with the social. Human beings were not repositories of culture; they were reflections of it. They also maintained it and repaired it. The locus of knowledge appeared to be not the individual but the social group. Since human beings and their knowledge were irreducibly social, they could not be imitated by an intelligent machine because a machine is an unsocialized, isolated thing made out of little bits of information, not a community or a member of society. Sargent saw classifier systems as models of an individual's brain; science studies scholars argued that intelligent machines are more usefully thought of as models of communities or societies.

By making the boundedly rational agents artificially intelligent, Sargent had succeeded in automating a very limited conception of learning and mental activity. By conceiving of knowledge as a stable entity that could be acquired and transferred and by deleting the social and the cultural, he was able to render it machine-readable and manipulable by a computer program. In effect, knowledge had been operationally redefined in artificial intelligence to mean "what can be programmed." Social scientists and artificial intelligence enthusiasts disagreed about what knowledge was, how it was produced, and what would be required to automate the manipulation of knowledge in a meaningful way (see Collins 1990; Forsythe 1993). The artificial intelligence community tended to think that the nature of knowledge was not problematic, that knowledge was either present or absent, and that it was universal. It treated knowledge as a purely cognitive phenomenon and tended to assume that it was conscious. Artificial intelligence proponents seemed to conceive of reasoning as a matter of following formal rules and assumed that thought and action were isomorphic. In contrast, social scientists considered knowledge highly problematic, more usefully thought of in terms of its potential and negotiated relevance, and emphasized the significance of local and situational knowledge and the importance of combining local and global knowledge. Social scientists viewed knowledge as being encoded in cultural, social, and organizational order and expected some knowledge to be partially accessible and some to be inaccessible to the conscious mind. They tended to think of reasoning in terms of meaning and viewed the relation between belief and action as highly problematic.

The intelligent machine was a useful and interesting tool, but social scientists considered thinking like Sargent's, that a tool was an actor, erroneous. Unless machines could become members of our society, an unlikely event according to social scientists, they could appear to mimic human acts only by developing more and more ramified behaviors. Ramification of behaviors made for a new and better tool, not a new and better person. If intelligent machines were used with too much uncritical charity, or if we started to think of ourselves as machines or model our behavior on their behavior, social scientists argued, not only would we lose sight of what we were, but the tools we made would not be good ones. Machines could mimic us only in those cases in which we preferred to do things in a machinelike way.

5.8   Conclusion

It is unlikely that Sargent knew much about the developments in philosophy of science. However, he did have an experience that changed his view of learning and acquainted him with these more recent cultural trends. The one thing that got his attention was having physicists disparage his "science." His visit at the Santa Fe Institute made him aware that time had passed him by, that solving Hamiltonians and optimal control models had become part of electrical engineering rather than physics. Instead, at the institute, physicists were playing around with computer simulations, imagining artificial life, talking indeterminacy and path dependence, disparaging reductionism, and trying to employ some of the metaphors of evolutionary biology. In short, they were exploring paths that no physicist had entered before.

There was open resistance to Sargent's image of human "rationality." Whereas he was using nineteenth-century psychophysics in the form of general equilibrium theory, the Santa Fe Institute was about late-twentieth-century physics. Though he did not fully embrace these new views, he did start using some of the Santa Fe ideas and techniques. Although classifier systems were generally considered to be about population thinking, Sargent found he had to restrict them to modeling an individual's brain. Furthermore, he insisted that classifiers always converged to conventional rational expectations by employing the notions of representative agents and completed arbitrage, which violated the spirit of the research at Santa Fe. We will have to await his next moves. He may be led to renounce general equilibrium theory and make further forced moves in the direction of allowing differentiation of actors, a social component to his image of learning, and so on. Or he could just drop bounded rationality, as he abandoned Lévy stable distributions.

How did Sargent end up at this point? Motivated by achieving what he would regard as conceptual integrity of theory and method, he made free moves to vector autoregressions, general equilibrium theory, and rational expectations. Asymmetry between agents and econometricians followed as one of the resistances in terms of forced moves from these tentative choices, since agents were supposed to know what was going on, while econometricians were learning about it. Rather than incorporating learning in this framework of free moves, Sargent came up with three resistances that would appear if agents were to learn as he himself did: First, there would in general be no known closed-form prediction formula. Second, the resulting time-series models would have time-varying coefficients and hence be nonstationary. Third, it was difficult to decide where to set the "dial of rationality" and how to build this dial setting into theoretical models.

Eventually, Sargent's process of accommodation led him to make the free move to adaptive rather than rational expectations. Since he wanted the adaptive agents to resemble econometricians, he ended up with an econometrically motivated interpretation of adaptive expectations as a forced move. However, he encountered a more troubling forced move in the fact that his free moves resulted in a very limited interpretation of learning by the agents: They still had to be quite smart. Furthermore, when agents extracted signals from endogenous variables by fitting first-order vector autoregressions, the prediction errors from these vector autoregressions would not be orthogonal to information lagged two or more periods.

Unhappy with this weak attempt at restoring symmetry among agents, economists, and econometricians, Sargent continued his process of accommodation when he made the free move to artificial intelligence rather than adaptive expectations. The eventual combination of free moves toward econometrics, neoclassical theory, and artificial intelligence called forth a different set of forced moves. With respect to econometrics, Sargent tried to show that artificial intelligence just implemented recursive least squares in various ingenious contexts. He thereby ignored the resistance that handing over some recursive least squares algorithms to agents was certainly not the same as having agents that were modeled as using classifier systems to make decisions. With respect to neoclassical theory, Sargent tried to make a case for having artificial agents teach economists how to learn about the world. Interestingly enough, the outcome of these forced moves was asymmetry between him and the agents in his models, on the one hand, and between economists and econometricians, on the other.

Sargent tried to link his interpretations of bounded rationality and artificial intelligence with those of Simon. However, this link turned out to be rather weak. Since Sargent wanted to restore symmetry by incorporating learning, he embraced neoclassical theory and parallel adaptive computing systems. At the same time, Simon's motivations and moves resulted in a dismissal of neoclassical theory and parallel systems. His interest in human decision making and foundations of rationality made him move to the serial symbol-processing approach instead.

By embracing artificial intelligence, Sargent made himself vulnerable to several arguments against using artificial intelligence. Some scientists used Gödel's incompleteness theorem and Turing's discovery of noncomputable mathematical functions to argue that the brain's behavior could not be simulated by a computer algorithm. Others countered that mathematical computability was neither necessary nor sufficient to produce a mind or that human beings simply made use of a fallible algorithm. Some epistemologists argued that if connectionism is true, commonsense psychology must be false and should be eliminated. Finally, according to historians and sociologists of scientific knowledge, human beings and their knowledge were irreducibly social and could therefore not be imitated by an intelligent machine because a machine is an unsocialized thing, not a community or a member of society.

We have to wait to see whether Sargent will move to a wholehearted acceptance of the spirit of Santa Fe and how he will deal with the subsequent forced moves and resistances. If the unpublished papers on Sargent's website (http://riffle.stanford.edu) are any indication, he is moving back to the combination of general equilibrium theory, vector autoregressions, and rational expectations (see Hansen and Sargent 1995b, 1996; Hansen, Sargent, and Tallarini 1996; Huang, Imrohoroglu, and Sargent 1996; Ljungqvist and Sargent 1996; Manuelli and Sargent 1992; Marcet, Sargent, and Seppälä 1996; Sargent 1996b; Sargent and Smith 1995). However, there is currently insufficient information to evaluate this move.

Appendix 5A: Adaptive Expectations

Consider a self-referential dynamic model in which the stochastic process for a vector z_t of state variables obeys the law

$$z_t = f(z_{t-1}, \varepsilon_t) \tag{5A.1}$$

where ε_t is a vector white noise. Suppose there are two classes of agents, a and b, that make decisions based partly on their perceptions represented by two matrices, β_a and β_b. These beliefs are based on observation of a subset of the state vector z_t. Suppose that expression (5A.1), which is the actual law of motion of the state vector, is influenced by the agents' decisions in the following way:

$$f = T(\beta_a, \beta_b) \tag{5A.2}$$

The "irrationality" in this model follows from the fact that the operator T is derived under the assumption that β_j, where $j = a, b$ is known with certainty. Under the rational expectations equilibrium

$$(\beta_a, \beta_b) = (S_a(\beta), S_b(\beta)) \tag{5A.3}$$

where (β_a, β_b) are the arbitrary perceptions and $(S_a(\beta), S_b(\beta))$ are the optimal perceptions. In order to study convergence to this equilibrium, agents are posited as least squares learners:

$$\beta_{jt} = s_j(\beta_{jt-1}, z_{t-1}, R_{jt-1}), \qquad j = a, b \tag{5A.4}$$
$$R_{jt} = r_j(R_{jt-1}, z_{t-1}), \qquad j = a, b$$

where R_{jt} is the sample moment matrix of the information available to agents of type j at time t. The system (z_t, β_t) is assumed to evolve according to (5A.4) and

$$z_t = f_t(z_{t-1}, \varepsilon_t) \tag{5A.5}$$

where

$$f_t = T(\beta_{at}, \beta_{bt}) \tag{5A.6}$$

Marcet and Sargent (1988, p. 169) argue that if $\{\beta_{at}, \beta_{bt}\}_{t=0}^{\infty}$ converges, it converges to a rational expectations equilibrium. They further illustrate how the local stability of the learning system is determined by the differential equation system

$$\frac{d}{dt}\begin{pmatrix} \beta_a \\ \beta_b \end{pmatrix} = \begin{bmatrix} S_a(\beta) - \beta_a \\ S_b(\beta) - \beta_a \end{bmatrix} = S(\beta) - \beta \tag{5A.7}$$

and the way global convergence is governed by the larger differential equation system

$$\frac{d}{dt}\begin{bmatrix} \beta'_a \\ \beta'_b \\ R_a \\ R_b \end{bmatrix} = \begin{bmatrix} R_a^{-1}M_{z_a}(\beta)[S_a(\beta) - \beta_a]' \\ R_b^{-1}M_{z_a}(\beta)[S_b(\beta) - \beta_b]' \\ M_{z_b}(\beta) - R_a \\ M_{z_b}(\beta) - R_b \end{bmatrix} \tag{5A.8}$$

For proofs and further discussion, see Marcet and Sargent (1988, 1989a, 1989b, 1989c, 1992).

CHAPTER 6

An Interview with Thomas Sargent

There is . . . a case in which it can be interesting to resort to the intention of the empirical author. There are cases in which the author is still living, the critics have given their interpretations of his text, and it can then be interesting to ask the author how much and to what extent he, as an empirical person, was aware of the manifold interpretations his text supported. At this point the response of the author must not be used to validate the interpretations of his text, but to show the discrepancies between the author's intention and the intention of the text. The aim of the experiment is not a critical one, but, rather, a theoretical one.

Umberto Eco, *Interpretation and Overinterpretation*, pp. 72–3

Monday, April 25, 1994

[Esther-Mirjam Sent] *I suppose you now know what the topic of my manuscript is. I started this research because I was very confused by your classes, because I wasn't quite sure what rational expectations modeling is all about and why I should be using it. When I started reading about the history of rational expectations, I found out that there were very many stories that could be told about the interpretation and development of rational expectations, and that historians of economic thought very often tried to paint a very simple picture. I then tried to get a deeper understanding by going down to the individual level of your research on rational expectations, and I realized that your interpretation of rational expectations kept changing. Rather than evaluating the character of your work through the glasses of an economic methodologist, I tried to tell a story that was much more complicated than the stories one often sees in the history of economic thought, with the eventual aim of getting a deeper understanding of your work, rational expectations theory, and macroeconomics. So that's what motivated me in writing this manuscript. Can I ask you a few questions?*

[Thomas Sargent] Sure.

I would like to give you a chance to elaborate further on the points I've made in my manuscript. First of all, why do you think rational expectations was developed? You seem to argue on the one hand that it was developed out of

163

general equilibrium theory, by making agents optimize over information as well as other things. However, in other instances you argue that it was developed because in Keynesian models governments were optimizing, and that agents should be optimizing as well. In yet other instances you argue that rational expectations modeling really led to general equilibrium theory.

That's fair. The first thing is that, right now, it's related to general equilibrium theory but it didn't come from it. Because if you take an Arrow–Debreu model there's really no need for rational expectations, because you don't have to forecast. That's what's essential to the equilibrium concept. Another thing is that there's a lot of lack of knowledge when you're developing something like this and that the people who developed rational expectations were not working in a general equilibrium tradition, in the Arrow–Debreu tradition. I would say that the tradition they were coming from, to the extent that they knew it, was either a Keynesian tradition or was an incomplete markets tradition. One of those two. And both of those traditions shared the feature that people were going to have to forecast, and furthermore, forecasts were really important in terms of the model. That's what Keynes said in words, and that was true, and became increasingly true in the models that were developed in the 1950s to 1960s. And your theories about what the forecasts were, were a really important part of the dynamics. People developing the first theories recognized that what theory you had was important in determining the dynamics. They were pretty dissatisfied with the theories that they had. And then, within that tradition, rational expectations is just going to come up sooner or later. It's just inevitable. I'll give you an example. Did you read Jorgenson's (1967) comment on Sidrauski's (1967) paper? I think that Sidrauski wrote this paper in 1967. Jorgenson says in his comment that Sidrauski has three prices floating around for the same thing. He's got a market price, he's got a shadow price, and he's got people's expectations. And Jorgenson says, "Why aren't they the same?" It's a brilliant comment, which doesn't use the term "rational expectations," but it's right in there.

It also seems that different researchers in rational expectations came to it from different backgrounds. Some people did start from the general equilibrium tradition, and others started from an econometric tradition.

I think most of the people were not coming from a general equilibrium tradition. What's true is that after rational expectations was developed, a lot of people got more interested in general equilibrium. Lucas and Prescott form an exception to this, somewhat. But even Lucas's (1972a) paper in the *Journal of Economic Theory* is not in the general equilibrium tradition. It's an overlapping generations model, and it's an incomplete markets model, where people do have to forecast. And the stuff with Prescott (Lucas and Prescott 1971), even though you can go back and do the equilibrium investment under uncertainty, even though you can go back and do that general equilibrium stuff, that's not how they did it. And what's interesting in that paper is that the way they formulate their equilibrium concept, with a fixed point, you can go back and give that a general equilibrium interpretation, but it's a concept whose power comes from applying it to models of incomplete markets. It's actually paradoxical because of the controversies that were going on, but rational expectations first emerged in its most interesting form in an incomplete markets context. Even though in lots of applications in the 1980s' real business cycle theories it's easiest to apply rational expectations in complete markets because then you can just throw away the forecasting problem and do general equilibrium.

Now what was your motivation for adopting rational expectations? Or what do you think was your general motivation in your research in the beginning?

I was just a straight Keynesian economist. And in those days, rational expectations were clearly sort of a next step. I could give you an example of my friend, a guy who's a Keynesian, Albert Ando. When I was just first out, I submitted a proposal for a little bit of money to do something on the term structure of interest rates, and I had a very crude version of rational expectations. And I remember riding in the car, and he described a much more ambitious version of rational expectations. Basically I had people using these autoregressions to forecast, and what he said was, "What you should be doing is you should be having them use the forecast from the whole model." And I just said, "I don't know how to do it." He said, "That's tough. But that's what you want to do." So, it was not an ideological thing. And some of its consequences weren't understood; it was more like a technical finishing up.

How would you generally characterize the motivation for your research? What are you after? What are you trying to achieve in your research?

I'd say most of the stuff that I'd say is real research is aimed at being marginal. And what I mean by that is you find someplace where there's a crack or a deficiency in what is known, but is very close to problems that are almost posed for you in the existing literature. It could be just a puzzle or a technical problem that's stopping people. That unglamorous activity is what I do most of the time, not that big picture stuff.

But isn't it the case that what you define as a problem depends on what your starting position is?

Absolutely. That's exactly why rational expectations stuff was developed by people within the Keynesian tradition. There were people trying to knock off and destroy the Keynesian tradition from the outside, who weren't sympathetic enough to it to learn it. And I mean it was in the monetarist tradition, or something like that. And the paradox is that, I would say what's ended up being perceived as the most destructive in Keynesian tradition is from its own children. You know? Because if you look at what, say, Lucas, Prescott, Wallace, and Barro were working on, those were all pieces of a Keynesian model, a high-tech Keynesian style.

Going back to your work on the term structure of interest rates in the late 1960s to early 1970s, how do you think probabilities should be interpreted? How can we measure them, as relative frequencies, or subjective probabilities, or classical probabilities?

I think I know what you're driving at. I don't have a global answer to that. Sometimes the fate of rational expectations is that you equate subjective and empirical frequencies. But I don't think that's always a good modeling strategy. I mean, I think it is sometimes. Sometimes rational expectations models are good and sometimes they're silent. And the question you ask is, "When is it a good idea to say that people can use them?" See, you have to say more about relative frequencies. You have to say relative frequencies from what period if you're a time-series person, like which ones do you use and what do you condition on. So if you think about people in Eastern Europe, the rules aren't clear, and people are trying to figure out what the rules are. Rational expectations has bits and pieces to say, but not as much as it does in a system that's already operating.

What do you think is the source of probability and uncertainty?

You mean in the world or in equations?

Why do we use error terms in our econometric equations? Is it because we're uncertain? Or is it because there's an inherent uncertainty in the world? Or is it just pragmatic? Is our interpretation of error terms limited by the techniques we're using?

[Long pause.] Well, all of the things you said are true. I mean, there are basically, you know, classical models of error terms, which actually rational expectations has extended. There's random stuff hitting agents and information opportunities, and the econometrician always sees a subset of it. The agent sees more than the econometrician, or the agents together see more, so that introduces an error. It's kind of a Shiller error, which you can use. In another interpretation, the econometrician has the wrong model. That introduces a complicated kind of error, which has been worked on by the specification analysis tradition. It's very hard. And those are the two main ones. But where the errors come from is a tough and embarrassing question for everybody. Especially for real business cycle people, because they want to interpret shocks very strictly.

Now you've done some work on Lévy stable distributions and infinite variance with Robert Blattberg (Blattberg and Sargent 1971) in the early 1970s. How did you become aware of Lévy stable distributions with infinite variance? Do you remember?

Sure. There were some beautiful central limit theorems. And also I was influenced by the work of Mandelbrot and Fama.

What about Richard Roll's (1970) suggestion that you should do some work on Lévy stable distributions with spectral analysis?

Well, you can't use spectral analysis. Well, you can but it depends on what you mean. Actually, that's the nicest way to do it. Fama and Roll (1971) have a paper in the *Journal of the American Statistical Association,* where they compute Pareto–Lévy distributions. You can do that. I forget how they did it, actually. You can do that using Fourier transforms, that's the best way. You can't do it analytically, as I recall. Yet for these Pareto–Lévy distributions, except when α is 2 or 1, you can't write down densities. But what you can do is write down characteristic functions, and you can use inverse Fourier transforms, and you can get very accurate distributions like that. But what you can't do is, you know, the spectrum doesn't exist, because second moments don't exist. Well, there's a way of calculating something like a spectrum by using these techniques called "windsorizing." You take something that doesn't have second moments, then you transform the data so that it does. It's a two-piece trick. What you do is you take outliers, you announce a range in advance, and then you take outliers and you move them in. That object does have second moments, then you calculate spectrum like that. These are like the α-trimmed mean. I can use that in the theoretical sense.

Did you think Lévy stable distributions were important when you were working on this topic, or was it just something to play around with?

It was both. [Laughs.] I thought they were important.

Then why did you stop working on the Lévy stable distributions?

[Long pause.] I'm trying to reconstruct it. I was working on other stuff. Actually, Peter Clark (1973) wrote a Ph.D. thesis which was published in *Econometrica,* and Chris Sims (1971b) had an article in the *Review of Economics and Statistics,* and Granger had an article in the *International Economic Review,*[1] and they described other ways to get these fat-tailed distributions that had finite variances. Basically, the idea of all of them was to mix normal distributions, and then you would get these leptokurtic ones, so it's hard to tell Pareto–Lévy from heteroscedasticity. That was their insight. And Peter Clark actually showed how to do a correction for heteroscedasticity, and once you did the correction, the kurtosis, it went way down. That stuff really influenced me. So, I mean, technically, doing those heteroscedasticity corrections is, if you can get by doing that since you can't always do that, it's a much more convenient way than using these estimators.

But one of the problems with distributions that have infinite variance is that you can't write down density functions, so you don't know what the statistical properties of your estimators are. Do you know more about the behavior of estimators if you assume a leptokurtic distribution?

See, I haven't kept up with the history of that, but those things became more important in the 1980s; people use these quantile regressions and so on for very similar reasons. Not just to protect yourself against Pareto but sort of for robustness. And that stuff is much easier to do now than it was when we were doing it. There also wasn't a lot of interest in it.

It seems like there was a lot of interest in it in the late 1960s, and that it slowly dwindled down in the mid-1970s or so.

Yes, but I don't know why. Everybody went to . . . First, it's a pain to do those estimators the way you want to, so you cut yourself off from a lot. But that's not the reason I stopped. I guess the answer is I was interested in other stuff, and also Peter Clark's thing really, really influenced me.

Well, let me move on to the late 1970s, when you started working with general equilibrium theory, and vector autoregressions, and a new interpretation of rational expectations. First of all, why were vector autoregressions important? Why did you decide to focus on those?

This is actually related to your earlier question. I guess the basic idea is when you're doing research, the biggest scarce resource is you and your brain. [Laughs.] So, vector autoregression is the invention of Chris Sims. But more generally, you know, there's a strong tradition in time-series statistics and econometrics of using linear models, so the basic idea is you set out from the beginning to ignore nonlinearities. So you just try to characterize linear structures. That goes back to Kolmogorov, Wiener, Wold. And one reason you do that is that it's easy relative to other things, so you can do it fast, so you can do lots of things, and you can learn a lot about it. And then the other is faith. It is completely faith that linear structures are going to capture most of the serial dependence. The world doesn't have to be that way, but there's evidence that it's not too bad. OK, so the reason is there's a theory developed since the Second World War, as in T. W. Anderson's (1971) book, that you can immediately buy into. And then what Sims did, basically building on the work of Box and Jenkins (1970) except taking it in another direction, made it very easy to compute these things. So then the natural thing is to try to build theoretical models that tie into that. Because Sims and Box and Jenkins, what they were doing wasn't economics; it was just pure statistics.

Is that why you chose general equilibrium theory?

Well, no, I came at it not from general equilibrium but from building these little rational expectations models. And I wasn't originally aware that they were kind of generally open to interpretation.

Did you become aware of it through the work of Lucas and Prescott?

Yes.

And you think that trying to link these statistical models to theoretical models is an important motivation in your work?

Yes. Actually, I'm naturally not keen on the fact that they're general equilibrium, to tell you the truth. What I mean by that is for lots of business cycle things is, you like to handle the knowledge with missing markets, and they're missing but not too many missing. But that gets technically hard.

And you get problems like the no-trade theorems as well if you use rational expectations and general equilibrium theory.

Yeah, those no-trade theorems are . . . yeah. Sometimes, yeah.

Do you feel uncomfortable having agents all be very similar in general equilibrium theory?

Well, they're not. In part of this stuff Lars [Hansen] and I have done, they don't have to be very similar. They can be pretty different. They can be quite different, because you can do these . . . I feel uncomfortable about a lot of things, but not . . . . Well, we spent some effort introducing heterogeneous agents, which is hard work, but the hard thing about it is the prediction of the amount of risk sharing that you get; it's too much. So the hard thing is to have a lot of heterogeneity, incomplete markets, but some markets. That's kind of a frontier now. It's helped some by computer technology, but not as much as you'd like. Lucas has this great line that all Arrow–Debreu general equilibrium models are alike. A line that says, it's a quote from Tolstoy, "All happy families are alike, and each unhappy family is different." And all Arrow–Debreu models are alike, to be true. And each incomplete markets model is a brand new thing. You've got to use new tricks.

How do you deal with policy recommendations in rational expectations and general equilibrium? You've discussed the problem that in order to make policy recommendations you have to assume that there was no rational expectations equilibrium.

Yeah. I don't know. [Sighs.] That's a hard problem. I don't make policy recommendations.

So you feel stronger about using rational expectations models than you do about making policy recommendations?

No, I mean there are paradoxes. The reason you want rational expectations models is to make policy recommendations. See, rational expectations is just something like taking derivatives. It doesn't deliver you a lot by itself, because you can have right wing or left wing or anything in the economics of rational expectations, which makes you more cautious about making policy recommendations.

But you still have the logical problem of not being able to make policy recommendations at all in rational expectations, right?

Yeah, this is a problem for game theory, too; it's the same problem. Like if you've got an equilibrium, that's it.

What do you think about game theory?

Well, let me put it this way. If Lucas and Prescott hadn't existed, macroeconomics would still be in about the same place, because if it had stayed where it was in the 1960s, then right now there would be this huge gap between macro and the rest of economic theory. Because our equilibrium concept would have been a lot different, and the whole point of rational expectations is to bring the equilibrium concept to basically the same place game theory is. Something like subgame perfection. And actually, if you use subgame perfection you have a model of the government. That's when there's no choice for policy. But most people back off a little bit, and then they start using game theory, and when they actually start using the thing, they talk about what's a good game to play. That's what they want to do.

We talked about this before, but how can you justify the error term with the general equilibrium theory? It seems like you started out trying to link theory and econometrics, and you were arguing that theory had no randomness in it while econometrics did have randomness in it. But if you have this framework of general equilibrium theory and vector autoregressions, you still just need to add the error term. There's no intrinsic source of the error term in general equilibrium theory.

OK, now Hansen and I have written papers where you can get error terms, so the basic idea is you have . . . You're right in saying that general equilibrium is a stochastic process, which you can also use as a mapping from the exogenous shocks, which you make up, onto the prices and quantities. And that mapping is a one-to-one mapping. So if the econometrician had the right model, and he saw all the shocks that are in the Arrow–Debreu contracts, then you're right, there's no error, you get R^2 of 1. So there's two ways of introducing error terms – classical ways – one is to assume that the econometrician is observing only a subset of prices and quantities, and it turns out that gives you a model of the error term that you can get by with. It's a very stringent model of the error term. And another is to assume some kind of measurement error. We've actually used it a little bit, but misspecification is hard because to get anywhere with it, you can't just say "misspecification," you have to have in mind two models. You have to have in mind a model which you think could be the true model and your model which is phony, because if you really knew what this other model was, you wouldn't be diddling around with the model you have. But the tradition is to basically ask yourself how you can craft procedures to protect yourself against various kinds of misspecification with what differences between your model and the true model. And Sims has written about this. And it turns out that you can use it to think about whether you should use filtered data or not.

This brings me to the question of how you feel about seasonal adjustment of data.

I used to have a strong opinion, but I changed my mind. I used to have the simple argument that you should use the same data that the agents are using, and the data are coming into them wrong, not seasonally adjusted. And Sims and I had a lot of arguments about that, and I was sure this was the one time he was wrong. Then Lars [Hansen] and I wrote this paper that was actually designed to show definitively that he was wrong, and it turned out that every example that we did turned in his favor. I mean, the thing was, we had models where, by using seasonally adjusted data and by using rational expectations econometrics, the econometrician protects himself against specification error that's sort of quarantined to the seasons. It's a hard argument to see unless you go through the details. And that's what convinced me to use seasonally adjusted data. Chris [Sims] didn't. It convinced me to be much more agnostic. It also convinced me to use Hodrick–Prescott filters. I used to be opposed to using Hodrick–Prescott filters. The same kind of argument can be used to rationalize Hodrick–Prescott filters, although it can't be used to rationalize the procedures Prescott used, it can be used to rationalize using the filtered data. That kind of shook me up, you know?

Do you feel that your coauthored work is different from the work you've done on your own?

It's a hard thing to do, actually. [Laughs.] Usually, if I write a paper, I write repeated papers with the same person, so then it's like a long-term contract. You do different amounts of work on different papers. But you basically have to agree very totally with the person about a given subject.

All right. Finally, let me move onto your latest work on incorporating learning and bounded rationality in macroeconomics, which is very fascinating. What are the problems with incorporating learning in rational expectations models?

Well, there are two kinds of learning. There's rational learning, which is basically just rational expectations where the environment's a little more uncertain. There's lots of work in that tradition, like Jovanovic, several of his papers (e.g., Jovanovic and Lach 1989; Jovanovic and Rafael 1989). And I just saw a paper by Jovanovic and Matsushima, which is a rational model of learning by doing, where it's all doing by statistical learning, the Kalman filter. It's a very pretty paper. You know, like Lucas's original model of the Phillips curve is a model of people rationally learning by doing signal extraction. But that's not what people mean by bounded rationality. The other tradition is this somehow trying to assign enough concreteness to this idea of boundary rationality to actually do something. And there's been a lot of work on that.

Do you see your work on learning with adaptive expectations in the first tradition?

No. That's in the second. And the reason is, is . . . yeah. This makes it low-brow work from the point of view of a rational expectations purist. The reason, I mean the stuff I did with Albert Marcet and with Ramon Marimon and Ellen McGrattan, it has that characteristic that the learning mechanism is at some level incompatible with the model that's generating the data, at a more or less subtle level, but it is incompatible. They are both incompatible. Well, the learning mechanism makes the data actually nonstationary. The agents are proceeding in some ways as if they are in a stationary environment. And their behavior in the aggregate over time is rendering the environment nonstationary, but they don't know that. But then when you rig things so that things are asymptotic, it's stationary in some sense, so they have a chance of being right or wrong.

But you need to rig it that way. It's not always the case that there is asymptotic stationarity.

Right.

And is the prediction formula the Kalman filter in that case?

It all depends on the application. This stuff Albert [Marcet] and I did, the stuff in the least squares learning tradition, has some interpretation like that. But in the artificial intelligence stuff you have to look harder to see a Kalman filter. It's there a lot of the time.

Why did you decide to incorporate learning?

For a bad reason. Actually, because it was in the air. I saw these nice papers by Margaret Bray (e.g., Bray 1982), and trying to generalize those a little bit turned out to be a very challenging technical problem. It turned out to be very hard to generalize it. So, when Albert [Marcet] and I first tried it, we couldn't do it. And then we couldn't let it go. But that's not a good reason to do research, because we didn't have an empirical puzzle we were after.

Do you think that's what good research is about, trying to solve empirical puzzles?

Yeah. Even though that's not what I was doing. It wasn't solving any empirical problems with rational expectations. I'll give you an example. Yeah, what I mean by that is, that's what's puzzling about this literature. It's very short on empirical applications, even though it's a literature that purports to be driven by realism. That's very puzzling. I mean, I've thought about using models of irrational learning methods to study events like regime changes and so on. Then someone showed me a paper a couple weeks ago, which is in the rational learning tradition, which has very interesting and powerful implications about regime changes that really seem to fit a set of observations which I never could understand before, like transition questions. Why do countries that have very high rates of inflation, if they're going to stabilize, they go [Snaps fingers.] like that? Whereas countries that have kind of moderate rates of inflation, they stabilize. The typical pattern is that they don't stabilize all at once. So this rational learning model really gets at why that pattern might emerge. See, I like that. That's the nice success, because there is this empirical puzzle out there.

So you wouldn't say that there was this empirical puzzle of regime changes and you wanted to deal with it, and that that's why you started working on adaptive expectations?

I was imitating a theorist, or something like that, which is what I am, I mean, what I'm good at. I just got engaged by this really hard puzzle without asking what's really going to be added to what Margaret Bray got.

Why did you incorporate learning with adaptive expectations, rather than using game theory or Bayesian learning?

Well, you see, Bayesian learning is a version of rational expectations, if you do it. There's a beautiful paper by Bray and Kreps (1987) that talks about these two traditions. Actually, they talk about contradictions involved with trying to build a rational model of learning about an equilibrium, and what they show is that as long as you stick to rationality and Bayesian conceptions, you get driven back to having to learn within an equilibrium, where everybody is . . . but not about an equilibrium. So this is a theme of some of Kreps's writings. If you want to talk about how people learn about an equilibrium, you have to go outside the rational expectations tradition. Yeah, and I'm sure he's right; he's right as a theoretical point; there's no question about it. What I question is whether or not it's going to pay off empirically. And I kind of doubt it, but that's attacking my own stuff.

And were you influenced by your visit to Santa Fe, when you started using classifier systems to incorporate learning? What did you think of your visit to the workshop there?

Yes. It was a lot of fun. It was great fun. I met some very interesting people.

Was it difficult to talk to the physicists about what kinds of models were being used in economics?

You know, see, it wasn't just physicists. There was this guy, a computer scientist, named John Holland. He's very easy to talk to, to listen to. I'll tell you what surprised me, well, we surprised each other is . . . you know, I'm not a mathematical economist. I'm pretty applied. Although there were some very good mathematical economists at that meeting, and at subsequent meetings. You know, when I got up there, and wrote down some math, I would write down, like we always do "for all t." Well, a physicist would get up there and they would just be very sloppy with their math. And to see a macroeconomist dotting the t's, you know, "for all t, such that. . . ." These guys were just, you know, it was amazing to see real scientists being much sloppier with math than lowly economists. That surprised both of us. But then, one thing that lots of the economists there stressed were the dynamics and the physicists live on dynamics. But there were different natures to our systems, in particular regarding the foresight component. We went around and around on that at first. And about the notion of equilibrium, the first couple days, when an economist said "equilibrium," the physicist thought something different. He thought we were talking about fixed points in different spaces. So a physicist, he would talk about an equilibrium, or some of the time it would be, not as the entire path, but as the rest point. But we were talking about the entire path. And there was no rest point except the path. But that got straightened out. And also how in our systems people were forecasting the future and how the future has an impact on stuff now; that was something right there, that kind of generated some thought.

Have you been back to Santa Fe since the economics workshop?

I've been a few times.

It seems as if the researchers at Santa Fe are still grasping for a general definition of what their complexity analysis is about. Do you have any sense of how the research that's being done at Santa Fe can be characterized?

It's not . . . . You know there's a number of individuals there with very different perspectives, and I don't think there's . . . . [There was an interruption at the door at this point.]

Do you think that classifier systems are very similar to least squares learning?

I just got a paper on that. In some ways it is; in some ways it isn't.

Well, in your book on bounded rationality you're trying to link the two, and you're trying to argue that a lot of artificial intelligence is really just recursive least squares.

Yeah. I think that's the line I push, which is not original. It's all a Euler equation. But that's not surprising, all right, because it's all based upon . . . that's what one of the physicists said the first day; they're similar whatever you're trying to prove.

But aren't genetic algorithms really very different from least squares learning?

Yeah, they are. They're global and they're not local.

And they're trying to search for new information and new ways of dealing with things, where that doesn't seem to happen in least squares learning.

Well, that's what they say, but what they're really doing is they're . . . The way I characterize them is by just thinking about the X space, so that when you use a genetic algorithm, you have to name the X space. You do, not the algorithm. And what it does is it hops around the space, and not in a local way. I mean, they can be good for some things.

And do you think that by using classifier systems you will always end up with a rational expectations equilibrium eventually?

No. You get trapped sometimes. There's no general theorems about that. I mean, it can happen. Also, when you ever set up a classifier system – I actually have this paper – you find out how much you're putting into it. [Laughs.] It starts looking just like you. Well, here's a paper by Lettau and Uhlig (1994).[2] So here's what these guys claim; so here's what they want to do; they want to know whether classifiers solved dynamic programming problems. It says, "We demonstrate in a robust example that the learnable decision function is in general not unique, not characterized by a strict ordering under the classifiers, and may not coincide with the decision function delivered by the solution to a dynamic programming problem even if that function is obtainable."

So did you have to play around with your model with Marimon and McGrattan (Marimon et al. 1990) to get a rational expectations outcome?

You mean did we have to weather some false starts in terms of setting up the classifiers? You know, I can't guarantee this, but I think that when we first set that up . . . . You see, we had these classifiers and they were proceeding sequentially; that's the part of us that's in there. We had rigged things. As I recall, in an earlier version of that, we had set things up and there was a problem. They were eating too much when they shouldn't have been, and it was because of the design of the classifier.

Arthur (1991) and Holland also built classifier systems which didn't converge to a rational expectations equilibrium.

You see, that's consistent with what Lettau and Uhlig are saying.

So do you think that adaptive computing is a threat to rational expectations or to the econometric techniques we're using or to general equilibrium theory?

No. I don't buy Hal White's line; I'm not on that side. Well, the way I think about it is a class of approximated functions; it's a way of handling nonlinearities. And you just estimate them by some version of nonlinear least squares. Just that observation takes you a long way to understanding them. So I view them as a marginal but useful addition to my kit of tools. The sense in which those things learn is the sense in which the standard errors go down if you update least squares.

But with updating least squares you still need to have very rational agents.

You mean if we attribute . . . . Somewhat, somewhat smart.

Do you expect to do more work in rational expectations? Even given all the problems that you yourself indicated, do you still think that's a better research agenda than bounded rationality?

They're at very different stages, so rational expectations and rational expectations econometrics now is a bunch of tools that you can use on applied problems and it's ready to go. It's like a 486 PC. You just buy it and you can use it. You know, it's just routinely used. People don't even mention it; they have no second thoughts. I'll give you an example. Sherwin Rosen's paper on farm economics, his paper on housing, which are very empirical papers, just do rational expectations right from the start (e.g., Rosen 1987; Rosen and Topel 1988). There's a lot of work like that. So I guess you would say it's a mature technology, so you can use it to do lots of stuff and a lot of problems have been resolved. Whereas this other thing, it's kind of not fair to compare them. In my statements that this bounded rationality stuff hasn't had empirical applications, that's partly because it's just gotten started. I mean, after Simon said it, there was almost no work on it.

So do you think that this work on parallel adaptive computing is closely linked to Simon's work on bounded rationality? He seems to criticize neoclassical economics and use serial symbol processing.

Yeah. I just don't know.

And do you think that what you see as an important research agenda depends on what you're interested in? Do you think that someone who is not interested in linking theory with data would have a different perspective on what kind of research agenda is more profitable?

I can give you my approach to research. It's that I'm an ant, and I'm supposed to do something. [Laughs.] I'm endowed by nature with certain little skills, and

I can help out with some little tasks. I don't have any big, global . . . . There are some guys who are capable of enlarging influence to the entire research agendas of other people. I have trouble figuring out what the hell to do the next six months myself. So I think if I work on some little niche that I'm capable of doing, like if I'm a second string catcher, doesn't mean I think that the guy who's playing second base is not doing the right thing. It's just a division of labor. It's getting more and more important.

But don't you think, continuing the ant analogy, that the obstacles an ant is going to run into depend on what the ant is after? Some ants are after just explaining the data, some ants are after linking data with theories, some ants are after having theories that have no ad hoc concepts in them. So depending on these interests, the ants would run into different obstacles.

Yeah. And the trick in any research is to have some compromise between what's doable and what's interesting. Lots of times you can write down things that are too hard for you to do.

But whether something's hard to do or interesting really depends on your bigger picture of your research.

Absolutely.

So what is your grand picture?

[Very long pause.] I don't spend a lot of time thinking about that.

Can you characterize how your approach to economics is different from Lucas's or Sims's or Wallace's approach?

I think you know it when you see it. I think a lot of people like it when they see, I mean, I certainly admire beautiful pieces of theory; I get most excited when they're useful. Even when I don't do it. I think of work with nice mathematics as beautiful. It would be beautiful even if it weren't applicable, but it often is applicable. But my looking at that stuff as something I think is pretty doesn't mean it's something I'm going to do or tell very many other people to try to do, because you have to be extremely lucky and smart to do something like that. That's like seeing a beautiful painting. I'm not going to go out and try to start painting. It's tricky. I see some of Sherwin Rosen's papers, a couple I've read recently, and they're very, you know, the technique . . . I could do the technique part easily, but there's a cleverness, there's a shrewdness and an economy of specification that's very pleasing.

Do you feel that you're still learning yourself?

Yes, that makes it fun. Yeah, I mean, being an academic, you don't have to grow up.

Well, let me not bother you any longer by asking questions. Thank you for taking time to answer them.

OK. OK, good.

CHAPTER 7

Conclusion

The Conclusion, in Which Nothing Is Concluded

Samuel Johnson, *The History of Rasselas,*
Chapter XLIX

Different people give different twists to the rise of rational expectations economics. Even one of the individual contributors, Sargent, entertained different interpretations of rational expectations in different periods. How can I offer a short conclusion in the face of this pluralism? My answer is to try to tie some of the loose ends together here by summarizing the argument, discussing the framework, and giving some suggestions for further research.

7.1   Summary

In terms of its content, the book comprises four case studies of how Sargent tried to satisfy his interest in conceptual integrity of neoclassical economic theory and econometrics during different historical periods. The first, Accommodating Randomness, is staged in the late 1960s to early 1970s. The second case study, Accommodating Prediction, takes place in the late 1970s to early 1980s. The third, Accommodating Symmetry, is set in the early to mid-1980s. The last, Accommodating Learning, takes place in the late 1980s to early 1990s. I should acknowledge that though chronology is used as a general ordering principle throughout this book, Sargent has sometimes gone back and forth between different justifications and interpretations of rational expectations during these different periods. Keeping this in mind, let me summarize the four case studies.

Sargent's community in the late 1960s to early 1970s consisted of his thesis adviser Meyer, his colleague Roll, and his student Blattberg. In this setting, as discussed in Chapter 2, Sargent made the initial decision to focus on the randomness of time-series econometrics, the determinism of neoclassical economic theory, the linking of theory and method with rational expectations, and the term structure of interest rates. The consequences of those decisions were the measurement and justification of randomness as found in econometrics, an econometrically motivated interpretation of rational expectations, and the importance of Lévy stable distributions. The problems he ran into were that for

Lévy stable distributions there was no general estimation method and the properties of estimators could be investigated only in an indirect way. He accommodated these problems by giving up Lévy stable distributions without explicit justification.

Wallace, Sims, and Hansen were Sargent's collaborators in the late 1970s to early 1980s, as discussed in Chapter 3. Influenced by his colleague Sims and a change in his economic environment, Sargent tried to employ rational expectations for restricting vector autoregressions and to use the acquired statistical information to construct a theoretical model. The trouble was that Sims's test was a necessary but not a sufficient condition for establishing strict exogeneity. Furthermore, Sargent's observational equivalence implied that the natural and nonnatural rate hypotheses both generated identical observable consequences and formed the basis of equally good forecasts. When Sargent tried to remedy these defects by collaborating with Hansen on general equilibrium models, he found that there were no neoclassical dynamics that commanded much consensus anywhere. In relying on convenience, Sargent obtained a very restricted environment for rational expectations agents and used engineering conceptions in his quest for a more scientific macroeconomics.

In the early to mid-1980s, as discussed in Chapter 4, Sargent was greatly influenced by Lucas. In this environment, he initially decided to focus on general equilibrium theory, vector autoregressions, and rational expectations. This led him to stress symmetry among agents, economists, and econometricians. However, he found that asymmetry appeared as a consequence of the no-trade theorems, incorporating information gathering, error term justification, making policy recommendations, and allowing for seasonal adjustment. Sargent tried to accommodate these problems and restore symmetry by adopting adaptive expectations and artificial intelligence.

Marcet, Marimon, McGrattan, and the Santa Fe Institute were part of Sargent's environment in the late 1980s to early 1990s, as discussed in Chapter 5. In these surroundings, Sargent first focused on rational expectations and moved to the combination of vector autoregressions, general equilibrium theory, and rational expectations. This resulted in asymmetry among agents, economists, and econometricians. Initially, Sargent used the lack of a closed-form prediction formula, the possibility of nonstationarity, and the arbitrary setting of the dial of rationality as arguments against restoring symmetry by incorporating learning. However, Sargent subsequently focused on adaptive rather than rational expectations. This reduced the asymmetry among agents, economists, and econometricians but still constituted a very limited interpretation of learning. Other consequences were an econometrically motivated interpretation of adaptive expectations, a still arbitrary setting of the dial of rationality, and prediction errors that were not orthogonal to information lagged 2 or more periods. Sargent tried to eliminate some of these consequences by finally adopting a version of artificial intelligence limited to convergence with representative agents. This left him with asymmetry between himself and agents and between economists and econometricians. Furthermore, it led him to make changes to econometric techniques and neoclassical economics.

Using the framework of interests, free moves, forced moves, and resistances, it is shown that Sargent entertained different justifications and interpretations of rational expectations in different periods. In the late 1960s to early 1970s, he used an econometrically motivated interpretation of rational expectations with a focus on restricting distributed lags. In the late 1970s to early 1980s, this emphasis changed to restriction of vector autoregressions. In the early to mid-1980s, Sargent focused on how rational expectations in a general equilibrium framework could lead to vector autoregressions. In the late 1980s to early 1990s, he tried to show convergence to rational expectations through learning with adaptive expectations or artificial intelligence. Sargent's choice of free moves was shown to be influenced by his social environment: Meyer, Roll, and Blattberg in the late 1960s to early 1970s; Wallace, Sims, and Hansen in the late 1970s to early 1980s; Lucas in the early to mid-1980s; and Santa Fe, Marcet, Marimon, and McGrattan in the late 1980s to early 1990s.

Another finding that follows from the framework was that Sargent had several ways of dealing with resistances. The resistance in the late 1960s to early 1970s was posed by the lack of a general estimation method for Lévy stable distributions. Sargent accommodated this resistance by ignoring this forced move and resistance, without explicit justification. In the late 1970s to early 1980s, he was faced with the resistance that without theory, Sims's test was a necessary but not a sufficient condition for establishing strict exogeneity. Furthermore, Sargent's analysis of observational equivalence implied that within any policy regime there were an infinite number of equally accurate representations of the data. These resistances led Sargent to change his free moves by incorporating theory. The trouble here was that he ended up with a very restricted environment as a result of his reliance on engineering conceptions in his search for neoclassical dynamics. In the early to mid-1980s, Sargent found that with symmetry among agents, economists, and econometricians, there would be no trade, no information gathering, no error term justification, no policy recommendations, and no seasonal adjustment. He tried to solve these problems by changing his free moves and incorporating learning. In the late 1980s to early 1990s, Sargent's resistance within the rational expectations framework was that the results of assuming symmetry among agents, economists, and econometricians were no known closed-form prediction formula, nonstationary, and an arbitrary setting of the dial of rationality. Sargent's accommodation consisted of changing his free moves and adopting adaptive expectations. But the resistances within this framework were a limited interpretation of learning and a still arbitrary setting of the dial of rationality. Sargent tried to deal with these by changing his free moves again, now by adopting artificial intelligence. However, new resistances appeared in the form of changing econometrics and neoclassical economics, asymmetry between Sargent and agents, asymmetry between economists and econometricians, and the possibility of nonconvergence. We have to wait to see how Sargent will deal with these difficulties.

Having summarized the content, I should explain why and how I set out to write this book.

7.2   Framework

What motivates the book is the argument that there is no generic science, as reflected by the fact that there is no universal interpretation of rational expectations. Depending on the focus, different stories can be constructed about the history of rational expectations. First, suppose data were the driving force. In that case, rational expectations arose out of the expiration of the Phillips curve or out of policy irrelevance. Second, let techniques be the main factor. Then, the availability of tools for optimal prediction and filtering led to rational expectations. Third, assume that rational expectations followed from existing theories. In that case, the focus would be on eliminating asymmetric agents and governments or on extending the optimization principle to the problem of expectations. Fourth, suppose that problems with existing theories were on center stage. In that case, rational expectations arose out of endogenizing expectations revisions, the possibility of making public predictions by focusing on consistent outcomes, or attempts to counter Simon's bounded rationality research program. Finally, let linking theory and econometrics be the driving force. Then rational expectations managed to link deterministic theories with random methods in an effort to restrict the distributed lags in decision rules or it was able to incorporate vector autoregressions.

Not only is it possible to tell many stories about the rise of rational expectations at the level of economic theory, which is often overlooked by orthodox philosophers and historians of economic thought, but in addition the pluralism does not disappear – and possibly increases – if we look at one rational expectations economist. Rather than analyzing these stories from an outsider's perspective and using outside standards such as progress to limit the focus, I attempt to provide a richer reading and deeper understanding of what was going on by focusing on the account of one of the central players in the rational expectations movement, Thomas Sargent. What were the alternatives available to him? What choices did he make? What were the consequences of those decisions? How did he accommodate undesirable consequences? The framework used to answer these questions was inspired by insights from the sociology of scientific knowledge. It started out with Sargent's interests, which were situated in and subject to change through scientific practice. I show how Sargent tried to extend culture to serve his interests and used his motivations as a standard for judging whether the extension of culture was successful or not. The free moves reflected the tentative choices Sargent made, carrying no guarantee of success. The forced moves served to elaborate the choices through conceptual, sociotechnical, and experimental practice. Sargent could accommodate resistances that appeared when the extension of culture was not successful by changing his interests, changing his free moves, or ignoring the forced moves.

Acknowledging that notions of universality and progress need to be problematized in an evaluation of economics, I have pictured economics as a field of emergent human and natural agency engaged by means of a dialectic of resistance and accommodation. I have used the framework of interests, moves, resistances, and accommodation to illustrate the emergence of continually changing interpretations of rational expectations in Sargent's work and to provide an internal criticism. The insight that Sargent ran into resistances in his attempts to satisfy his interests can be used to resist his analysis. Sargent quietly abandoned Lévy stable distributions when they turned out to be too threatening. He resorted to convenient engineering metaphors in his quests for a more scientific macroeconomics. He was unable to retain symmetry within the rational expectations framework. In response, he used a very limited interpretation of standard genetic algorithms. Rather than imposing my standards, I illustrate that Sargent was unable to meet his own standards. I believe that this kind of analysis provides an interesting alternative to the many different, simple, and equally (un)compelling stories about the rational expectations revolution that have been circulating in the history of thought community up until now.

An additional attraction of the approach used in analyzing Sargent's work throughout is that there is a symmetry in the treatment of the "interests" of Sargent and the "interests" of the agents in his model, as mentioned briefly in Chapter 1. Hands (1994b) notes: "[W]hile economists do not normally use the term 'interests,' they do in fact explain economic behavior on the basis on the 'interests' of the agents involved" (p. 81). In fact, Pickering, the father of the framework composed of interests, free moves, forced moves, resistances, and accommodation, posits individual scientists as behaving essentially in the way that economic agents act. According to Hands, Pickering's scientists "make intentional choices on the basis of their beliefs and desires" (p. 85). Furthermore, Hands indicates that Pickering "has been criticized precisely because [his work] characterizes the behavior of scientists in the way that a neoclassical economist would characterize individual behavior" (p. 84). Whereas it is standard in economics to explain human behavior in terms of exogenous reasons why agents act, I use a similar approach to open up insights into how Sargent acts. Whereas Sargent has endowed his agents with neoclassical behavior, I characterize his behavior in a neoclassical economic way. The fact that that is precisely the symmetry that Sargent eventually sought to achieve strengthens the arguments for using Pickering's framework. I should admit that my attraction to the framework may also be explained by the fact that I am both a historian and an economist.

This brings me back to the fact that, though I initially felt hostile to Sargent as a result of the classes I took from him, I have come to the realization, as mentioned in Chapter 1, that Sargent and I seem to be fascinated by very similar things, struggling with very similar issues, and having very similar concerns. We are both wondering how we can model human behavior, of economic agents in Sargent's case and of economists in mine. However, there is a difference in that Sargent tends to abstract human behavior out of context, whereas I try to make it more concrete by focusing on Sargent himself. Whereas Sargent's research was driven by a somewhat vague notion of conceptual integrity, I have tried to contextualize this idea. In situating Sargent and making him an instantiation rather than a generic actor, I have tried to bring human behavior out in the open. Let me close by touching on some of the issues discussed in the previous chapters to illustrate that my concerns seem to be very similar to Sargent's.

Accommodating Randomness discusses Sargent's struggle with infinite variance. Similarly, I have been trying to discover in what sense Sargent's moves were random or caused, free or forced, unbounded or bounded. Accommodating Prediction analyzes how Sargent was dissatisfied with his attempts to find regularities in history without dependence on abstract theory and how he searched for a framework in general equilibrium theory. Similarly, I feel unable to tell Sargent's tale without a framework and have searched for theory in science studies. In addition, Sargent's search for convenience left him with a very restricted world. Similarly, I have come to the realization that contextualization can be nasty and my analysis is therefore conveniently restricted to Sargent. Thus, we both seem to understand that convenience is context-dependent and that therefore an analysis of human behavior is fraught with contingency. Accommodating Symmetry discusses Sargent's attempts to establish symmetry among agents, economists, and econometricians. Similarly, I attempt to create symmetry between Sargent and me by modeling him as he models economic agents. However, just like Sargent, I encounter the paradox of symmetry in that Sargent and I can neither be the same nor be very different. Finally, Accommodating Learning analyzes how Sargent sought to make everyone boundedly rational through learning. Similarly, I place bounds on Sargent's rationality and track his learning process through the use of the framework of interests, free moves, forced, moves, resistances, and accommodation.

7.3   Final Comments

Though I not only focus on internal processes but also provide a wider perspective on Sargent's work through discussions of philosophy, science studies, physics, engineering, and artificial intelligence, the contextualization is somewhat limited by the necessity that a lot of space must be devoted to analyzing the progress of Sargent's research. Though I give a sense of how Sargent was influenced by his social environment, the next questions to ask are what determined Sargent's social environment and how Sargent influenced that environment. Though I illustrate Sargent's different interpretations of the rational expectations hypothesis, his history will have to be coupled reciprocally with those of Lucas, Sims, and Wallace, among others.[1] To get an even richer reading and deeper understanding, issues like these will have to be further explored. Though I have taken the first steps in that direction, the journey is far from over.

Notes

Chapter 1

1 Though Sargent (1996a, p. 540) noted: "From today's standpoint, it is evident that the rational expectations revolution was impartial in the rough treatment it handed out to participants on both sides of the monetarist–Keynesian controversies raging in the 1960's, and it is puzzling to comprehend the reluctance with which many leading Keynesian economists initially greeted rational expectations methods."

2 I should note that the more specific claim is that policies that alter nominal aggregate demand do not affect real variables. It was later argued that this claim follows not from rational expectations, except to the degree that rational expectations prevents money illusion from encouraging people to make real mistakes, but from the classical dichotomy built into the notion of continuous market clearing. In fact, in his interview with Klamer (1983), Sargent said, "The neutrality proposition was an important element in my work six or seven years ago, but not recently. . . . Some people, however . . . took the neutrality proposition more seriously than [Wallace and I] did" (p. 70).

3 In particular, making policy recommendations required that the government had better information than everyone else or was able always to do the unexpected and catch people off guard.

4 According to some it is not at all clear that the hypothesis of rational expectations is derivable from general assumptions of rationality. Hahn (1986, p. 281) points out that to jump from "the respectable proposition that an agent will not persist in expectations which are systematically disappointed" to the proposition that "agents have expectations which are not systematically disappointed [is a] non sequitur of a rather obvious kind." Janssen (1993, p. 142) shows that the rational expectations hypothesis "is an aggregate hypothesis that cannot unconditionally be regarded as being based on [methodological individualism]."

5 Static expectations may be regarded as a special case of adaptive expectations in which the adjustment parameter is set equal to unity (see, e.g., Nerlove 1958).

6 I should note that Carnegie Mellon University came into being in 1967, after the merger of the Carnegie Institute of Technology and the Mellon Institute. Our narrative therefore shifts from the Carnegie Institute to Carnegie Mellon.

7 In his personal letter dated October 30, 1996, Richard Roll, who was also at Carnegie Mellon at that time, remembers many discussions with Lucas, Sargent, Simon, Meltzer, and later others such as Prescott, in which Roll was the advocate of rationality and hence efficient information processing by agents, and the others were generally skeptical. Though Muth had left Carnegie Mellon before Roll arrived, Roll knew Muth's (1960, 1961) papers well, because his fellow students and professors at

Chicago had used it as one element in constructing their ideas about market efficiency. Roll believes that the embracing of Muth's ideas would not have happened so quickly, and certainly not with the same actors, if the finance literature had not come to the attention of the Carnegie economists by virtue of the interdisciplinary environment. This claim could be elaborated in yet another story about the rise of rational expectations economics.

8 Lucas (1976) noted that if the estimated coefficients of observable equations implicitly contain policy parameters that have entered through their role as predictors of the future, these parameters will change when a new policy is adopted. The Lucas critique is discussed in more detail in Chapter 3.

9 Sargent (1976b) showed that models compatible with the natural rate hypothesis and those incompatible with it could both generate the very same causal relations. This point is analyzed in Chapter 3.

10 I should also note that these stories are revisited in more detail in the following chapters.

11 This is nicely illustrated in the following statement by Woolgar (1988b, pp. 12–13): "[T]here is no essential difference between science and other forms of knowledge production; . . . there is nothing intrinsically special about 'the scientific method;' indeed, even if there is such a thing as 'the scientific method,' much scientific practice proceeds in spite of its canons rather than because of them. . . . It is not that science has its 'social aspects,' . . . but that science is itself constitutively social."

12 In the same interview, Sargent also said, "It's a fruitful enterprise to link dynamic theories with econometrics" (Klamer 1983, p. 74).

13 That is to say, Sargent's rational expectations economics was technically rather than politically motivated. This point is discussed in Chapter 3.

14 This illuminating perspective on scientific culture and practice is proposed by Pickering (1992, pp. 4–5).

15 Also see Klamer's (1983) interview with Sargent: "The research I'm involved in has this momentum. . . . Even though there's a lot of uncertainty, you can see what the next step is" (p. 78).

16 Also see Klamer's (1983) interview with Sargent: "There are technical problems in taking [the next step]" (p. 78).

17 Sargent also said: "There are surprises in how it comes out" (Klamer 1983, p. 78).

18 This suggests that there is some path dependence in Sargent's dialectic of resistance and accommodation. However, though chronology is used as a general ordering principle in the following chapters, it should be acknowledged that Sargent has sometimes gone back and forth.

19 In addition, it echoes Merz and Knorr Cetina's (1997a) analysis of theoretical physics in terms of "deconstruction, variation, 'doing examples', modelling and, finally, thought alliances between subjects" (p. 73).

20 I should note that Pickering refers to the British usage of the word "mangle," meaning a clothes wringer.

21 In a sense, I am adopting three languages: the participant's language (Sargent's report in his own language through the use of quotations), observation language (a clarification of Sargent's report in my language), and explanatory language (an account

of the balance of human and nonhuman agency and the emergent structure of Sargent's research using the dialectic of resistance and accommodation). For more on this, see Gale and Pinnick (1997) and Merz and Knorr Cetina (1997b).

22 Again, I should acknowledge that though chronology is used as a general ordering principle in the following chapters, Sargent has sometimes gone back and forth.

23 This is also the interpretation Sargent stressed in his talk during the luncheon honoring the 1995 Nobel Laureate in Economics, Robert Lucas, at the 1997 Allied Social Science Association meetings.

Chapter 2

1 Other forms include psychological, theological, and logical determinism.

2 Dupré (1993) names this view "probabilistic uniformitarianism."

3 This is where Earman (1986) and Weatherford (1991) depart; Dupré (1993) travels on and identifies this step as probabilistic catastrophism.

4 I choose not to discuss the propensity interpretation in order to avoid getting mixed up in the still very lively debate over this rendition. I should also note that the different interpretations are not necessarily incompatible but have chosen to focus on different aspects. More thorough discussions of probability theory can be found in Cohen (1989), Daston (1988), Fine (1973), Kyburg (1969), and Weatherford (1982).

5 I am here not making any claims about the reasonableness of this conviction, as I am just trying to situate Sargent's work in its economic landscape.

6 Note that the narrative of the concept of subjective probability as the foundation for the Bayesian approach to statistics falls outside the scope of this text.

7 I highlight only the aspects of Lévy distributions that are needed to get a perspective on Sargent's work and refer the reader to Zolotarev (1986) for a more thorough general discussion.

8 Examples occur in economics: see, e.g., Mandelbrot (1963a) for Pareto's law of income distribution; see, e.g., Mandelbrot (1963b) for the variation of speculative prices; see, e.g., Mandelbrot (1965) for the problem of industrial concentration.

9 The normal law had been invented by De Moivre and applied by Laplace to statistical matters but was best known after Gauss as the law governing the distribution of errors from true values in astronomical and geodetic observations.

10 The characteristic function of a random variable X is defined by Ee^{itX}. Thus if the distribution function of X is $F(\bullet)$, the characteristic function is $\int_{-\infty}^{\infty} e^{itX} \, dF(X)$.

11 DuMouchel (1971) used a multinomial approximation to the likelihood function to find approximate maximum likelihood estimators.

12 Paulson, Holcomb, and Leitch (1975) minimized some function through iterative renormalization. Koutrouvelis (1980, 1981) extended Wiener's regression-type method to the four-parameter case.

13 For a survey of all these methods, see Akgiray and Lamoureux (1989) and Zolotarev (1986).

14 Theoretical determinism is closely linked to computability.

15 Samuelson (1965) marked a turning point in the discussion of the distinction between determinism and randomness in neoclassical economics. By claiming that the

neoclassical model gives rise to a martingale, he tried to introduce randomness while preserving some of the law-governedness of the economy.

16 Telephone interviews with Robert Blattberg on March 12, 1993, and Richard Roll on May 24, 1993.

17 See Taylor (1974) for an attempt to understand MSAE estimation better and to link it to already well-understood formalisms of linear programming. The essential ingredient in the proof of unbiasedness is symmetry of the error term. If the independent variables are symmetrical about their respective means, unbiasedness of the estimator does not require the distribution of the error term to be symmetrical. However, this is a very restricted case.

18 Personal letter from Roll dated October 30, 1996. I should also note that Roll's dissertation won the Irving Fisher award in 1969.

19 Personal letter from Roll dated October 30, 1996.

20 Ibid.

21 Telephone interview with Roll on May 24, 1993.

22 Later evidence of the importance of stable Lévy distributions included commodity futures, foreign currencies, and Treasury bills. For an excellent review of the recent studies on stock prices, see Akgiray and Booth (1988). The reader can find a short survey of recent evidence in other areas in Gribbin, Harris, and Lau (1992).

23 Personal letter from Roll dated October 30, 1996.

24 Notice how Roll used an ontic interpretation of probabilism – arguing that chance is an irreducible part of the natural phenomena we are investigating – while trying to save some determinism, arguing that the random variables are individually unimportant. Chance would then disappear in the large numbers.

25 Since there does not seem to be a universally accepted notation for the parameters in the characteristic function, I use Roll's notation.

26 I should note that the introduction of discrete distributional models to deal with fat tails ultimately occurred.

27 Telephone interview with Roll on May 24, 1993.

28 Mandelbrot and Taqqu (1979) show how R/S analysis can be used to test for the presence of very long nonperiodic statistical dependence and to estimate the intensity of that dependence. The main virtue of the statistic R/S is its robustness with respect to the marginal distribution. It is equally effective when the underlying data or random processes are Gaussian or extremely far from Gaussian.

29 I should note that Granger and Hatanaka try to make a case for the fact that just as it is useful to discuss the correlation coefficient for nonnormal statistical variables, so it is similarly useful to use spectral techniques on economic data although there is a certain amount of evidence that economic processes are not normal, having too much mass in the tails. This case is not very convincing since spectral analysis deals exclusively with second moments and is paralyzed if the second moments do not exist.

30 The analysis of the problem of minimizing the sum of absolute values of deviations goes back as far as Fourier's proposal in the 1820s to use an iterative procedure similar to the simplex method. In 1955, Charnes, Cooper, and Ferguson (1955) showed that a certain management problem involving a minimization of absolute values

could be transformed to standard linear programming form by employing the device of representing a deviation as the difference between two nonnegative variables. For a further discussion of the history of this estimator, see Fisher (1961).

31 Telephone interview with John Meyer on May 21, 1993.

32 In her e-mail message dated November 2, 1996, Deirdre McCloskey, a fellow classmate of Sargent's at Harvard, recalls that Sargent was quiet and unimpressive as a graduate student and that the other students (who were not of course in a very good position to observe his actual work) did not as she recalls think of him as any kind of future star.

33 Also see Sargent (1996a, p. 537): "Friedman and his students had pioneered the use of distributed lags in macroeconomic contexts." For more work on distributed lags, see, e.g., Anderson (1979), Griliches (1967), Jorgenson (1963), Lucas (1972b), Muth (1960, 1961), Nerlove (1967), Sargent (1971b), and Sims (1971a).

34 Note that this ignores the fact that spectral analysis is compromised in the presence of Lévy stable distributions with infinite variance.

35 Notice how the first reason – the epistemic interpretation – amounts to attributing randomness to human ignorance, thus saving determinism. The second reason – the ontic interpretation – comes very close to admitting indeterminism.

36 A similar argument can be found in Cootner (1964, p. 337): "If [Mandelbrot] is right . . . almost without exception, past econometric work is meaningless. Surely, before consigning centuries of work to the ashpile, we should like to have some assurance that all our work is truly useless."

37 As an aside, Sargent worked with Neil Wallace at the National Bureau of Economic Research, the University of Minnesota, and the Federal Reserve Bank of Minneapolis. In Klamer (1983), both Sargent and Townsend mention that Wallace taught them how to attack problems. In my interview with him on November 16, 1992, Wallace made a case for a budget view of decisions made by economists. He argued for giving their work a rationale that makes sense in terms of the idea that there is a time limit to answer a question and only a certain budget to expend.

38 In his personal letter dated October 30, 1996, Roll argues that the difference between his and Sargent's costs derives from the fact that he was a pragmatic financial engineer, whereas Sargent was arguing (Roll thinks incorrectly) that theoretical insights could be more easily obtained with a simplification, even though it is fundamentally unsound and would ultimately have to be replaced.

39 Note that for lack of universal standards I am not making any judgments about the different motivations of Roll and Sargent.

40 Witness the combination of the idea of rational expectations with vector autoregressive models. This connection is discussed further in the next chapter.

41 Personal letter from Roll dated October 30, 1996. Roll notes that he also thought this was plausible but that he never saw evidence that completely supported normality. He further mentions that he too has not paid much attention to stable laws since the late 1970s and that this has occurred even though finance is somewhat better equipped than economics to deal with stable law generalizations of finite variance models.

42 See, e.g., Mandelbrot (1973, pp. 158–9): "When the lognormal is very skewed, its

'small sample' properties are extremely erratic, and calculations of sample distributions are very complicated. Thus, the reputed 'tameness' of the lognormal is entirely based on its asymptotics, and in practice has little value."

Chapter 3

1 In particular, Sargent became an associate professor at the University of Minnesota in September 1971 and was promoted to full professor in July 1975. He spent a year as the Ford Foundation visiting professor at the University of Chicago from September 1976 until June 1977. Furthermore, the University of Chicago awarded him the Mary Elizabeth Morgan Prize for Excellence in Economics in 1979.

2 Or order can be created!

3 Whether this characterization does justice to the practice of physics is a question I want to raise but leave unanswered as it would require a long detour.

4 According to Hausman (1984), these possibilities do not reveal any fundamental difficulties. He puts a lot of trust in the ability of a social theorist to "factor in" the reactions of those who become aware of any particular theory and claims that there is in principle no difficulty here at all.

5 This dates back to Comte.

6 Vocal skeptics of the possibility of prediction in economics were found among Frank Knight, Oskar Morgenstern, and the Austrians, such as Hayek, who maintained that as soon as one abandons the subjective point of view and attempts to think of economics as if it were a natural science, one loses sight of the essence of the subject.

7 Hands (1990) also mentions the literature surrounding sunspot equilibria. Here, the idea is that economic fundamentals move in a deterministic fashion whereas economic agents believe that prices and quantities are affected by irrelevant random factors (e.g., sunspots). These expectations are postulated to be self-fulfilling, and, hence, one gets sunspot equilibria and an inherent unpredictability in the market. Such results are very ironic since the self-fulfilling expectations lead to unpredictability. See, e.g., Azariadis (1981) and Cass and Shell (1983).

8 It is interesting to note that Grunberg, Modigliani, and Simon were all at the Carnegie Institute of Technology during the early 1950s. Self-reference may have been an important concern at Carnegie because of the connection between Gödel's theorem and the paradoxes of logic in computer theory.

9 In fact, Muth was first a graduate student and then briefly a faculty member at Carnegie, collaborated with Modigliani on the Planning and Control of Industrial Operations project (see Holt et al. 1960), and explicitly acknowledged the Grunberg–Modigliani paper as a direct ancestor in Muth (1961). Furthermore, Simon (1982b, p. 608) notes, "More recently, the question of the self-consistency of predictions has arisen again in connection with the so-called rational expectations theories of economic behavior under uncertainty."

10 I should note that despite the prestigious attention the question of public prediction has received historically, it currently does not seem to be a topic of much interest within the philosophy and methodology of economics. Hands (1990) attributes this to the decline of logical positivism: "When logical positivism reigned supreme,

questions such as the self-falsifying nature of public predictions which emphasizes the possible differences between the empirical testability of theories in social science and their natural science counterparts seemed to be more important than they do today in the post-positivist era" (p. 221).

11 Also see Marcet and Sargent (1992, p. 139): "A rational expectations equilibrium is a fixed point of a particular mapping from beliefs to outcomes. When agents have an arbitrarily given set of beliefs about the laws of motion of the economy, their behavior causes the actual laws of motion to be determined. We can think of people's behavior collectively as inducing a mapping from their believed laws of motion to the actual laws of motion for the economy. A rational expectations equilibrium is a fixed point of that mapping, which is a set of beliefs about laws of motion that is consistent with realized outcomes." This claim comes awfully close to Grunberg and Modigliani's fixed point argument. Further see Sargent (1987a, p. 402): "[T]he observation that an equilibrium implicitly solves a social welfare problem . . . enables the modelbuilder to replace a complicated 'fixed point' problem with a maximization problem."

12 Also see Sargent (1996a, p. 537): "At the AEA meetings in 1966, Dale Jorgenson discussed Miguel Sidrauski's paper about the optimum quantity of money and asked why, in Sidrauski's dynamic model, there appeared three distinct prices for money: its value in exchange, the (rate of change of its) expected future value, and a shadow price of money. Wouldn't a consistent presentation of the theory equate these prices?"

13 Also see Sargent (1993, pp. 6–7): "[I]f perceptions of the environment, including perceptions about the behavior of other people, are left unrestricted, then models in which people's behavior depends on their perceptions can produce so many outcomes that they are useless as instruments for generating predictions." Further see Hansen and Sargent (1980).

14 According to Sargent (1996a), part of this was due to the tension resulting from the fact that the size of the comprehensive models required a decentralized research strategy "that worked against things fitting together" (p. 537n).

15 Sargent (1996a) recalled that there was "an intense and respectful dialogue between Christopher Sims and Neil Wallace. . . . Somehow, Sims and Wallace created an atmosphere that attracted several generations of researchers and teachers" (p. 545).

16 Sargent and Wallace do spend some time trying to justify rational expectations, though. See, e.g., Sargent and Wallace (1976, p. 209): "Several reasons can be given for using the hypotheses of rational expectations. . . . [I]t offers one reason, but probably not the only reason, that macroeconometric models fail tests for structural change. . . . A second reason . . . is that in estimating econometric models it is a source of identifying restrictions. . . . A third reason . . . is that it accords with the economist's usual practice of assuming that people behave in their own best interests."

17 Specifically, Sargent and Wallace incorporated the Lucas aggregate supply curve and the rational expectations hypothesis in their IS-LM models.

18 Furthermore, systematic fiscal policy would not affect current real output or employment and would affect these variables in the long run only to the extent that by manipulating the composition of the given output level it could affect investment and

hence future aggregate supply. Moreover, random or nonsystematic components of monetary and fiscal policies would typically only increase the uncertainty and fluctuations in the economy.

19 Also see Sargent (1996a, p. 543): "Time has broken the 1970s perception . . . of a close connection between 'rational expectations' and 'neutrality' or 'policy ineffectiveness'." Further see Parkin's (1996) interview with Sargent: "The logic of the policy irrelevance result has nothing to say about the effects of government policies that work through avenues other than by inducing errors in people's forecasts" (p. 652).

20 Also, Alan Blinder said in his interview with Klamer (1983, p. 159), "[Sargent] doesn't come to these economic views from a rigidly maintained ideological position."

21 In particular, Sargent was involved with systems analysis as a staff member and acting director at the Economics Division of the office of the assistant secretary of defense from February 1968 until December 1969.

22 I should note that the objections that Hoover lists are ones that were pretty well seen immediately on publication of Sargent and Wallace's paper.

23 The key assumption in their model is that there is some limit to the amount of government debt that the public will hold as a proportion of national income. For a summary of Sargent and Wallace's argument, see Hoover (1988, pp. 73–80).

24 I should note that Sargent's embarrassment here refers mostly to Sargent and Wallace (1975, 1976). Also see Klamer (1983, p. 62): "When I think back to how [Wallace and I] were struggling with this rational expectations stuff, lots of it is pretty funny because we didn't do things in the cleanest way." Further see Sargent (1987a, p. xviii): "It is true that there were other, more elegant routes toward that end, through general equilibrium theory or optimal growth theory, but those were not the routes that Wallace and I took. (While Neil Wallace and I were struggling with Keynesian models, Robert E. Lucas, Jr., and Edward C. Prescott were mostly traveling along these alternative and more direct routes.)"

25 Sims started at Harvard in 1963, a year before Sargent, and was graduated in 1968, the same year as Sargent. While Sims was at Minnesota from 1970 until 1990, Sargent was there from 1971 until 1987.

26 For work on vector autoregressions, see, e.g., Hansen and Hodrick (1980), Hansen and Sargent (1991a), Sargent (1979b), Shiller (1979), and Sims (1980a).

27 There are two general strategies for focusing on vector autoregressions. One method employs so-called index models as described by Brillinger (1975); Priestley, Rao, and Tong (1974); and Sargent and Sims (1977). The idea here is that the dynamic interactions among all variables are forced to be entirely intermediated through a small number of variables termed "indexes." Another, less complicated and more easily implemented method was developed by Litterman (1979), who introduced restrictions directly.

28 Sargent (1981a) also appealed to economic data: "Since time series of economic data usually have the properties of high own-serial correlation and various patterns of cross-serial correlation, it seems that there is potential for [specifications] . . . that roughly reproduce the serial correlation and cross-serial correlation in a given collection of time series measuring market outcomes" (p. 215).

29 As before, the trouble was that using this statistical technique required the avail-

ability of algorithms for the estimators of the parameters. These were not available for most Lévy stable distributions. What happened is that almost every economist dropped infinite variance and infinite dependence in the time domain, and the focus of attention changed to using elaborate econometric techniques based on linear Gaussian processes instead.

30 In her e-mail message dated November 2, 1996, Deirdre McCloskey, a former class-mate of Sargent's, suggests that Sargent's later fascination with math may have arisen from an emotional predisposition to be precise, precise, precise. She also no-ticed this trait in Robert Lucas, a colleague of hers for five or six years at Chicago in the late 1970s.

31 Also see Klamer's (1983) interview with Sargent: "The language is probably new to macroeconomics, but not completely new in other areas of economics or in other ar-eas of statistics and probability theory. . . . I think it's too bold to say that we invented it" (pp. 64–5).

32 Forecasting of the time-series model, by and large, is better than that of large-scale simultaneous equation models, but the time-series model usually fails to forecast the turning points of business cycles.

33 Interestingly enough, though never publicly acknowledged by Lucas, Sargent (1996a) indicated that he played an essential role in bringing this paper to life: "On a Friday early in April 1973, I organized a small conference on rational expectations at Ford Hall at the University of Minnesota. On Saturday morning, I received a phone call from Rita Lucas relaying a request from Bob, who was playing baseball, that I return to Ford Hall to search for an important folder Bob had misplaced. I found a file containing a handwritten draft of 'Econometric Policy Evaluation' and mailed it to Bob" (p. 539n).

34 Sims (1980a), for example, argued that in order to identify the parameters of large macroeconomic models, econometricians had typically placed a vast number of ar-bitrary restrictions on the structure of the estimated equations. He challenged this whole line of activity and rejected all identifying restrictions as "incredible."

35 This still begs the question of what "good dynamic economic theory" is. Also see Sargent and Sims (1977, p. 46), whose criticism of existing econometric models was that "very little of the *a priori* theory embodied in macroeconometric models is based explicitly on models of the behavior of individuals [and that] very little of the the-ory embodied in such models is explicitly stochastic." Hence, for Sargent, good dy-namic economic theory implied finding a basis in individual behavior and incorpo-rating randomness.

36 Others, when confronted with the apparent inadequate modeling particularly of price relations and financial sector behavior, continually announced that "the" key vari-able that would set matters right had finally been located. See, e.g., Eckstein (1976).

37 See Zellner and Palm (1974) for a synthesis of univariate stochastic autoregressive and moving average processes with structural models.

38 The resistances following from this move are the topic of the next chapter.

39 See, e.g., Sims (1980a). Dynamic elaboration of single-equation regression to pro-duce the error correction models associated with Hendry and his colleagues was the other response by econometricians to the evidence.

40 Also see Sargent and Sims (1977, p. 47): "Rather than reduce the dimensionality of our models by restricting particular equations *a priori,* as in the standard methodology, we proceed by imposing simplifying conditions which are symmetric in the variables."

41 Theoretical restrictions such as 0 restrictions on the coefficients and cross-equation restrictions are not imposed on the coefficient matrices.

42 Since I do not want to get too wrapped up in the technical details, let me explain the two general strategies in this area very briefly in this note. One method employs index models as described by Brillinger (1975); Priestley, Rao, and Tong (1974); and Sargent and Sims (1977). The idea here is that the dynamic interactions among all variables are forced to be entirely intermediated through a small number of variables, indexes. Also see Sargent and Sims (1977, pp. 47–8): "Their attractiveness as statistical devices for restricting the dimensionality of vector time series models is not the only feature which draws us toward experimenting with index models. Certain theoretical macroeconomic models can be cast in index-model form. These include a class of models pioneered by Lucas as well as simple macroeconomic models which seem to us to reflect the pattern of quantitative thinking about the business cycle of many macroeconomists, 'Keynesian' as well as 'monetarist.'" Another, less complicated and more easily implemented, method was developed by Litterman (1979), who introduced restrictions directly. Even more so than with index models, these restrictions are admitted at the outset not to be based on dynamic economic theory. There is evidence that Litterman's procedures produce forecasts of many macroeconomic variables that are competitive with those produced outside the estimation periods by various of the better known of the large structural macroeconometric models.

43 Sargent (1977b, p. 213) summarizes his and Sims's position in the following way: "[I]n the context of building large economy-wide models, we do mean to question whether existing theory really provided the reliable identifying restrictions needed to carry out structural estimation. It is our opinion that the identifying restrictions used in macroeconomic models are sufficiently questionable to make the exploration of alternative modeling strategies worthwhile." Also see Sargent and Sims (1977, pp. 45–7).

44 In particular, causal order is obtained through Wold causal chains or block recursive orderings.

45 Although a lot of current research focuses on cointegration, that technique was not considered by Sargent and Sims.

46 Also see Sargent (1977a, p. 60): "Empirical tests by Wallace and me typically indicated substantial evidence of feedback from money creation to inflation. Cagan's model under rational expectations predicts a particular extreme version of such a pattern: it predicts that inflation 'causes' (in Granger's sense) money creation with no reverse feedback (or 'causality') from money creation to inflation. Cagan's model with rational expectations thus seems to provide one way of explaining the Granger-causal structure exhibited in the data."

47 See, e.g., Klamer's (1983) interview with Sargent: "What we do is actually a child of the enterprise in which the Cowles Commission was involved, both in terms of its

econometric challenge and in terms of its theoretical challenge" (p. 67). The econometric challenge is the focus of this and the following section. The theoretical challenge is the focus of sections 3.4 and 3.5.

48 Although Roll and Sargent had showed in the early 1970s that the term structure of interest rates exhibits infinite variance, as discussed in the previous chapter, Sargent worked with the term structure of interest rates in this paper under the assumption that variance is finite. See Sargent (1976a, p. 208): "The key elements of the model . . . are: (a) a drastic version of the natural unemployment rate hypothesis; (b) the expectations theory of the term structure of interest rates, and (c) the assumption that the public's expectations are 'rational.'" Also: "[Unemployment] is an indeterministic, covariance-stationary process. . . . [The error terms] are serially uncorrelated with mean zero and finite variance" (p. 214).

49 Sargent is referring to Hansen and Sargent (1980).

50 Some assumptions, such as an underlying structural coefficient matrix that is lower triangular, are needed to use vector autoregressions for policy analysis. The triangular solution is unsatisfactory, however, insofar as the model was intended to prevent the need for such assumptions about structure. See Epstein (1987, pp. 205–22) for more on this issue.

51 Further see Parkin's (1996) interview with Sargent: "Economics is interesting because of the opportunities that it affords for unleashing one's natural curiosity about history, society, mathematics, and statistics. It is especially attractive to people with an interest in understanding what it takes to improve the governmental and business arrangements that we live with" (p. 653).

52 Their conclusions shed an interesting light on their view of the impact of evidence in economics. See Neftci and Sargent (1978, p. 317): "The marginal significance levels are such that a true believer in the invariance across regimes of [the neutrality proposition] would probably not find the evidence sufficiently negative to change his beliefs; a true believer in the invariance of [the Keynesian model] would have to be rather more pigheaded in order not to have the evidence change his views."

53 It is interesting to note that whereas Sargent and Sims's work had been against the spirit of the Cowles Commission, Tobin believed that Sargent's new approach was "not different from the spirit of the Cowles Commission econometrics 40 years ago" (Klamer 1983, pp. 107–8).

54 In his interview with Klamer (1983, p. 62), Sargent said: "I don't really work much with Lucas. I spent a year at Chicago. I took two courses from him. He's a very good teacher. I learn from him. I read his papers. He's been a big influence on me." Also, see Sargent (1980, p. 107n): "This paper is an exercise that was undertaken to practice some of the methods that were taught by R. E. Lucas, Jr., in his Economics 337 class at the University of Chicago in the spring of 1977." However, Lucas said in his interview with Klamer (1983, p. 34), "Tom and I talk quite a bit. I think that we influence each other a lot."

55 According to Sargent (1996a), this set him "on a path that transformed macroeconomics" (p. 538).

56 Also see Sargent (1996a, p. 540): "Keynesians lost the technical high ground, and were never to recover from it."

57 Also see Sargent in Klamer (1983, p. 68): "What we mean by equilibrium is essentially two things. First, we set out to explain data on prices and quantities resulting
from the interaction of individual decisions; that's the key thing together with the
notion that markets clear in some sense." Further see Sargent (1981a, p. 215): "The
basic idea is to interpret a collection of economic time series as resulting from the
choices of private agents interacting in markets assumed to be organized along well-
specified lines. The private agents are assumed to face nontrivial dynamic and stochastic optimization problems. This is an attractive assumption because the solutions
of such problems are known to imply that the chosen variables . . . can exhibit serial
correlation and cross-serial correlation. Since time series of economic data usually
have the properties of high own-serial correlation and various patterns of cross-serial correlations, it seems that there is potential for specifying dynamic preferences,
technologies, constraints, and rules of the market game that roughly reproduce the
serial correlation and cross-serial correlation patterns in a given collection of time
series measuring market outcomes. If this can be done in such a fashion that the free
parameters of preferences, technologies, and constraints are identifiable econometrically, it is then possible to interpret the collection of time series as the outcome of
a well-specified dynamic, stochastic equilibrium model."

58 Also see Sargent (1987c, p. 77): "Lucas and Prescott's model took a big step toward
integrating theory and econometrics by generating an explicit mapping from economic parameters . . . to the population moments of observable sequences of
economic time series."

59 Rapping corroborates this story in Klamer (1983, p. 225): "Tom Sargent was at
Carnegie Mellon when Lucas and I were writing [our] paper. He came from Harvard and stayed for a year. . . . He did not pay much attention to what Bob and I were
doing. He did not talk with Lucas much. . . . He must have been aware of the fac-
tions at Carnegie at that time. He was considered part of the Harvard group. The
Chicago people tended to have reservations about liberals, and the Harvard people
were liberals."

60 Also see Klamer's (1983) interview with Sargent: "The only reason why it hadn't
been done was technical. We didn't know the right techniques, such as filtering procedures to construct models with rational expectations" (p. 65).

61 After graduation, Hansen spent a few years at Carnegie Mellon University and became professor at the University of Chicago in 1982. Sargent also joined the faculty
of the University of Chicago in July 1991.

62 Hansen and Sargent (1991g) is an earlier draft of this manuscript. Most references
here are to the later version.

63 Also see Hansen and Sargent (1982, p. 265): "The purpose of the present paper is to
describe optimal estimation procedures in the case in which y is not strictly exogenous, in which the agents' decision variable in general Granger-causes the forcing
variable y and in which full-blown maximum likelihood procedures are thought to
be undesirable or inapplicable."

64 This reflects the change in focus in time-series econometrics from distributed lags
to vector autoregressions mentioned earlier.

65 Also see Nerlove (1967) and Nerlove, Grether, and Carvalho (1979).

66 See Hansen and Sargent (1983b, p. 377): "This paper reconsiders the aliasing problem of identifying the parameters of a continuous time stochastic process from discrete time data." Also see Hansen and Sargent (1991d, 1991e, 1991f) and Hansen,
Heaton, and Sargent (1991).

67 I should qualify this by noting that some of Sims's later work has witnessed a move
to structural vector autoregressions and to development of models that provide interpretations of them.

68 See Sargent (1984, p. 408): "I continue to attribute to Sims a line of argument which
he disowns." Also see Sargent (1984, p. 414): "I find persuasive the preceding defense of empirical work in the style of Sims. . . . While that work is 'atheoretical' in
terms of restrictions that it actually imposes on estimated vector autoregressions, it
has foundations in terms of a deep and consistent application of rational expectations dynamic theory."

69 I should note that these approaches also found their inspiration in engineering.

70 For example, Alain Lewis (1985, 1992a, 1992b) employs recursion theory to analyze recursively representable choice functions and general equilibrium models in
the domain of countable families of finite sets. For nontrivial recursively representable choice functions found in decision theory, Lewis shows that they are not
recursively solvable, and that implies that they cannot be recursively realized in a
uniform way through machines or algorithms and therefore are not computable.
Lewis concludes that choice functions consequently cannot exist in any meaningful
constructive sense. Lewis further notes that the problems are worse for general equilibrium models than for choice functions because the complexity of the realization
of these models can be no less than the complexity of the realization of the choice
functions for each type of agent.

71 See Hansen and Sargent (1996, p. 2): "Two computational problems have left much
of this promise unrealized. The first is Bellman's 'curse of dimensionality,' which
usually makes dynamic programming a costly procedure for systems with even small
numbers of state variables. The second problem is that after a dynamic program has
been solved and the equilibrium Markov process computed, the vector autoregression implied by the theory has to be computed by applying classic projection formulas to a large number of second moments of the stationary distribution associated
with that Markov process. Typically, each of these computational problems can be
solved only approximately."

72 According to Sargent (1996a), part of the reason for the delayed impact of Muth's
work was that he used classical procedures: "Muth framed his analysis in terms of
objects from the classical literature on forecasting time series unfamiliar to most
macroeconomists" (p. 537).

73 According to Sargent (1996a), part of the appeal of the work of Lucas and Prescott
was that they "showed how to apply recursive methods to build equilibria" (p. 538;
also see pp. 542–3).

74 Further see Sargent (1996b, p. 15): "Extending the range of problems susceptible
to recursive methods has been one of the major tasks and accomplishments of

macroeconomic theory since 1970." Or see Sargent (1996b, p. 179): "We describe classes of problems in which the dynamic programming and Kalman filtering algorithms are formally equivalent. . . . By exploiting their equivalence, we reap double dividends from any results that apply to one or the other problem." Notice the use of dividends here and recall the analysis of the problems associated with this kind of metaphor in the previous chapter. A similar discussion reappears at the end of this section and in Chapter 5.

75 Also see Parkin's (1996) interview with Sargent: "I find that it is easy to communicate with other scientists because we speak the same statistical and mathematical language" (p. 650).

76 Linear-quadratic versions can also be found, for example, in Sargent's (1987a) model of investment under uncertainty, Salemi and Sargent's (1979) and Sargent's (1977a) versions of Cagan's model of portfolio balance during hyperinflations, and Sargent's (1978b) rational expectations version of Friedman's permanent income theory of consumption. The two unpublished manuscripts by Hansen and Sargent (1996) and Sargent (1996b) also make extensive use of this setup.

77 This setup also made sure that the solution was bounded (see Sargent 1987a, p. 199).

78 Oddly enough, Simon was a staunch critic of rational expectations economics. For more on Simon's criticism of the rational expectations hypothesis, see Chapter 5.

79 See, e.g., Anderson, Hansen, McGrattan, and Sargent (1996, pp. 176–81): "We now apply a standard trick. . . . Using the well-known certainty equivalence property . . . we zero out the uncertainty without altering the optimal control law." It should be noted that risk sensitivity causes ordinary certainty equivalence to fail. For those cases, Hansen, Sargent, and Tallarini (1996) found another convenient solution technique: "Although ordinary certainty equivalence fails, the model is solved conveniently as a two-person linear-quadratic game. In effect, one of the players imputes a 'pessimistic view' about shocks" (p. 3). They call this the "pessimistic form of certainty equivalence." Also see Huang, Imrohoroglu, and Sargent (1996, p. 16).

80 I should note that the assumption of covariance stationarity can be relaxed somewhat, provided other restrictive assumptions are made.

81 For instance, Robert Solow observed in his interview with Klamer (1983, pp. 142–3): "I have two problems with Sargent's . . . work. Problem one: The methods that he proposes to introduce . . . are excessively heavy artillery. . . . Problem two: . . . [E]ven the authors of the papers don't tend to believe in their results. They are writing these papers to get across the message that it can be done technically; that's all." In my interview with Simon on May 30, 1997, he said that rational expectations agents must live in a linear-quadratic world.

82 But what about distributions that do not have second moments? What about Blattberg and Sargent's (1971, p. 502) "body of evidence which suggests that many economic variables have infinite variances"? As in the previous chapter, we see Sargent silently abandon Lévy stable distributions. Following developments in mathematics, engineering, and econometrics, he ignored the problems associated with constructing statistical estimators under stable laws and tamed randomness by assuming that variances are finite.

83 The applications of variational calculus to engineering can be divided into three

broad categories: First, we find problems that require the determination of some best design or strategy, where "best" has a well-defined sense. In this context, engineers have applied "classical" control to problems in aerodynamics, thermodynamics, and hydrodynamics. Second, engineers have used methods of approximating certain differential equations by direct calculations based on the variational "analog" to differential equations. Third, engineers have found that variational formulations are useful in finding approximate solutions.

84 Richard Bellman and Stuart Dreyfus were research associates at the RAND Corporation. As an interesting aside, the humanistic philosopher Hubert Dreyfus, Stuart Dreyfus's brother, has launched several attacks on the artificial intelligence research undertaken by some of the other RAND associates and was later joined by his brother in these attacks (Dreyfus 1992; Dreyfus and Dreyfus 1986; McCorduck 1979, pp. 180–205; Simon 1991, p. 274). Furthermore, Stuart Dreyfus later also turned against his work with Bellman: "[When] one tries, like Stuart and Richard Bellman, to find optimal algorithms, the result fails to capture the insight and ability of the expert decision-maker" (Dreyfus and Dreyfus 1986, p. 10).

85 Also see Bellman (1957, p. ix): "The adjective 'dynamic,' however, indicates that we are interested in processes in which time plays a significant role, and in which the order of operations may be crucial. However, an essential feature of our approach will be the reinterpretation of many static processes as dynamic processes in which time can be artificially introduced." Just as Sargent ultimately added uncertainty as an afterthought, Bellman eventually added time in this manner.

86 Also see Bellman (1984, p. 138): "The main mathematical activity of the mathematics division [at the RAND Corporation] was the theory of games, under the influence of von Neumann who visited from time to time. This is a mathematical theory of competition and one expected that it would be quite useful for the Air Force. . . . Of great interest at RAND was the question of target selection in the U.S.S.R."

87 Although attempts have been made to claim that game theory is a natural extension of general equilibrium theory, convincing arguments have shown that the two programs are opposed (see Rizvi 1994).

88 The technique used here is dynamic programming, which solves the infinite horizon problem by a sequence of finite horizon problems where the horizon is increased by one time period in each iteration. An alternative approach, the doubling algorithm, also solves the infinite horizon problem by backward induction but increases the horizon by double the number of time periods in each iteration (see Anderson, Hansen, McGrattan, and Sargent 1996, pp. 194–7; Hansen and Sargent 1996, p. 170–2).

Chapter 4

1 This discussion is postponed because it deserves extra attention in that it sheds light on my perspective.

2 I should also note that these problems of self-referentiality deflate the "scientific" pretensions of the use of economic metaphors in philosophy of science (see, e.g., Bartley 1990; Goldman and Shaked 1991; Kitcher 1993; Radnitzky and Bartley 1987; Radnitzky and Bernholz 1987).

3 According to Sargent (1996a) the general equilibrium interpretation of rational ex-

pectations thrust macroeconomics "toward a pre-determined destiny: it would be inconceivable for macroeconomics nowadays not to use . . . equilibrium concepts" (p. 538). In particular, "[t]he 'rational expectations revolution' promoted the practical application to macroeconomic time series of an equilibrium concept consistently incorporating individual rationality" (p. 539). Also see Sargent (1993, p. 7): "Another reason for embracing rational expectations is that the consistency condition can be interpreted as describing the outcome of a process in which people have optimally chosen their perceptions. . . . Insisting on the disappearance of all such unexploited possibilities is a feature of all definitions of equilibrium in economics."

4 Also see Parkin's (1996) interview with Sargent: "The [rational expectations] revolution was about building macroeconomics on the same foundation as microeconomics, a foundation grounded in the idea that people make rational choices and interact in markets that coordinate those choices. Viewed in this way, the revolution was inevitable" (p. 651).

5 In the same paper, Sargent (1996a) denied a connection between rational expectations economics and monetarism: "The links to monetarism in Lucas's [research] were incidental to the methodology of the rational expectations program but integral to the substance of Lucas's own research program" (p. 544).

6 Also see Klamer's (1983) interview with Sargent: "[T]he recent developments are really an inevitable consequence of the logical development of Keynesian economics" (p. 65). This is also the interpretation Sargent stressed in his talk during the luncheon honoring the 1995 Nobel Laureate in Economics, Robert Lucas, at the 1997 ASSA meetings. He further claimed that Hurwicz was the first to discuss rational expectations in 1949, but that this idea was not picked up.

7 Since it is not necessary to dwell on these stories for the purpose of Sargent's narrative, the reader is referred to Hands and Mirowski (forthcoming) for more insights into these stories and the argument that they are inconsistent.

8 Walras had visualized this market equilibrium as established through tâtonnement by an imaginary auctioneer announcing successive sets of prices until the market clears.

9 I should note that Edgeworth's "recontracting" process is not just an alternative rationalization of perfect competition. His primary interest was not in the limiting case of perfect competition but in the indeterminacy of imperfect competition.

10 For simplicity, I limit my case to an exchange economy. However, matters get worse, not better, by the introduction of production (see Kirman 1992; Ingrao and Israel 1990).

11 In order not to become overly entangled in this subplot, I state only the results in this part of the case and refer the reader to Rizvi (1991) for a more detailed argument.

12 Also see Sargent (1987c, p. 76): "[R]ational expectations possesses the defining property that the forecasts made by agents within the model are no worse than the forecasts that can be made by the economist who has the model." Further see Sargent (1987a, p. 440): "We implement the hypothesis of rational expectations by assuming that agents' expectations about unknown random variables equal the linear least squares projections on certain information sets to be specified." And see Sargent in Jordan, Meltzer, Schwartz, and Sargent (1993, p. 210): "[R]ational expectations . . . is the idea that the agents in the model could forecast at least as well as the econometricians who had the model, and as well as the government that was using the model."

13 This transformation is discussed in Chapter 5.

14 Further see Sargent in Jordan, Meltzer, Schwartz, and Sargent (1993, p. 211): "Paul Milgrom and Nancy Stokey and Jean Tirole have shown that in the context of a whole class of models in which differentially informed agents are trading an asset for speculative purposes, rational expectations implies that there will be no trade and no volume, but that the price will immediately adjust to a level that reveals everybody's private information. . . . These models work rational expectations very hard in a subtle way."

15 It could be argued that Sargent was not bothered by this earlier because he believed in a distinction between "context of discovery" and "context of justification." However, this does presume a lot of familiarity with prior contemporary notions of philosophy of science.

16 See Hansen and Sargent (1991f, p. 219): "[W]e want to estimate models in which optimizing economic agents make decisions at finer time intervals than the interval of time between the observations used by the econometrician." Also see Hansen and Sargent (1995b, p. 4): "[B]ecause they wanted to inform monetary policy (which is executed hourly), economists at the Federal Reserve wanted to estimate weekly, daily, or even continuous time models."

17 Notice the link between Sargent's use of the term "force" and the interpretation of forced moves in our framework of analysis.

18 Lucas and Sargent (1981) also note that the "model misspecification route seems less likely to deliver error terms with the good statistical properties – namely, certain orthogonality properties" (p. xxii). Also see Hansen and Sargent (1990).

19 This is known as the epistemic interpretation of error term justification, which stands in contrast to the ontic or sampling justification. This route is followed by Hansen and Sargent (1982, 1983a, 1991a, 1991c, 1991d); Hansen, Roberds, and Sargent (1991); and Sargent and Sims (1977). For more specifics, see Hansen and Sargent (1991a, p. 6; 1991c, pp. 45–6).

20 See Sargent (1987a, p. 334): "These specifications are motivated by an idea of Shiller . . . who used an iterated projections argument to show that when private agents are assumed to observe more information relevant for forecasting than does the econometrician, the error thereby induced in the equation of interest to the econometrician remains orthogonal to part of the econometrician's information set. These orthogonality conditions can restrict the variables observable to the econometrician and provide a sufficient basis for estimating and testing the model." Also see Hansen and Sargent (1991c, p. 46). The idea of replacing the information set with a subset, thereby adding an error term, was suggested by Shiller in his study of the term structure of interest rates. Recall that Chapter 2 discusses the focus of Sargent's early work on the term structure of interest rates.

21 Taking this idea to the limit, economic agents perceive and process information in continuous time, whereas econometricians only have discrete time data. This is known as the problem of aggregation over time.

22 Also see Hansen and Sargent (1980, p. 93): "[This] imposes substantial structure on the error term and limits the freedom of the econometrician in certain respects to be described. Together with variants of 'errors in variables' models, these models are about the only plausible models of error processes that we can imagine."

23 In particular, Sargent developed two models of the error term that can be constructed
    this way: One model results from assuming that the econometrician has time series
    but never observes the random processes; in the second model it is assumed that the
    econometrician possesses only observations on subsets of the information variables
    that private agents use to forecast.
24 See Sargent (1989, pp. 251–2): "[I]f only error-ridden data exist for the variables of
    interest, then more steps are needed to extract parameter estimates. In effect, we re-
    quire a model of the data reporting agency, one that is workable enough that we can
    determine the mapping induced jointly by the dynamic economic model and the
    measurement process to the probability law for the measured data. The model cho-
    sen of the data collection agency is an aspect of an econometric specification that
    can make big differences in inferences about the economic structure." Errors-in-
    variables have never been taken seriously by neoclassical econometrics, because
    they display very little interest in the process of the generation of their data.
25 According to Sargent (1989, p. 253n): "This simplifies the setup." Note again how
    Sargent alluded to convenience, as discussed in the previous chapter.
26 Muth advocated that economists stop working with models that predicted that econo-
    metricians could forecast better than people who lived in the model: "The dichotomy
    between the agents within the model, who experience fluctuations but no uncer-
    tainty, and an econometrician, who interprets those fluctuations as reflecting uncer-
    tainty, is striking. The situation depicted in these models in effect turns on its head
    a situation that Muth sought to correct" (Evans et al. 1993, p. 706). Also see Sargent
    (1993, p. 21): "Rational expectations equilibrium . . . typically imputes to the peo-
    ple inside the model much more knowledge about the system that they are operat-
    ing in than is available to the economist or econometrician who is using the model
    to try to understand their behavior. In particular, an econometrician faces the prob-
    lem of estimating probability distributions and laws of motion that the agents in the
    model are assumed to know. Further, the formal estimation and inference procedures
    of rational expectations econometrics assume that the agents in the model already
    know many of the objects that the econometrician is estimating."
27 In some of his discussions, Sargent couches the argument in terms of a dynamic
    game, justifying this with the claim that the "rational expectations revolution" in
    macroeconomics consists of a broad collection of research united mainly by an aim
    to respect the principle of strategic interdependence. Under the view that models are
    used as a vehicle for giving the government advice for improving its strategy rela-
    tive to the one used historically, the idea is that a new and different game is to be rec-
    ommended for the future, namely, the solution of the dominant player game under
    study. Another view is that models are positive descriptions of historical government
    behavior rather than a source of recommendations for new policy. See Sargent (1984,
    1987c) and Lucas and Sargent (1981, pp. xi–xl).
28 This asymmetry in the former view is also addressed in Sargent (1984, p. 411): "This
    setup envisions that government behavior may have been guided by different princi-
    ples during the sample period than are hypothesized to guide it during the future. Dur-
    ing the sample period, there is permitted to be an asymmetry between the principle

guiding the government's strategy, which is arbitrarily (if generally) specified, and that guiding agents, which is purposeful. However, for computing the optimal government policy strategy for the future, this possible asymmetry of behavior is removed, and both private agents and the government are supposed to be purposeful. (*Some* such difference in government behavior between the sample period and the hypothetical future *must* be posited by anyone recommending a change in the government's strategy.)"

29 This contradiction only appears in attempts to put the formal results to use: "In formal work, this contradiction is evaded by regarding analyses of policy interventions as descriptions of different economies, defined on different probability spaces. . . . The contradiction mentioned in the text surfaces when attempts are made to put these formal results to partial use by speaking of regime changes that are imagined to occur suddenly in real time" (Sargent 1984, p. 413n).

30 This conundrum was discussed by Sargent and Wallace (1976) and by Sargent (1984, 1987a) and forms the basis for Sims's challenge to rational expectations econometrics. See Sargent (1984, p. 411): "I interpret Sims as objecting to the assumed asymmetry between private agents' behavior and government behavior during the estimation period. Sims's view is that the asymmetry should be eliminated by assuming that government agents as well as private agents have behaved as rational expectations intertemporal optimizers during the sample period." This perspective underlied Sims's interest in estimating vector autoregressions without imposing restrictions from dynamic economic theory.

31 Also see Sargent (1987a, p. 436n): "The dynamic systems under study are full of self-referential aspects, which threaten to draw the analyst into the system. A consequence of such self-reference is that neither of the views mentioned in the text is free of logical contradictions."

32 Although Sargent (1987b) praised the convenience and internal consistency of general equilibrium models, he ignored the logical inconsistency that appears when they are used for making policy recommendations: "General equilibrium models form a convenient context for analyzing such alternative government policies, because their construction requires feasible contingency plans for government actions, explicitly and completely spelled out, as well as a set of consistent assumptions about private agents' perception of the government's plans. A related attraction of general equilibrium models is their internal consistency" (p. 1). This denial is also found in one of Sargent's (1986) main publications on policy: "The hope is that . . . observations on an economy operating under a single set of rules can be interpreted and used to make predictions about how the economy would behave under brand new rules. Possessing the ability to do this is a sine qua non for scientific and quantitative evaluation of alternative government rules" (p. 13).

33 Also see Klamer's (1983) interview with Sargent: "I claim that rational expectations is terribly fruitful. . . . The reason is that it changes the way you think about policy. . . . [I]t forces you to think about what's going on in Washington" (p. 75). Note Sargent's use of the word "force" here and its connection with the term "forced move."

34 Notice that whether or not a move is inevitable – or forced – depends on motivation and free moves.

35 Also see Sargent (1992, p. 671n): "Macroeconomists who are policy advisors confront the problem that if their advice is likely to be considered seriously, then they should model themselves as participants in the very dynamic interactions that they are studying."

36 Sims and many statisticians were strong advocates of using seasonally adjusted data.

37 See Sargent (1978c, p. 691n): "The argument advanced in the text is predicated on the assumption of stationarity."

38 See Sargent (1978c, p. 362): "If the model is true, these restrictions are predicted to hold for the raw unadjusted data. Therefore, the model should be tested by using unadjusted data."

39 See Sargent (1987a, p. 336): "Unless the seasonal components are thought mainly to reflect measurement errors that are unrelated to economic activity, seasonal adjustment is typically misleading."

40 See Sargent (1978c, p. 691n): This "argument has several elements, one of which is a desire to have procedures that are robust to departures from stationarity together with the suspicion that departures from stationarity are in some sense most likely at the seasonal frequencies." Also see Sargent (1978c, p. 361): They "have set down a neat statistical model that can be used to rationalize the use of seasonally adjusted data. Their model [is] essentially an error in variable model. . . . However, we seem to lack a plausible economic model that is capable of generating [such] a statistical model." Further, see Hansen and Sargent (1993, pp. 21–2): "Other writers responded that the argument for using seasonally unadjusted data assumes that the model is correctly specified, and asserted that admitting the possibility of approximation error would alter the situation. [They] said that if the approximation error were particularly bad with respect to the seasonal components of a model, better estimates of at least a subset of economically relevant parameters might be attained by using seasonally adjusted data and giving up the pretense of accurately modeling all frequencies."

41 Many symmetries can also be expressed as impossibility theorems, or statements of what is and is not covered by a theory. The theory purports to find certain phenomena impossible within its ambit.

42 Jean Piaget has made a case for the difficulty of discovering what is conserved in the world. Children do not start to order and categorize until a certain age and until then they cannot tell what is fixed and what is changing. They need to learn to sort out the relevant invariances in a large set of invariances.

43 Mirowski (1989a, p. 397) takes this argument further: "Under the mandate of causal explanation, invariance and sameness are assigned by human institutions. . . . Hence, the possibility arises that causal explanation requires invariance, but plausible invariance requires institutional stability, and institutional stability in turn is derived from physical metaphor."

44 Bloor defines the sociology of scientific knowledge by the following four tenets: First, it should be causal, that is, concerned with the conditions that bring about belief or states of knowledge. Naturally, there will be other types of causes apart from social ones that will cooperate in bringing about belief. Second, it would be impar-

tial with respect to truth and falsity, rationality or irrationality, success or failure. Both sides of these dichotomies will require explanation. Third, it would be symmetrical in its style of explanation. The same types of cause would explain, say, true and false beliefs. Finally, it would be reflexive. In principle its patterns of explanation would have to be applicable to sociology itself. Like the requirement of symmetry this is a response to the need to seek general explanations. It is an obvious requirement of principle because otherwise sociology would be a standing refutation of its own theories.

45 Note also that there is an implicit causal determinism of this view, which appears to clash with the notion of an interest as an active construction of the social world.

46 Collins and Yearly (1992a, 1992b) introduced the notion of hyperactivity in an attempt to ridicule the actor–network approach.

47 For complete derivation and further explanation, see Hansen and Sargent (1980, pp. 94–101).

Chapter 5

1 In addition, Sargent left the University of Minnesota to become a senior fellow at the Hoover Institute at Stanford University in March 1987. Furthermore, he became the David Rockefeller Professor of Economics at the University of Chicago in July 1991. Sargent (1996a, p. 545n) recalled: "The University of Chicago really took off as a rational expectations training institution with the arrival of Hansen and Townsend from Minnesota via Carnegie Mellon."

2 A large amount of the scientists' and economists' time was taken up learning about each other's interpretation of language: "From William Brock's summary and José Scheinkman's and Thomas Sargent's discussion of the concept of the Arrow–Debreu economy, we learned that even theories which appeal to the concept of 'equilibrium' do not necessarily avoid the apparently random fluctuations in the course of time which are characteristic of driven dynamical systems in physics. In physics, these are called 'non-equilibrium' systems; a liberal education on the various meanings of the word 'equilibrium' was a bracing experience for all" (Anderson et al. 1988, p. 265). See Weintraub (1991, pp. 99–112) for the evolution in meaning of the word "equilibrium" in economics.

3 See Klamer's (1983, pp. 33–4) interview with Lucas: "Tom [Sargent] needs to make some technical set-up costs before he wants to talk about something. . . . I remember a seminar . . . [during which] Tom made some point and the speaker didn't seem to understand it. . . . At the end, he just handed the speaker a piece of paper with a bunch of equations on it and said, 'Here's what I was trying to say.' . . . [T]he speaker said, 'This is Sargent's idea of a conversation' and laughed. I think it's just that Tom thinks he can get things settled on a more technical level."

4 Further see Sargent (1981a, p. 236): "[S]ince we simply do not know how to compute optimum decision rules under the assumption that agents [are learning], no consistent estimators of the underlying parameters have been proposed that incorporate agents' learning . . . in the optimal way, to say nothing of expressions for the associated asymptotic covariance matrices."

5 It could be argued that the distinction between context of discovery and context of justification was replaced in this interpretation of rational expectations without learning by the distinction between regime changes and stationary stability.

6 Also see Sargent (1981a, p. 235): "If the initial prior were to be estimated, this would substantially complicate the estimation problem and add to the number of parameters."

7 In Klamer's (1983) interview, Sargent said: "People who take [Simon's] criticism seriously end up doing . . . more difficult rational expectations" (p. 79). As we see in section 5.5, Sargent did think eventually that he had taken Simon's criticism seriously.

8 Marcet and Sargent (1989c), though, indicate that it can also occur that there exists no equilibrium under least squares learning, even though there exists a continuum of rational-expectations equilibria.

9 Further see Sargent in Jordan, Meltzer, Schwartz, and Sargent (1993, p. 212): "If you take exactly the environment that is described in a no-trade-theory model, and you replace the hypothesis of rational expectations with the assumption that agents are [learning], and you start them off almost having rational expectations, then you can destroy the no-trade result and get a model in which there is volume of trade among heterogeneously informed agents."

10 Also see Parkin's (1996) interview with Sargent: "[Rational expectations theories] don't have much to say about situations in which the rules and social institutions are ill-formed and under discussion" (p. 653).

11 In fact, Sargent himself had used rational expectations models to analyze regime changes (see, e.g., Parkin 1996, pp. 651–2; Sargent and Velde 1995; Sargent 1986).

12 Also see Parkin's (1996) interview with Sargent: "In the last fifteen years, some economists have started studying how people learn about the economic world" (p. 652).

13 See Sargent (1993, p. 166): "Marcet and Sargent's examples are in the adaptive control tradition of assuming that agents use dynamic programming to compute an optimal decision rule, that they know the parameters of their return function and the parametric form of the transition function, but that they lack knowledge of the parameters of the transition function."

14 Also see Sargent (1991, pp. 246–7): "The equilibrium is then defined and computed as the fixed point of the mapping from perceived ARMA processes to actual ARMA processes that is induced by agents' behavior and market clearing. It is the inclusion of the moving-average components in agents' perceptions and of lagged innovations to agents' information in the state vector that enables us to formulate the equilibrium as a fixed point of a finite-dimensional operator."

15 Also see Marimon, McGrattan, and Sargent (1990, p. 330n): "The way in which we model agents as searching for rewarding decision rules attributes much less knowledge and rationality to them than is typical in the literature on least-squares learning in the context of linear rational expectations models."

16 Holland is referring to Hansen and Sargent (1981a).

17 I should note that Sargent also coauthored a survey article on neural networks in which he devoted large amount of space to an analysis of different versions of classifier systems (see Cho and Sargent 1996).

18 Since the mathematics of classifier systems is fairly complicated, I limit myself to a verbal description.

19 Also see Marimon, McGrattan, and Sargent (1990, p. 330): "A classifier system is a collection of potential decision rules, together with an accounting system for selecting which rules to use. The accounting system credits rules generating good outcomes and debits rules generating bad outcomes. The system is designed to select a 'co-adaptive' set of rules that work well over a range of situations that an agent typically encounters."

20 "Learning" in classifier systems has a quite different meaning from that in rationalistic theories like Bayesian learning theory. In the rationalistic view, the world is composed of definite objects, properties, and relations, and "learning" is the process whereby an agent forms a mental model of the world that correctly describes these features. Learning in classifier systems is about acquiring circumstance-specific behavioral propensities that function together to achieve a reward. That is, the agent is learning how to reap rewards, rather than how to describe the world. In the process, an agent may or may not develop descriptive categories, causal theories, and so forth, and even if she does, there is no presumption that these categories and theories match some objective features "out there," nor would their worth to an agent depend on whether or not they did so.

21 See Arthur (1991, pp. 358–9): "We can indeed design artificial learning agents and calibrate their 'rationality' to replicate human behavior. Not only does the learning behavior of our calibrated agents vary in the way human behavior varies as payoffs change from experiment to experiment in this repeated multichoice context, but it also reproduces two stylized facts of human learning well-known to psychologists: that with frequency-dependent payoffs humans meliorate rather than optimize; and there is a threshold in discrimination among payoffs below which humans may lock in to suboptimal choices. Most usefully perhaps, the calibrated algorithm has a convenient dynamic representation that can be inserted into theoretical models."

22 Personal e-mail message from McGrattan dated October 9, 1996.

23 McGrattan corroborates this in her e-mail message of October 9, 1996. She was attracted to the study of learning because she saw learning as a way of selecting equilibria, a means of computing equilibria, and an illustration of convergence to rational expectations equilibria.

24 Janssen (1993, p. 132) criticized this approach: "[I]n most models in this learning literature, no distinction is made between the subjective expectations of different agents. . . . [I]n order to give individualistic foundations for an aggregate relationship (hypothesis) it does not suffice to assume the existence of one representative individual."

25 See Cho and Sargent (1996, p. 443): "[W]e adduce several examples that show neural networks to be fruitful sources of 'functional forms' for conveniently representing equilibria; for formulating ways of computing them; and for studying their stability." Also see Cho and Sargent (1996, pp. 462–3). McGrattan corroborates this in her e-mail message October 9, 1996, in which she indicates that she and her coauthors found that their learning agents learned pretty fast. She also notes that for anyone who

wants to consider learning models as an alternative, it will have to be the case that learning occurs slowly.

26 Also see Sargent (1992, p. 671): "Furthermore, when one examines the structure of many adaptive learning algorithms, they closely resemble iterative algorithms for computing equilibria. . . . Where is the line between a learning algorithm and an equilibrium computation algorithm?" Further see Sargent (1993, pp. 1–2, 4, 155).

27 See Lane (1993b, p. 186n): "Of course, it is not particularly surprising that Marimon, McGrattan, and Sargent agents do not speculate, since to do so, they would have to form linked chains of actions – and these are unlikely to emerge without system rules that promote them, like triggered chaining operations."

28 See Arthur (1991, p. 359): "To the degree that the algorithm replicated human behavior, it indicates that human learning most often adapts its way to an optimal steady state. . . . But it also shows that humans systematically underexplore less-known alternatives, so that learning may sometimes lock in to an inferior choice when payoffs to choices are closely clustered, random, and difficult to discriminate among. Thus the question of whether human learning adapts its way to standard economic equilibria depends on the perceptual difficulty of the problem itself."

29 See Palmer, Arthur, Holland, LeBaron, and Tayler (1994, p. 270): "Instead of the R[ational] E[xpectations] approach, we propose an inductive model in which we start with agents who have little knowledge or reasoning ability. The agents trade on the basis of internal models or rules that are initially very poor. By observing the success or failure of these internal models the agents can improve them, select among alternatives, and even generate totally new rules. Thus over time their behavior becomes more sophisticated, and they become able to recognize and exploit many patterns in the market. . . . The inductive approach provides a dynamical picture of a market and avoids most of the . . . problems of RE theory. It is also inherently closer to the way humans typically make decisions in complex situations."

30 See Palmer et al. (1994, p. 273): "In all, our models of a stockmarket can reproduce the major features . . . of real markets, including dynamical and non-equilibrium phenomena. It does not require – and indeed rejects – the restrictive assumptions of rational expectations theory."

31 See Arthur (1991, p. 358): "How might we use calibrated agents to represent actual human adaptive behavior in other standard neoclassical models? My paper in progress with Holland, Palmer, and Tayler explores convergence to rational expectations equilibrium using calibrated agents in an adaptive . . . stock market. We find that the calibrated agents learn to buy and sell stock appropriately, and that the stock price indeed converges to small fluctuations around the rational expectations value. However, we also find that speculative bubbles and crashes occur – a hint that under realistic learning technical analysis may emerge." Also see Arthur (1992, 1993) and Lane (1993b).

32 Also see Sargent (1993, p. 22): "The intent of the 'bounded rationality' program is to work the methodology of science doubly hard because . . . it will use models that are populated by artificial people who behave like working scientists."

33 Also see Sargent (1993, p. 4): "On the credit side of the ledger . . . [is] . . . these models' . . . suggestion, through the literatures on parallel and genetic algorithms, of new gadgets and statistical methods for econometricians."

34 The stochastic approximation algorithm can be used to implement the least squares formulas recursively and can be interpreted as a stochastic Newton algorithm (see Sargent 1993, pp. 41–2).

35 Also see Sargent (1993, p. 22n): "In economics, procedures for revising theories in the light of data are typically informal, diverse, and implicit." Snippe (1986, p. 434) concurs: "[I]t is very doubtful whether . . . rational expectations can be expected to be successful . . . for this would require the logic of choice to be capable of providing indications as to the best route to satisfactory knowledge. Unfortunately, awareness of the problems associated with induction should make us acknowledge that no belief in such a route can be logically justified."

36 More detail is provided by Sargent (1993, pp. 168–9): "There are problems of arbitrariness and need for prompting, with a concomitant sensitivity of outcomes to details of adaptive algorithms. There is the extreme simplicity of learning tasks typically assigned in the models compared even with the econometric learning tasks assigned in econometric classes. . . . [T]here is the shortage of results on rates of convergence, and the need severely to restrict the distribution of agents' beliefs in order to get tractable models. . . . [A]pplied econometricians have supplied us with almost no evidence about how adaptive models might work empirically."

37 Sargent (1992, pp. 670–1) also alluded to a potential asymmetry: "If we obtain convergence results by shrewdly selecting from among the wide range of algorithms that are 'adaptive,' there is a danger that when we do manage to obtain convergence results, other advocates of bounded rationality may say that our algorithms are too smart. Is it really in the spirit of 'bounded rationality' to head straight for the literatures on adaptive control and simulated annealing?"

38 Also see Sargent (1993, pp. 4–5): "The essay ends near where it started, with a difference between the behavior of econometricians and the agents in their models. As I have interpreted it, the bounded rationality program wants to make the agents in our models more like the econometricians who estimate and use them. Given the compliment ('imitation is the sincerest form of flattery'), we might expect macroeconometricians to rush to implement such models empirically. There has been no rush, maybe for the reason that many macroeconometricians are in the market for methods for reducing the number of parameters to explain data, and such a reduction is not what bounded rationality promises."

39 Interestingly enough, Sargent said in his interview with Klamer (1983), "It remains to be seen whether Simon's criticism is constructive or useful in the sense . . . that someone builds on it. No one has yet" (p. 79). As we see here, Sargent thought that he eventually did build on Simon's criticism.

40 In contrast, Sargent's "main exercise was to construct equilibria sustained by simple neural networks, and to study how much the restriction on strategies reduced the set of equilibrium outcomes" (Cho and Sargent 1996, pp. 462–3).

41 In contrast, Sargent "regarded bounded rationality as a constraint on computational capabilities" (Cho and Sargent 1996, p. 462).

42 Recall that Holland's classifiers consist of a basic rule-based system along with a bucket brigade algorithm and a genetic algorithm.

43 I should note that Penrose's reliance on Gödel to refute artificial intelligence is

routinely dismissed by many scientists in artificial intelligence and cognitive science.

44 Simon (1967) complained, "in the philosophical literature, the adequacy of proposed formalisms has too often been tested only against simple hypothetical cases, often contrived to be paradoxical, but none the less contrived" (p. 33).

45 According to Callebaut (1993, p. 24): "Kuhn not only caused us to give up one sort of rationality – the a priori, categorical sort – but . . . also opened our eyes to the more elusive but much more important thing that has sometimes been called instrumental rationality, which is embodied in the scientific enterprise as a collective undertaking."

Chapter 6

1 I could not track down this reference; however, I did find Granger and Orr (1971).

2 I should note that the set of classifiers in their classifier system is constant, because it lacks a genetic algorithm.

Chapter 7

1 In fact, Pickering (1995b) argues that disciplinary history must be problematized since it is part and parcel of the history of the world. Though I welcome this suggestion, I have doubts about the feasibility of such a project.

References

Akgiray, Vedat and G. Geoffrey Booth. 1988: The Stable-Law Model of Stock Returns. *Journal of Business and Economic Statistics* 6 (1), pp. 51–7.

―――― and Christopher G. Lamoureux. 1989: Estimation of Stable-Law Parameters: A Comparative Study. *Journal of Business and Economic Statistics* 7 (1), pp. 85–93.

Amemiya, Takeshi. 1985: *Advanced Econometrics.* Cambridge, MA: Harvard University Press.

Anderson, Brian D.O. and John B. Moore. 1979: *Optimal Filtering.* Englewood Cliffs, NJ: Prentice-Hall.

Anderson, Evan W., Ellen R. McGrattan, Lars P. Hansen, and Thomas J. Sargent. 1996: Mechanics of Forming and Estimating Dynamic Linear Economies. In Hans M. Amman, David A. Kendrick, and John Rust (eds.), *Handbook of Computational Economics, Volume 1.* Amsterdam: Elsevier Science, pp. 171–252.

Anderson, Paul A. 1979: Help for the Regional Economic Forecaster: Vector Autoregression. *Federal Reserve Bank of Minneapolis Quarterly Review* 3 (3), pp. 2–7.

Anderson, Philip W., Kenneth J. Arrow, and David Pines. (eds.) 1988: *The Economy as an Evolving Complex System.* Santa Fe Institute Studies in the Sciences of Complexity, *Volume 5.* Redwood City, CA: Addison-Wesley.

Anderson, Theodore W. 1971: *The Statistical Analysis of Time Series.* New York: John Wiley and Sons.

Arthur, W. Brian. 1991: Designing Economic Agents That Act Like Human Agents: A Behavioral Approach to Bounded Rationality. *American Economic Review* 81 (2), pp. 353–9.

――――. 1992: On Learning and Adaptation in the Economy. *Santa Fe Institute Working Paper 92-07-038.*

――――. 1993: On Designing Economic Agents That Behave Like Human Agents. *Journal of Evolutionary Economics* 3 (1), pp. 1–22.

Arrow, Kenneth J. 1978: The Future and the Present in Economic Life. *Economic Inquiry* 16 (2), pp. 157–69.

―――― and Gerard Debreu. 1954: Existence of an Equilibrium for a Competitive Economy. *Econometrica* 22 (3), pp. 265–90.

Ashmore, Malcolm. 1989: *The Reflexive Thesis.* Chicago: University of Chicago Press.

Aubert, Karl E. 1982: The Role of Mathematics in the Exploration of Reality: Comments on a Paper by Herbert A. Simon. *Inquiry* 25 (3), pp. 353–9.

Azariadis, Costas. 1981: Self-Fulfilling Prophecies. *Journal of Economic Theory* 25 (3), pp. 380–96.

Barro, Robert J. 1976: Rational Expectations and the Role of Monetary Policy. *Journal of Monetary Economics* 2 (1), pp. 1095–117.

Barrow, John D. 1992: *Pi in the Sky: Counting, Thinking, and Being.* Boston: Little, Brown.

Bartlett, Maurice S. 1966: *Stochastic Processes.* Cambridge: Cambridge University Press.

Bartley, William W. 1990: *Unfathomed Knowledge, Unmeasured Wealth.* LaSalle, IL: Open Court.

Bechtel, William and Adele A. Abrahamsen. 1991: *Connectionism and the Mind: An Introduction to Parallel Processing in Networks.* Oxford: Basil Blackwell.

Begg, David K.H. 1982: *The Rational Expectations Revolution in Macroeconomics.* Baltimore: Johns Hopkins University Press.

Bellman, Richard E. 1957: *Dynamic Programming.* Princeton, NJ: Princeton University Press.

———. 1984: *Eye of the Hurricane: An Autobiography.* Singapore: World Scientific.

——— and Stuart E. Dreyfus. 1962: *Applied Dynamic Programming.* Princeton, NJ: Princeton University Press.

Berreby, David. 1993: Chaos Hits Wall Street. *Discover* (March), pp. 76–84.

Binmore, Ken G. 1985: Equilibria in Extensive Games. *Economic Journal* 95 (378), pp. 51–9.

———. 1987: Modeling Rational Players. Part I. *Economics and Philosophy* 3 (2), pp. 179–214.

———. 1988: Modeling Rational Players. Part II. *Economics and Philosophy* 4 (1), pp. 9–55.

Blattberg, Robert and Thomas J. Sargent. 1971: Regression with Non-Gaussian Stable Disturbances: Some Sampling Results. *Econometrica* 39 (3), pp. 501–10.

Bloor, David. 1991: *Knowledge and Social Imagery,* 2nd ed. London and Boston: Routledge and Kegan Paul.

Blume, Lawrence E., Margaret M. Bray, and David Easley. 1982: Introduction to the Stability of Rational Expectations Equilibrium. *Journal of Economic Theory* 26 (2), pp. 313–17.

Booker, Lashlon. 1987: Improving Search in Genetic Algorithms. In Lawrence D. Davis (ed.), *Genetic Algorithms and Simulated Annealing.* New York: Pittman, pp. 61–73.

Box, George E.P. and Gwilym M. Jenkins. 1970: *Time Series Analysis, Forecasting, and Control.* San Francisco: Holden-Day.

———, Gwilym M. Jenkins, and Gregory C. Reinsel. 1994: *Time Series Analysis.* Englewood Cliffs, NJ: Prentice-Hall.

Bray, Margaret M. 1982: Learning, Estimation, and Stability of Rational Expectations. *Journal of Economic Theory* 26 (3), pp. 318–39.

———. 1983: Convergence to Rational Expectations Equilibrium. In Roman Frydman and Edmund S. Phelps (eds.), *Individual Forecasting and Aggregate Outcomes: "Rational Expectations" Examined.* Cambridge: Cambridge University Press, pp. 123–32.

——— and David Kreps. 1987: Rational Learning and Rational Expectations. In George

Feiwel (ed.), *Arrow and the Ascent of Modern Economic Theory.* New York: New York University Press, pp. 597–625.

Brillinger, David R. 1975: *Time Series: Data Analysis and Theory.* New York: Holt, Rinehart, and Winston.

Buck, Roger. 1963: Reflexive Predictions. *Philosophy of Science* 30 (4), pp. 359–69.

Buiter, Willem H. 1980: The Macroeconomics of Dr. Pangloss: A Critical Survey of the New Classical Macroeconomics. *Economic Journal* 90 (357), pp. 34–50.

Caballero, Ricardo J. 1992: A Fallacy of Composition. *American Economic Review* 82 (5), pp. 1279–92.

Cagan, Philip. 1956: The Monetary Dynamics of Hyperinflation. In Milton Friedman (ed.), *Studies in the Quantity Theory of Money.* Chicago: University of Chicago Press, pp. 25–117.

Callebaut, Werner (ed.). 1993: *Taking the Naturalistic Turn or How Real Philosophy of Science Is Done.* Chicago: University of Chicago Press.

Callon, Michel and Bruno Latour. 1992: Don't Throw the Baby Out with the Bath School! A Reply to Collins and Yearly. In Andrew Pickering (ed.), *Science as Practice and Culture.* Chicago: University of Chicago Press, pp. 343–68.

Cass, David and Karl Shell. 1983: Do Sunspots Matter? *Journal of Political Economy* 91 (2), pp. 193–227.

Charnes, A., W.W. Cooper, and R.O. Ferguson. 1955: Optimal Estimation of Executive Compensation by Linear Programming. *Management Science* 1 (2), pp. 138–50.

Cho, In-Koo and Thomas J. Sargent. 1996: Neural Networks for Encoding and Adapting in Dynamic Economies. In Hans M. Amman, David A. Kendrick, and John Rust (eds.), *Handbook of Computational Economics, Volume 1.* Amsterdam: Elsevier Science, pp. 441–70.

Chow, Gregory C. 1981: *Econometric Analysis by Control Methods.* New York: John Wiley and Sons.

Clark, Peter B. 1973: A Subordinated Stochastic Process Model with Finite Variance for Speculative Prices. *Econometrica* 41 (1), pp. 135–55.

Cohen, L. Jonathan. 1989: *An Introduction to the Philosophy of Induction and Probability.* New York: Clarendon.

Coddington, Alan. 1975: Creaking Semaphone and Beyond. *British Journal of Philosophy of Science* 26 (2), pp. 151–63.

———. 1976: Keynesian Economics: The Search for First Principles. *Journal of Economic Literature* 14 (4), pp. 1258–73.

Collins, Harry M. 1990: *Artificial Experts: Social Knowledge and Intelligent Machines.* Cambridge, MA: MIT Press.

———. 1992: *Changing Order: Replication and Induction in Scientific Practice.* Chicago: University of Chicago Press.

——— and Steven Yearly. 1992a: Epistemological Chicken. In Andrew Pickering (ed.), *Science as Practice and Culture.* Chicago: University of Chicago Press, pp. 301–26.

——— and ———. 1992b: Journey into Space. In Andrew Pickering (ed.), *Science as Practice and Culture.* Chicago: University of Chicago Press, pp. 369–89.

Cooley, Thomas F. and Stephen F. LeRoy. 1985: Atheoretical Macroeconometrics: A Critique. *Journal of Monetary Economics* 16 (3), pp. 283–308.

Cooper, J. Phillip and Charles R. Nelson. 1975: The *Ex Ante* Prediction Performance of the St. Louis and FRB–MIT–PENN Econometric Models and Some Results on Composite Predictors. *Journal of Money, Credit, and Banking* 7 (1), pp. 1–32.

Cootner, Paul H. (ed.). 1964: *The Random Character of Stock Market Prices*. Cambridge, MA: MIT Press.

Crevier, Daniel. 1993: *AI: The Tumultuous History of the Search for Artificial Intelligence*. New York: Basic Books.

Danziger, Kurt. 1985: The Origins of the Psychological Experiment as a Social Institution. *American Psychologist* 40 (2), pp. 133–40.

——— . 1987: Social Context and Investigative Practice in Early Twentieth-Century Psychology. In Mitchell G. Ash and William R. Woodward (eds.), *Psychology in Twentieth-Century Thought and Society*. Cambridge: Cambridge University Press, pp. 13–33.

——— . 1988: A Question of Identity. In Jill G. Morawski (ed.), *The Rise of Experimentation in American Psychology*. New Haven, CT: Yale University Press, pp. 35–52.

——— . 1990: *Constructing the Subject: Historical Origins of Psychological Research*. Cambridge: Cambridge University Press.

Daston, Lorraine. 1988: *Classical Probability in the Enlightenment*. Princeton, NJ: Princeton University Press.

Davidson, Paul. 1982–3: Rational Expectations: A Fallacious Foundation for Studying Crucial Decision-Making Processes. *Journal of Post-Keynesian Economics* 5 (2), pp. 182–207.

——— . 1988: A Technical Definition of Uncertainty and the Long-Run Non-Neutrality of Money. *Cambridge Journal of Economics* 12 (3), pp. 329–37.

——— . 1991: Is Probability Theory Relevant for Uncertainty? A Post Keynesian Perspective. *Journal of Economic Perspectives* 5 (1), pp. 129–43.

Davies, Paul C.W. 1989: *The New Physics*. Cambridge: Cambridge University Press.

Day, Richard H. and Gunnar Eliasson (eds.). 1986: *The Dynamics of Market Economies*. Amsterdam: Elsevier Science.

——— and Vernon L. Smith (eds.). 1993: *Experiments in Decision, Organization, and Exchange*. Amsterdam: North-Holland.

Debreu, Gerard. 1959: *The Theory of Value*. New Haven, CT: Yale University Press.

——— . 1974: Excess Demand Functions. *Journal of Mathematical Economics* 1 (1), pp. 15–23.

DeCanio, Stephen. 1979: Rational Expectations and Learning from Experience. *Quarterly Journal of Economics* 93 (1), pp. 47–57.

Dennett, Daniel C. 1978: *Brainstorms*. Cambridge, MA: MIT Press.

Depew, David J. and Bruce H. Weber. 1995: *Darwinism Evolving: Systems Dynamics and the Genealogy of Natural Selection*. Cambridge, MA: MIT Press.

De Vaney, Arthur. 1996: Putting a Human Face on Rational Expectations: A Book Review. *Journal of Economic Dynamics and Control* 20 (5), pp. 811–17.

Devletoglou, Evangelos. 1961: Correct Public Prediction and the Stability of Equilibrium. *Journal of Political Economy* 69 (2), pp. 142–61.

Dobell, A. Rodney and Thomas J. Sargent. 1969: The Term Structure of Interest Rates in Canada. *Canadian Journal of Economics* 2 (1), pp. 65–77.

Dow, Sheila C. 1985: *Macroeconomic Thought: A Methodological Approach*. New York: Basil Blackwell.

Dreyfus, Hubert L. 1992: *What Computers Still Can't Do*. Cambridge, MA: MIT Press.

——— and Stuart E. Dreyfus. 1986: *Mind over Machine: The Power of Human Intuition and Expertise in the Era of the Computer*. New York: Free Press.

DuMouchel, William H. 1971: *Stable Distributions in Statistical Inference*. Unpublished Ph.D. thesis. Yale University, Department of Statistics.

Dupré, John. 1993: *The Disorder of Things: Metaphysical Foundations of the Disunity of Science*. Cambridge, MA: Harvard University Press.

Earman, John. 1986: *A Primer on Determinism*. Dordrecht: D. Reidel.

Eatwell, John, Murray Milgate, and Peter Newman (eds.). 1989: *The New Palgrave: General Equilibrium*. New York: W.W. Norton.

Eberlein, Ernst and Murad S. Taqqu (eds.). 1986: *Dependence in Probability and Statistics*. Boston: Birkhäuser.

Eckstein, Otto (ed.). 1976: *Parameters and Policies in the U.S. Economy*. Amsterdam: North-Holland.

Edgeworth, Francis Ysidro. 1881: *Mathematical Physics: An Essay on the Application of Mathematics to the Moral Sciences*. London: C. Kegan Paul; reprinted New York: A.M Kelley, 1967.

Egedi, Massimo, Robin Marris, Herbert Simon, and Riccardo Viale. 1992: *Economics, Bounded Rationality and the Cognitive Revolution*. Brookfield, VT: Edward Elgar.

Epstein, Roy J. 1987: *A History of Econometrics*. Amsterdam: North-Holland.

Evans, George W., Seppo Honkapohja, and Thomas J. Sargent. 1993: On the Preservation of Deterministic Cycles When Some Agents Perceive Them to Be Random Fluctuations. *Journal of Economic Dynamics and Control* 17 (5–6), pp. 705–21.

Falkenburg, Brigitte. 1988: The Unifying Role of Symmetry Principles in Particle Physics. *Ratio* 1 (2), pp. 113–34.

Fama, Eugene F. 1963: Mandelbrot and the Stable Paretian Hypothesis. *Journal of Business* 36 (4), pp. 420–9.

——— . 1965: The Behavior of Stock-Market Prices. *Journal of Business* 38 (1), pp. 34–105.

——— and Richard Roll. 1971: Parameter Estimates for Symmetric Stable Distributions. *Journal of the American Statistical Association* 66 (334), pp. 331–8.

Farmer, J. Doyne and John J. Sidorowich. 1987: Predicting Chaotic Time Series. *Physical Review Letters* 59 (8), pp. 845–8.

——— and ——— . 1988: Can New Approaches to Nonlinear Modeling Improve Economic Forecasts? In Philip W. Anderson, Kenneth J. Arrow, and David Pines (eds.), *The Economy as an Evolving Complex System*. Redwood City, CA: Addison-Wesley, pp. 99–115.

Feller, William. 1966: *An Introduction to Probability Theory and Its Applications, Volume II*. New York: John Wiley and Sons.

——— . 1971: *An Introduction to Probability Theory and Its Applications, Volume I*, 3rd ed. New York: John Wiley and Sons.

Fine, Terrence L. 1973: *Theories of Probability.* New York: Academic Press.

Fisher, Walter D. 1961: A Note on Curve Fitting with Minimum Deviations by Linear Programming. *Journal of the American Statistical Association* 56 (294), pp. 359–62.

Fleming, Wendell H. and Raymond W. Rishel. 1975: *Deterministic and Stochastic Optimal Control.* Berlin: Springer-Verlag.

Forsythe, Diana E. 1993: Engineering Knowledge: The Construction of Knowledge in Artificial Intelligence. *Social Studies of Science* 23 (3), pp. 445–77.

Freedman, David H. 1993: Enter the Market Merlins. *Forbes* 152 (October 25 Supplement), pp. 38–41.

Friedman, Benjamin M. 1979: Optimal Expectations and the Extreme Information Assumptions of "Rational Expectations" Macromodels. *Journal of Monetary Economics* 5 (1), pp. 23–41.

Friedman, Daniel and John Rust (eds.). 1991: *The Double Auction Market: Institutions, Theories, and Evidence.* Reading, MA: Addison-Wesley.

Friedman, Milton. 1968: The Role of Monetary Policy. *American Economic Review* 58 (1), pp. 1–17.

Frost, Peter A. and Thomas J. Sargent. 1970: Money-Market Rates, the Discount Rate, and Borrowing from the Federal Reserve. *Journal of Money, Credit, and Banking* 2 (1), pp. 56–82.

Frydman, Roman. 1982: Towards an Understanding of Market Processes: Individual Expectations, Learning, and Convergence to Rational Expectations Equilibrium. *American Economic Review* 72 (4), pp. 652–68.

———— and Edmund S. Phelps (eds.). 1983: *Individual Forecasting and Aggregate Outcomes: "Rational Expectations" Examined.* Cambridge: Cambridge University Press.

Galatin, Malcolm. 1976: Optimal Forecasting in Models with Uncertainty When the Outcome Is Influenced by the Forecast. *Economic Journal* 86 (342), pp. 278–95.

Gale, George and Cassandra L. Pinnick. 1997: Stalking Theoretical Physicists: An Ethnography Flounders: A Response to Merz and Knorr Cetina. *Social Studies of Science* 27 (1), pp. 113–23.

Galison, Peter. 1994: The Ontology of the Enemy: Norbert Wiener and the Cybernetic Vision. *Critical Inquiry* 21 (1), pp. 228–66.

Gans, Joshua S. 1990: Time and Economics: Reflections on Hawking. *Methodus* (December 1990), pp. 80–1.

Geanakoplos, John. 1989: Arrow–Debreu Model of General Equilibrium. In John Eatwell, Murray Milgate, and Peter Newman (eds.), *The New Palgrave: General Equilibrium.* New York: W.W. Norton, pp. 43–61.

Geertz, Clifford. 1988: *Works and Lives: The Anthropologist as Author.* Stanford, CA: Stanford University Press.

Gigerenzer, Gerd and David J. Murray. 1987: *Cognition as Intuitive Statistics.* Hillsdale, NJ: Lawrence Erlbaum.

————, Zeno Swijtink, Theodore Porter, Lorraine Daston, John Beatty, and Lorenz Krüger. 1989: *The Empire of Chance.* Cambridge: Cambridge University Press.

Glauber, Robert R. and John R. Meyer. 1964: *Investment Decisions, Economic Forecasting, and Public Policy.* Boston: Harvard Business School.

Goldberg, David E. 1989: *Genetic Algorithms in Search, Optimization, and Machine Learning.* Reading, MA: Addison-Wesley.

Goldman, Alvin I. and Moshe Shaked. 1991: An Economic Model of Scientific Activity and Truth Acquisition. *Philosophical Studies* 63 (1), pp. 31–55.

Golubitsky, Martin and Ian Stewart. 1992: *Fearful Symmetry.* London: Penguin Books.

Granger, Clive W.J. 1969: Investigating Causal Relations by Econometric Models and Cross-Spectral Methods. *Econometrica* 37 (3), pp. 424–38. Reprinted in Robert E. Lucas and Thomas J. Sargent (eds.), 1981: *Rational Expectations and Econometric Practice.* Minneapolis: University of Minnesota Press, pp. 371–86.

———. 1994: Forecasting in Economics. In Neil A. Gershenfeld and Andreas S. Weigend (eds.), *Time Series Prediction: Forecasting the Future and Understanding the Past.* Reading, MA: Addison-Wesley, pp. 529–38.

——— and Michio Hatanaka. 1964: *Spectral Analysis of Economic Time Series.* Princeton, NJ: Princeton University Press.

——— and Paul Newbold. 1986: *Forecasting Economic Time Series.* Orlando, FL: Academic Press.

——— and Daniel Orr. 1971: Infinite Variance and Research Strategy in Time-Series Analysis. *Econometrica* 39 (4), pp. 67–8.

——— and Timo Teräsvirta. 1993: *Modeling Nonlinear Economic Relationships.* Oxford: Oxford University Press.

Grether, David M., R. Mark Isaac, and Charles R. Plott (eds.). 1989: *The Allocation of Scarce Resources.* Boulder, CO: Westview Press.

Gribbin, Donald W., Randy W. Harris, and Hon-Shiang Lau. 1992: Futures Prices Are Not Stable-Paretian Distributed. *Journal of Futures Markets* 12 (4), pp. 475–87.

Griliches, Zvi. 1967: Distributed Lags: A Survey. *Econometrica* 35 (1), pp. 16–40.

Grünbaum, Adolf. 1956: Historical Determinism, Social Activism, and Predictions in the Social Sciences. *British Journal for the Philosophy of Science* 7 (27), pp. 236–40.

Grunberg, Emile. 1986: Predictability and Reflexivity. *American Journal of Economics and Sociology* 45 (4), pp. 475–88.

——— and Franco Modigliani. 1954: The Predictability of Social Events. *Journal of Political Economy* 62 (6), pp. 465–78.

Guzzardi, Walter. 1978: The New Down-to-Earth Economics. *Fortune* (December 21), pp. 72–9.

Hahn, Frank H. 1986: Review of Arjo Klamer, "Conversations with Economists." *Economics and Philosophy* 2 (2), pp. 275–82.

Hakansson, Nils H., J. Gregory Kunkel, and James A. Ohlson. 1982: Sufficient and Necessary Conditions for Information to Have Social Value in Pure Exchange. *Journal of Finance* 37 (5), pp. 1169–81.

Hall, Robert E. 1978: Stochastic Implications of the Life Cycle–Permanent Income Hypothesis: Theory and Evidence. *Journal of Political Economy* 86 (6), pp. 971–87.

Hands, D. Wade. 1985: Karl Popper and Economic Methodology: A New Look, *Economics and Philosophy* 1 (1), pp. 83–99.

———. 1990: Grunberg and Modigliani, Public Predictions and the New Classical Macroeconomics. *Research in the History of Economic Thought and Methodology* 7, pp. 207–23.

————. 1992: *Testing, Rationality and Progress.* Lanham, MD: Rowman and Little-field.

————. 1994a: Blurred Boundaries. *Studies in History and Philosophy of Science* 25 (5), pp. 751–72.

————. 1994b: The Sociology of Scientific Knowledge. In Roger E. Backhouse (ed.), *New Directions in Economic Methodology.* London: Routledge, pp. 75–106.

————. 1996: Economics and Laudan's Normative Naturalism: Bad News from Instrumental Rationality's Front Line. *Social Epistemology* 10 (2), pp. 137–52.

————. 1997: Caveat Emptor: Economics and Contemporary Philosophy of Science. *Philosophy of Science* 64, *Proceedings.*

———— and Philip E. Mirowski. forthcoming: A Paradox of Budgets: The Postwar Stabilization of American Neoclassical Demand Theory. *History of Political Economy* 30, *special issue.*

Hansen, Lars P., John Heaton, and Thomas J. Sargent. 1991: Faster Methods for Solving Continuous Time Recursive Linear Models of Dynamic Economies. In Lars P. Hansen and Thomas J. Sargent (eds.), *Rational Expectations Econometrics.* Boulder, CO: Westview Press, pp. 177–208.

———— and Robert J. Hodrick. 1980: Forward Exchange Rates as Optimal Predictors of Future Spot Rates: An Econometric Analysis. *Journal of Political Economy* 88 (5), pp. 829–53.

————, William Roberds, and Thomas J. Sargent. 1991: Time Series Implications of Present Value Budget Balance and of Martingale Models of Consumption and Taxes. In Lars P. Hansen and Thomas J. Sargent (eds.), *Rational Expectations Econometrics.* Boulder, CO: Westview Press, pp. 121–62.

———— and Thomas J. Sargent. 1980: Formulating and Estimating Dynamic Linear Expectations Models. In Robert E. Lucas and Thomas J. Sargent (eds.), 1981: *Rational Expectations and Econometric Practice.* Minneapolis: University of Minnesota Press, pp. 91–125. Reprinted from *Journal of Economic Dynamics and Control* 2 (1), pp. 7–46.

———— and ————. 1981a: Linear Rational Expectations Models for Dynamically Interrelated Variables. In Robert E. Lucas and Thomas J. Sargent (eds.), 1981: *Rational Expectations and Econometric Practice.* Minneapolis: University of Minnesota Press, pp. 127–56.

———— and ————. 1981b: A Note on Wiener–Kolmogorov Prediction Formulas for Rational Expectations Models. *Economics Letters* 8 (3), pp. 255–60.

———— and ————. 1982: Instrumental Variables Procedures for Estimating Linear Rational Expectations Models. *Journal of Monetary Economics* 9 (3), pp. 263–96.

———— and ————. 1983a: Aggregation over Time and the Inverse Optimal Predictor Problem for Adaptive Expectations in Continuous Time. *International Economic Review* 24 (1), pp. 1–20.

———— and ————. 1983b: The Dimensionality of the Aliasing Problem in Models with Rational Spectral Densities. *Econometrica* 51 (2), pp. 377–87.

———— and ————. 1990: Recursive Linear Models of Dynamic Economies. *National Bureau of Economic Research Working Paper No. 3479.*

———— and ————. 1991a: Introduction. In Lars P. Hansen and Thomas J. Sargent (eds.), *Rational Expectations Econometrics.* Boulder, CO: Westview Press, pp. 1–12.

———— and ————. 1991b: Lecture Notes on Least Squares Prediction Theory. In Lars P. Hansen and Thomas J. Sargent (eds.), *Rational Expectations Econometrics.* Boulder, CO: Westview Press, pp. 13–44.

———— and ————. 1991c: Exact Linear Expectations Models: Specification and Estimation. In Lars P. Hansen and Thomas J. Sargent (eds.), *Rational Expectations Econometrics.* Boulder, CO: Westview Press, pp. 45–76.

———— and ————. 1991d: Two Difficulties in Interpreting Vector Autoregressions. In Lars P. Hansen and Thomas J. Sargent (eds.), *Rational Expectations Econometrics.* Boulder, CO: Westview Press, pp. 77–120.

———— and ————. 1991e: Prediction Formulas for Continuous Time Linear Rational Expectations Models. In Lars P. Hansen and Thomas J. Sargent (eds.), *Rational Expectations Econometrics.* Boulder, CO: Westview Press, pp. 209–18.

———— and ————. 1991f: Identification of Continuous Time Rational Expectations Models from Discrete Time Data. In Lars P. Hansen and Thomas J. Sargent (eds.), *Rational Expectations Econometrics.* Boulder, CO: Westview Press, pp. 219–36.

———— and ————. 1991g: *Recursive Linear Models of Dynamic Economies.* Unpublished Manuscript. University of Chicago and Hoover Institution.

———— and ————. 1993: Seasonality and Approximation Errors in Rational Expectations Models. *Journal of Econometrics* 55 (1–2), pp. 21–55.

———— and ————. 1995a: Discounted Linear Exponential Quadratic Gaussian Control. *IEEE Transactions on Automatic Control* 40 (5), pp. 968–71.

———— and ————. 1995b: *An Appreciation of A.W. Phillips.* Unpublished Manuscript. University of Chicago and Hoover Institution.

———— and ————. 1996: *Recursive Linear Models of Dynamic Economies.* Unpublished Manuscript. University of Chicago and Hoover Institution.

————, Thomas J. Sargent, and Thomas D. Tallarini. 1996: *Risk, Pessimism, and General Equilibrium.* Unpublished Manuscript. University of Chicago, Hoover Institution, and Carnegie Mellon University.

———— and Kenneth J. Singleton. 1982: Generalized Instrumental Variables Estimators of Nonlinear Rational Expectations Models. *Econometrica* 50 (5), pp. 1269–86.

Hausman, Daniel M. (ed.). 1984: *The Philosophy of Economics.* Cambridge: Cambridge University Press.

Hawking, Stephen W. 1988: *A Brief History of Time: From the Big Bang to Black Holes.* New York: Bantam Books.

Henshel, Richard L. 1982: The Boundary of the Self-Fulfilling Prophesy and the Dilemma of Social Prediction. *British Journal of Sociology* 33 (4), pp. 511–28.

Herrnstein, Richard J. 1991: Experiments on Stable Suboptimality in Individual Behavior. *American Economic Review* 81 (2), pp. 360–4.

Hickman, Bert G. (ed.). 1972: *Econometric Models of Cyclical Behavior.* New York: Columbia University Press.

Hodges, Andrew. 1983: *Alan Turing: The Enigma.* New York: Simon and Schuster.

Hofstadter, Douglas R. 1979: *Gödel, Escher, Bach: An Eternal Golden Braid.* New York: Basic Books.

Holland, John H. 1995: *Hidden Order: How Adaptation Builds Complexity.* Reading, MA: Addison-Wesley.

——— and John H. Miller. 1991: Artificial Adaptive Agents in Economic Theory. *American Economic Review* 81 (2), pp. 365–70.

Holt, Charles C., Franco Modigliani, John F. Muth, and Herbert A. Simon. 1960: *Planning Production, Inventories, and Work Force.* Englewood Cliffs, NJ: Prentice-Hall.

Hoover, Kevin D. 1988: *The New Classical Macroeconomics.* New York: Basil Blackwell.

Hsu, Der-Ann, Robert B. Miller, and Dean W. Wichern. 1974: On the Stable Paretian Behavior of Stock-Market Prices. *Journal of the American Statistical Association* 69 (345), pp. 108–13.

Huang, He, Selahattin Imrohoroglu, and Thomas J. Sargent. 1996: *Two Computations to Fund Social Security.* Unpublished Manuscript. University of Chicago, University of Southern California, and Hoover Institution.

Ingrao, Bruna and Giorgio Israel. 1990: *The Invisible Hand.* Cambridge, MA: MIT Press.

Janssen, Maarten C.W. 1993: *Microfoundations: A Critical Inquiry.* London: Routledge.

Jordan, Jerry L., Allan H. Meltzer, Anna J. Schwartz, and Thomas J. Sargent. 1993: Milton, Money, and Mischief: Symposium and Articles in Honor of Milton Friedman's 80th Birthday. *Economic Inquiry* 31 (2), pp. 197–212.

Jorgenson, Dale W. 1963: Capital Theory and Investment Behavior. *American Economic Review* 53 (2), pp. 247–59.

——— . 1967: Comment on Sidrauski's Rational Choice and Patterns of Growth in a Monetary Economy. *American Economic Review* 57 (2), pp. 557–9.

Jovanovic, Boyan and Saul Lach. 1989: Entry, Exit, and Diffusion with Learning by Doing. *American Economic Review* 79 (4), pp. 690–9.

——— and Rob Rafael. 1989: The Growth and Diffusion of Knowledge. *Review of Economic Studies* 56 (4), pp. 569–82.

Judge, George G., William E. Griffiths, R. Carter Hill, Helmut Lütkepohl, and Tsoung-Chao Lee. 1985: *The Theory and Practice of Econometrics,* 2nd ed. New York: John Wiley and Sons.

——— , ——— , ——— , ——— , and ——— . 1988: *Introduction to the Theory and Practice of Econometrics,* 2nd ed. New York: John Wiley and Sons.

Kailath, Thomas. 1980: *Linear Systems.* Englewood Cliffs, NJ: Prentice-Hall.

Kalman, Rudolf E. 1960: A New Approach to Linear Filtering and Prediction Problems. *Journal of Basic Engineering* 82 (March), pp. 35–45.

——— and R.W. Koepcke. 1959: The Role of Digital Computers in the Dynamic Optimization of Chemical Reactors. *Proceedings of the Western Joint Computer Conference,* pp. 107–16.

Kantor, Brian. 1979: Rational Expectations and Economic Thought. *Journal of Economic Literature* 17 (4), pp. 1422–41.

Kemp, Murray C. 1962: Economic Forecasting When the Subject of the Forecast Is Influenced by the Forecast. *American Economic Review* 52 (3), pp. 492–6.

Keuzekamp, Hugo A. 1991: A Precursor to Muth: Tinbergen's 1932 Model of Rational Expectations. *Economic Journal* 101 (408), pp. 1245–53.

Keynes, John Maynard. 1936: *The General Theory of Employment, Interest, and Money.* London: Macmillan.

Kim, Kyun. 1988: *Equilibrium Business Cycle Theory in Historical Perspective.* Cambridge: Cambridge University Press.

Kirman, Alan P. 1992: Whom or What Does the Representative Individual Represent? *Journal of Economic Perspectives* 6 (2), pp. 117–36.

———. 1993: Ants, Rationality, and Recruitment. *Quarterly Journal of Economics* 108 (1), pp. 137–56.

Kitcher, Philip. 1993: *The Advancement of Science.* New York: Oxford University Press.

Klamer, Arjo. 1983: *Conversations with Economists.* Savage, MD: Rowman & Littlefield.

Klein, Judy L. 1995: *A Funny Thing Happened on the Way to Equilibrium: The Interplay of Economic Theory and Time Series Analysis from 1890 to 1938.* Manuscript Presented at the ASSA meetings.

Koutrouvelis, Ioannis A. 1980: Regression-Type Estimation of the Parameters of Stable Laws. *Journal of the American Statistical Association* 75 (372), pp. 918–28.

———. 1981: An Iterative Procedure for the Estimation of the Parameters of Stable Laws. *Communications in Statistics – Simulation and Computation* 10 (1), pp. 17–28.

Koza, John R. 1992: *Genetic Programming: On the Programming of Computers by Means of Natural Selection.* Cambridge, MA: MIT Press.

Kuhn, Thomas S. 1962: *The Structure of Scientific Revolutions.* Chicago: University of Chicago Press.

Kwakernaak, Huibert and Raphael Sivan. 1972: *Linear Optimal Control Systems.* New York: John Wiley and Sons.

Kyburg, Henry E. 1969: *Probability Theory.* Englewood Cliffs, NJ: Prentice-Hall.

Lakatos, Imre. 1976: *Proofs and Refutations.* Cambridge: Cambridge University Press.

Lane, David A. 1993a: Artificial Worlds and Economics. Part I. *Journal of Evolutionary Economics* 3 (2), pp. 89–107.

———. 1993b: Artificial Worlds and Economics. Part II. *Journal of Evolutionary Economics* 3 (3), pp. 177–97.

Latour, Bruno. 1987: *Science in Action.* Cambridge, MA: Harvard University Press.

———. 1992: One More Turn after the Social Turn. In Ernan McMullin (ed.), *The Social Dimensions of Science.* Notre Dame, IN: University of Notre Dame Press, pp. 272–94.

Laudan, Larry. 1979: Historical Methodologies: An Overview and Manifesto. In Peter D. Asquith and Henry E. Kyburg (eds.), *Current Research in Philosophy of Science.* East Lansing, MI: Philosophy of Science Association.

———. 1984: *Science and Values: The Aims of Science and Their Role in Scientific Debate.* Berkeley: University of California Press.

———. 1987: Progress or Rationality? The Prospects for Normative Naturalism. *American Philosophical Quarterly* 24 (1), pp. 19–31.

Lee, Susan. 1984: The Un-Managed Economy. *Forbes* (December 17), pp. 147–58.

Lettau, Martin and Harald Uhlig. 1994: *Rules of Thumb and Dynamic Programming.* Unpublished Manuscript, Princeton Department of Economics.

Lewis, Alain A. 1985: On Effectively Computable Realizations of Choice Functions. *Mathematical Social Sciences* 10 (1), pp. 43–80.

———. 1992a: On Turing Degrees of Walrasian Models and a General Impossibility Result in the Theory of Decision-Making. *Mathematical Social Sciences* 24 (2–3), pp. 141–71.

———. 1992b: Some Aspects of Effectively Constructive Mathematics That Are Relevant to the Foundations of Neoclassical Mathematical Economics and the Theory of Games. *Mathematical Social Sciences* 24 (2–3), pp. 209–35.

Levacic, Rosalind and Alexander Rebman. 1982: *Macroeconomics: An Introduction to Keynesian–Neoclassical Controversies.* London: Macmillan.

Litterman, Robert B. 1979: Techniques of Forecasting Using Vector Autoregressions. *Research Department Working Paper 115.* Federal Reserve Bank of Minneapolis, Minnesota.

——— and Thomas J. Sargent. 1979: Detecting Neutral Price Level Changes and Effects of Aggregate Demand with Index Models. *Research Department Working Paper 125.* Federal Reserve Bank of Minneapolis, Minnesota.

Ljungqvist, Lars and Thomas J. Sargent. 1996: *The European Unemployment Dilemma.* Unpublished Manuscript. Federal Reserve Bank of Chicago, Hoover Institution, and University of Chicago.

Lucas, Robert E. 1972a: Expectations and the Neutrality of Money. *Journal of Economic Theory* 4 (2), pp. 103–24.

———. 1972b: Econometric Testing of the Natural Rate Hypothesis. In Otto Eckstein (ed.), *The Econometrics of Price Determination.* Washington, DC: Board of Governors of the Federal Reserve System, pp. 50–9.

———. 1973: Some International Evidence on Output–Inflation Tradeoffs. *American Economic Review* 63 (3), pp. 326–34.

———. 1975: An Equilibrium Model of the Business Cycle. *Journal of Political Economy* 83 (6), pp. 1113–44.

———. 1976: Econometric Policy Evaluation: A Critique. In Karl Brunner and Alan H. Meltzer (eds.), *The Phillips Curve and Labor Markets,* Carnegie-Rochester Conference Series on Public Policy, Volume 1. Amsterdam: North-Holland, pp. 19–46.

———. 1987: *Models of Business Cycles.* Oxford: Basil Blackwell.

——— and Edward C. Prescott. 1969: Price Expectation and the Phillips Curve. *American Economic Review* 59 (3), pp. 342–50.

——— and ———. 1971: Investment under Uncertainty. *Econometrica* 39 (5), pp. 659–81.

——— and ———. 1974: Equilibrium Search and Unemployment. *Journal of Economic Theory* 7 (2), pp. 188–209.

——— and Leonard A. Rapping. 1969a: Real Wages, Employment, and Inflation. *Journal of Political Economy* 77 (5), pp. 721–54.

——— and ———. 1969b: Price Expectations and the Phillips Curve. *American Economic Review* 59 (3), pp. 342–50.

———— and Thomas J. Sargent. 1979: After Keynesian Macroeconomics. *Federal Reserve Bank of Minneapolis Quarterly Review* 3 (Spring), pp. 1–16. Reprinted in Robert E. Lucas and Thomas J. Sargent (eds.). 1981: *Rational Expectations and Econometric Practice*. Minneapolis: University of Minnesota Press, pp. 295–320.

———— and ————. 1981: Introduction. In Robert E. Lucas and Thomas J. Sargent (eds.), *Rational Expectations and Econometric Practice*. Minneapolis: University of Minnesota Press, pp. xi–xl.

Lycan, William G. 1991: Homuncular Formalism Meets PDP. In William Ramsey, Stephen P. Stich, and David E. Rumelhart (eds.), *Philosophy and Connectionist Theory*. Hillsdale, NJ: Lawrence Erlbaum, pp. 259–86.

Mandelbrot, Benoit B. 1963a: New Methods in Statistical Economics. *Journal of Political Economy* 71 (5), pp. 421–40.

————. 1963b: The Variation of Certain Speculative Prices. *Journal of Business* 36 (4), pp. 394–419.

————. 1965: Very Long-Tailed Probability Distributions and the Empirical Distribution of City Sizes. In Fred Massarik and Philburn Ratoosh (eds.), *Explorations in Behavioral Science*. Homewood, IL: Richard D. Irwin, pp. 322–32.

————. 1969: Long-Run Linearity, Logically Gaussian Process, H-Spectra and Infinite Variances. *International Economic Review* 10 (1), pp. 82–111.

————. 1973: Comments on "A Subordinated Stochastic Process Model with Finite Variance for Speculative Prices" by Peter K. Clark. *Econometrica* 41 (1), pp. 157–9.

————. 1987: Towards a Second Stage of Indeterminism in Science. *Interdisciplinary Science Reviews* 12 (2), pp. 117–27.

———— and Murad S. Taqqu. 1979: Robust R/S Analysis of Long-Run Serial Correlation. Proceedings of the 42nd Session of the International Statistical Institute, Manila. *Bulletin of the International Statistics Institute* 48 (2), pp. 69–104.

Mannheim, Karl. 1936: *Ideology and Utopia: An Introduction to the Sociology of Knowledge*. New York: Harcourt, Brace.

Mantel, Rolf R. 1976: Homothetic Preferences and Community Excess Demand Functions. *Journal of Economic Theory* 12 (2), pp. 197–201.

Manuelli, Rodolfo and Thomas J. Sargent. 1992: *Alternative Monetary Policies in a Turnpike Economy*. Unpublished Manuscript. Stanford University, Hoover Institution, and University of Chicago.

Marcet, Albert and Thomas J. Sargent. 1986: Convergence of Least Squares Learning Mechanisms in Self-Referential Linear Stochastic Models. *Hoover Institution Working Papers in Economics E-86-33*.

———— and ————. 1988: The Fate of Systems with "Adaptive" Expectations. *American Economic Review* 78 (2) pp. 168–72.

———— and ————. 1989a: Convergence of Least Squares Learning Mechanisms in Self-Referential Linear Stochastic Models. *Journal of Economic Theory* 48 (2), pp. 337–68.

———— and ————. 1989b: Convergence of Least Squares Learning in Environments with Hidden State Variables and Private Information. *Journal of Political Economy* 97 (6), pp. 1306–22.

————— and ————— . 1989c: Least Squares Learning and the Dynamics of Hyperinflation. In William Barnett, John Geweke, and Karl Shell (eds.), *Economic Complexity: Chaos, Sunspots, and Nonlinearity.* Cambridge: Cambridge University Press, pp. 119–37.

————— and ————— . 1992: The Convergence of Vector Autoregressions to Rational Expectations Equilibrium. In Alessandro Vercelli and Nicola Dimitri (eds.), *Macroeconomics: A Strategic Survey.* Oxford: Oxford University Press, pp. 139–64.

—————, Thomas J. Sargent, and Juha Seppälä. 1996: *Optimal Taxation without State-Contingent Debt.* Unpublished Manuscript. University Pompeu Fabra, Hoover Institution, and University of Chicago.

Marimon, Ramon, Ellen McGrattan, and Thomas J. Sargent. 1989: Money as a Medium of Exchange in an Economy with Artificially Intelligent Agents. *Hoover Institution Working Papers in Economics E-89–28.*

—————, ————— , and ————— . 1990: Money as a Medium of Exchange in an Economy with Artificially Intelligent Agents. *Journal of Economic Dynamics and Control* 14 (2), pp. 329–74.

Massarik, Fred and Philburn Ratoosh (eds.). 1985: *Explorations in Behavioral Science.* Homewood, IL: Richard D. Irwin.

McCallum, Bennett T. 1979a: The Current State of the Policy Ineffectiveness Debate. *American Economic Review* 69 (2), pp. 240–5.

————— . 1979b: Rational Expectations and Macroeconomic Stabilization Policy. *Journal of Money, Credit, and Banking* 12 (4), pp. 716–46.

McCorduck, Pamela. 1979: *Machines Who Think.* San Francisco: W.H. Freeman.

McCulloch, J. Huston. 1986: Simple Consistent Estimators of Stable Distribution Parameters. *Communications in Statistics – Simulation and Computation* 15 (4), pp. 1109–36.

McKenzie, Lionel W. 1954: On Equilibrium in Graham's Model of World Trade and Other Competitive Systems. *Econometrica* 22 (2), pp. 147–61.

McMullin, Ernan. 1992: Introduction: The Social Dimensions of Science. In Ernan McMullin (ed.), *The Social Dimensions of Science.* Notre Dame, IN: University of Notre Dame Press, pp. 1–26.

Merton, Robert K. 1936: The Unanticipated Consequences of Purposive Social Action. *American Sociological Review* 1 (6), pp. 894–904.

————— . 1948: The Self-Fulfilling Prophecy. *The Antioch Review* 8 (2), pp. 193–210.

————— . 1960: *Social Theory and Social Structure,* rev. ed. Glencoe, IL: Free Press.

Merz, Martina and Karin Knorr Cetina. 1997a: Deconstruction in a "Thinking" Science: Theoretical Physicists at Work. *Social Studies of Science* 27 (1), pp. 73–111.

————— and ————— . 1997b: Floundering or Frolicking – How Does Ethnography Fare in Theoretical Physics? (and What Sort of Ethnography?): A Reply to Gale and Pinnick. *Social Studies of Science* 27 (1), pp. 123–31.

Milgrom, Paul and Nancy Stokey. 1982: Information, Trade and Common Knowledge. *Journal of Economic Theory* 26 (1), pp. 17–27.

Miller, Preston J. 1994: Introduction. In Preston J. Miller (ed.), *The Rational Expectations Revolution.* Cambridge, MA: MIT Press, pp. xiii–xvii.

Minford, Patrick and David Peel. 1983: *Rational Expectations and the New Macroeconomics.* New York: Basil Blackwell.

Mirowski, Philip E. 1988: *Against Mechanism.* Totowa, NJ: Rowman and Littlefield.

———. 1989a: *More Heat Than Light.* Cambridge: Cambridge University Press.

———. 1989b: 'Tis a Pity Econometrics Isn't an Empirical Endeavor: Mandelbrot, Chaos, and the Noah and Joseph Effects. *Recherche Economiche* 43 (1–2), pp. 76–99.

———. 1989c: The Probabilistic Counter-Revolution, or How Stochastic Concepts Came to Neoclassical Economic Theory. *Oxford Economic Papers* 41 (1), pp. 217–35.

———. 1990: From Mandelbrot to Chaos in Economic Theory. *Southern Economic Journal* 57 (2), pp. 289–307.

———. 1993a: What Could Mathematical Rigor Mean? Three Reactions to Gödel in Mid-20th Century Economics. *History of Economics Review* 20 (Summer), pp. 41–60.

———. 1993b: *What Econometrics Can and Can't Tell Us about the Historical Actors.* Unpublished Working Paper. University of Notre Dame, Department of Economics.

———. 1994: Review of Herbert Simon, "Economics, Bounded Rationality, and the Cognitive Evolution." *Southern Economic Journal* 60 (3), pp. 786–7.

———. 1996a: The Economic Consequences of Philip Kitcher. *Social Epistemology* 10 (2), pp. 153–70.

———. 1996b: Do You Know the Way to Santa Fe? In Steve Pressman (ed.), *Interactions in Political Economy.* London: Routledge, pp. 13–40.

———. 1997: On Playing the Economics Trump Card in the Philosophy of Science: Why It Didn't Work for Michael Polanyi. *Philosophy of Science* 64, *Proceedings.*

Mishkin, Frederick S. 1983: *A Rational Expectations Approach to Macroeconometrics.* Chicago: University of Chicago Press.

Monfort, Alain and R. Rabemananjara. 1990: From a VAR to a Structural Model, with an Application to the Wage–Price Spiral. *Journal of Applied Econometrics* 5 (3), pp. 203–28.

Morgan, Mary S. 1990: *The History of Econometric Ideas.* Cambridge: Cambridge University Press.

Morgenstern, Oskar. 1928: *Wirtschaftsprognose, Eine Untersuchung Ihrer Voraussetzungen und Möglichkeiten.* Vienna: Julius Springer.

Mulkay, Michael. 1979: *Science and the Sociology of Knowledge.* London: George Allen and Unwin.

Munz, Peter. 1985: *Our Knowledge of the Growth of Knowledge: Popper or Wittgenstein.* London: Routledge.

Muth, John F. 1960: Optimal Properties of Exponentially Weighted Forecasts. *Journal of the American Statistical Association* 55 (290), pp. 299–306.

———. 1961: Rational Expectations and the Theory of Price Movements. *Econometrica* 29 (3), pp. 315–35.

Neftci, Salih and Thomas J. Sargent. 1978: A Little Bit of Evidence on the Natural Rate Hypothesis from the U.S. *Journal of Monetary Economics* 4 (2), pp. 315–19.

Nelson, Charles R. 1972: The Prediction Performance of the FRB–MIT–Penn Model of the U.S. Economy. *American Economic Review* 62 (5), pp. 902–17.

Nerlove, Marc L. 1958: Adaptive Expectations and Cobweb Phenomena. *Quarterly Journal of Economics* 72 (2), pp. 227–40.

———. 1967: Distributed Lags and Unobserved Components in Economic Time

Series. In William J. Fellner (ed.), *Ten Economic Studies in the Tradition of Irving Fisher.* New York: John Wiley and Sons, pp. 127–69.

————, David M. Grether, and José L. Carvalho. 1979: *Analysis of Economic Time Series: A Synthesis.* New York: Academic Press.

Neumann, John von, and Oskar Morgenstern. 1944: *Theory of Games and Economic Behavior.* Princeton, NJ: Princeton University Press.

Newton, George C. 1952a: Compensation of Feedback Control Systems Subject to Saturation. Part I. *Journal of the Franklin Institute* 254 (4), pp. 281–96.

————. 1952b: Compensation of Feedback Control Systems Subject to Saturation. Part II. *Journal of the Franklin Institute* 254 (5), pp. 391–413.

————, Leonard A. Gould, and James F. Kaiser. 1957: *Analytical Design of Linear Feedback Controls.* New York: John Wiley and Sons.

Niehans, Jürg. 1990: *A History of Economic Theory.* Baltimore: Johns Hopkins University Press.

Øftsi, Audun, and Dag Østerberg. 1982: Self-Defeating Predictions and the Fixed-Point Theorem: A Refutation. *Inquiry* 25 (3), pp. 331–52.

Packard, Norman H. 1988: Dynamics of Development: A Simple Model for Dynamics Away from Attractors. In Philip W. Anderson, Kenneth J. Arrow, and David Pines (eds.), *The Economy as an Evolving Complex System.* Redwood City, CA: Addison-Wesley, pp. 169–76.

Palmer, R.G., W. Brian Arthur, John H. Holland, Blake LeBaron, and Paul Tayler. 1994: Artificial Economic Life: A Simple Model of a Stockmarket. *Physica D* 75, pp. 264–74.

Parkin, Michael. 1996. Talking with Thomas J. Sargent. In Michael Parkin, *Economics,* 3rd ed. Reading, MA: Addison-Wesley, pp. 650–3.

Paulson, A.S., E.W. Holcomb, and R.A. Leitch. 1975: The Estimation of the Parameters of Stable Laws. *Biometrika* 62 (1), pp. 163–70.

Penrose, Roger. 1989: *The Emperor's New Mind: Concerning Computers, Minds, and the Laws of Physics.* New York: Penguin Books.

Pesaran, M. Hashem and Ron Smith. 1992: The Interaction between Theory and Observation in Economics. *The Economic and Social Review* 24 (1), pp. 1–23.

Phelps, Edmund S. 1967: Phillips Curves, Expectations of Inflation, and Optimal Unemployment over Time. *Economica* 34 (3), pp. 254–81.

———— et al. 1970: *Microeconomic Foundations of Employment and Inflation Theory.* New York: W.W. Norton.

Pickering, Andrew. 1992: From Science as Knowledge to Science as Practice. In Andrew Pickering (ed.), *Science as Practice and Culture.* Chicago: University of Chicago Press, pp. 1–26.

————. 1993: The Mangle of Practice: Agency and Emergence in the Sociology of Science. *American Journal of Sociology* 99 (3), pp. 559–89.

————. 1995a: Beyond Constraint: The Temporality of Practice and the Historicity of Knowledge. In Jed Z. Buchwald (ed.), *Scientific Practice: Theories and Stories of Doing Physics.* Chicago: University of Chicago Press, pp. 42–55.

————. 1995b: *The Mangle of Practice: Time, Agency, and Science.* Chicago: University of Chicago Press.

——— and Adam Stephanides. 1992: Constructing Quaternions: On the Analysis of Conceptual Practice. In Andrew Pickering (ed.), *Science as Practice and Culture.* Chicago: University of Chicago Press, pp. 139–67.

Pool, Robert. 1989: Strange Bedfellows. *Science* 245, pp. 700–3.

Precious, Mark. 1987: *Rational Expectations, Non-Market Clearing, and Investment Theory.* Oxford: Clarendon Press.

Press, S. James. 1972: Estimation in Univariate and Multivariate Stable Distributions. *Journal of the American Statistical Association* 67 (340), pp. 842–6.

Priestley, M.B., T. Subba Rao, and Howell Tong. 1974: Applications of Principal Components and Factor Analysis in the Identification of Multi-Variable Systems. *IEEE Transactions on Automatic Control* AC-19 (6), pp. 730–4.

Radnitzky, Gerard and William W. Bartley (ed.). 1987: *Evolutionary Epistemology, Rationality, and the Sociology of Knowledge.* La Salle, IL: Open Court.

——— and Peter Bernholz (eds.). 1987: *Economic Imperialism: The Economic Approach Applied outside the Field of Economics.* New York: Paragon House.

Ramsey, William, Stephen P. Stich, and Joseph Garon. 1991: Connectionism, Eliminativism, and the Future of Folk Psychology. In William Ramsey, Stephen P. Stich, and David E. Rumelhart (eds.), *Philosophy and Connectionist Theory.* Hillsdale, NJ: Lawrence Erlbaum, pp. 199–228.

Resnick, Mitchel. 1994: Learning about Life. *Artificial Life* 1 (1–2), pp. 229–41.

Ringer, Fritz K. 1992: The Origins of Mannheim's Sociology of Knowledge. In Ernan McMullin (ed.), *The Social Dimensions of Science.* Notre Dame, IN: University of Notre Dame Press, pp. 47–66.

Rizvi, S. Abu Turab. 1991: Specialisation and the Existence Problem in General Equilibrium Theory. *Contributions to Political Economy* 10, pp. 1–10.

———. 1994: Game Theory to the Rescue? *Contributions to Political Economy* 13, pp. 1–28.

Roll, Richard. 1970: *The Behavior of Interest Rates.* New York: Basic Books.

Rosen, Joe. 1975: *Symmetry Discovered: Concepts and Applications in Nature and Science.* Cambridge: Cambridge University Press.

———. 1983: *A Symmetry Primer for Scientists.* New York: John Wiley and Sons.

———. 1990: Fundamental Manifestations of Symmetry in Physics. *Foundations of Physics* 20 (3), pp. 283–307.

Rosen, Sherwin. 1987: Dynamic Animal Economies. *American Journal of Agricultural Economics* 69 (3), pp. 547–57.

——— and Robert H. Topel. 1988: Housing Investment in the United States. *Journal of Political Economy* 96 (4), pp. 718–40.

Rossetti, Jane. 1990: *Deconstructing Economic Texts.* Ann Arbor, MI: UMI Dissertation Services.

Rothschild, Kurt. 1964: Cobweb Cycles and Partially Correct Forecasting, *Journal of Political Economy* 72 (3), pp. 300–5.

Rubinstein, Mark. 1975: Security Market Efficiency in an Arrow–Debreu Economy. *American Economic Review* 65 (5), pp. 812–24.

Runciman, Walter G. (ed.). 1978: *Max Weber: Selections in Translation.* Cambridge: Cambridge University Press.

Salemi, Michael K. and Thomas J. Sargent. 1979: The Demand for Money during Hyperinflation under Rational Expectations. II. *International Economic Review* 20 (3), pp. 741–58.

Samuelson, Paul A. 1965: Proof That Properly Anticipated Prices Fluctuate Randomly. *Industrial Management Review* 6 (2), pp. 41–9.

Sargent, Thomas J. 1968: Interest Rates in the Nineteen-Fifties. *Review of Economics and Statistics* 50 (2), pp. 164–72.

———. 1969: Commodity Price Expectations and the Interest Rate. *Quarterly Journal of Economics* 83 (1), pp. 127–40.

———. 1971a: Expectations at the Short End of the Yield Curve: An Application of Macaulay's Test. In Jack M. Guttentag (ed.), *Essays on Interest Rates,* Volume 2. New York: Columbia University Press, for the NBER, pp. 391–412.

———. 1971b: A Note on the "Accelerationist" Controversy. *Journal of Money, Credit, and Banking* 3 (3), pp. 721–5. Reprinted in Robert E. Lucas and Thomas J. Sargent (eds.) *Rational Expectations and Econometric Practice.* Minneapolis: University of Minnesota Press, pp. 33–8.

———. 1972: Rational Expectations and the Term Structure of Interest Rates. *Journal of Money, Credit, and Banking* 4 (1), pp. 74–97.

———. 1973: What Do Regressions on Inflation Show? *Annals of Economic and Social Measurement* 2 (3), pp. 289–301.

———. 1976a: A Classical Macroeconometric Model for the United States. *Journal of Political Economy* 84 (2), pp. 207–37. Reprinted in Robert E. Lucas and Thomas J. Sargent (eds.). 1981: *Rational Expectations and Econometric Practice.* Minneapolis: University of Minnesota Press, pp. 521–51.

———. 1976b: The Observational Equivalence of Natural and Unnatural Rate Theories of Macroeconomics. *Journal of Political Economy* 84 (3), pp. 631–40.

———. 1977a: The Demand for Money during Hyperinflations under Rational Expectations. I. *International Economic Review* 18 (1), pp. 59–82. Reprinted in Robert E. Lucas and Thomas J. Sargent (eds.). 1981: *Rational Expectations and Econometric Practice.* Minneapolis: University of Minnesota Press, pp. 429–52.

———. 1977b: Response to Gordon and Ando. In Christopher A. Sims (ed.), *New Methods in Business Cycle Research: Proceedings from a Conference.* Federal Reserve Bank of Minneapolis, pp. 213–17.

———. 1978a: Rational Expectations, Econometric Exogeneity, and Consumption. *Journal of Political Economy* 86 (4), pp. 673–700.

———. 1978b: Estimation of Dynamic Labor Demand Schedules under Rational Expectations. *Journal of Political Economy* 84 (2), pp. 207–37. Reprinted in Robert E. Lucas and Thomas J. Sargent (eds.). 1981: *Rational Expectations and Econometric Practice.* Minneapolis: University of Minnesota Press, pp. 463–500.

———. 1978c: Comments on "Seasonal Adjustment and Multiple Time Series Analysis" by Kenneth F. Wallis. In Arnold Zellner (ed.), *Seasonal Analysis of Economic Time Series.* Washington, DC: U.S. Department of Commerce, pp. 361–4.

———. 1978d: A Note on Maximum Likelihood Estimation of the Rational Expectations Model of the Term Structure. *Federal Reserve Bank of Minneapolis Staff Report No. 26.*

230   **References**

———— . 1979a: A Note on Maximum Likelihood Estimation of the Rational Expectations Model of the Term Structure. *Journal of Monetary Economics* 5 (1), pp. 133–43. Reprinted in Robert E. Lucas and Thomas J. Sargent (eds.). 1981: *Rational Expectations and Econometric Practice*. Minneapolis: University of Minnesota Press, pp. 453–62.

———— . 1979b: Estimating Vector Autoregressions Using Methods Not Based on Explicit Economic Theories. *Federal Reserve Bank of Minneapolis Quarterly Review* 3 (3), pp. 8–15.

———— . 1979c: Causality, Exogeneity, and Natural Rate Models: Reply to C.R. Nelson and B.T. McCallum. *Journal of Political Economy* 87 (2), pp. 403–9.

———— . 1979d: *Macroeconomic Theory*. Boston: Academic Press.

———— . 1980: 'Tobin's q' and the Rate of Investment in General Equilibrium. In Karl Brunner and Alan H. Meltzer (eds.), *Carnegie-Rochester Conference Series on Public Policy 12*. Amsterdam: North-Holland, pp. 107–54.

———— . 1981a: Interpreting Economic Time Series. *Journal of Political Economy* 89 (2), pp. 213–48.

———— . 1981b: *Lecture Notes on Filtering, Control, and Rational Expectations*. Unpublished Manuscript. University of Minnesota, Minneapolis.

———— . 1982: Beyond Demand and Supply Curves in Macroeconomics. *American Economic Review* 72 (2), pp. 382–9.

———— . 1983: An Economist's Foreword to Prediction and Regulation by Linear Least-Square Methods. In Peter Whittle, *Prediction and Regulation by Linear Least-Square Methods,* 2nd rev. ed. Minneapolis: University of Minnesota Press, pp. v–vii.

———— . 1984: Autoregressions, Expectations, and Advice (with Discussion). *American Economic Review* 74 (2), pp. 408–21.

———— . 1985: Energy, Foresight, and Strategy. In S. Rao Aiyagari and Thomas J. Sargent (eds.), *Energy, Foresight, and Strategy*. Washington, DC: Johns Hopkins University Press, pp. 1–13.

———— . 1986: *Rational Expectations and Inflation*. New York: Harper and Row.

———— . 1987a: *Macroeconomic Theory,* 2nd ed. Boston: Academic Press.

———— . 1987b: *Dynamic Macroeconomic Theory*. Cambridge, MA: Harvard University Press.

———— . 1987c: Rational Expectations. In John Eatwell, Murray Milgate, and Peter Newman (eds.), *The New Palgrave*. London: Macmillan, pp. 76–85.

———— . 1988: *Linear Optimal Control, Filtering, and Rational Expectations*. Unpublished Manuscript. Stanford University, Hoover Institution.

———— . 1989: Two Models of Measurements and the Investment Accelerator. *Journal of Political Economy* 97 (2), pp. 251–87.

———— . 1991: Equilibrium with Signal Extraction from Endogenous Variables. *Journal of Economic Dynamics and Control* 15 (2), pp. 245–74.

———— . 1992: Review of "Game Theory and Economic Modeling" by David M. Kreps. *Journal of Political Economy* 100 (3), pp. 665–72.

———— . 1993: *Bounded Rationality in Macroeconomics*. Oxford: Oxford University Press.

————. 1996a: Expectations and the Nonneutrality of Lucas. *Journal of Monetary Economics* 37 (3), pp. 535–48.

————. 1996b: *Recursive Macroeconomic Theory.* Unpublished Manuscript. University of Chicago and Hoover Institution.

———— and Christopher A. Sims. 1977: Business Cycle Modeling without Pretending to Have Too Much a Priori Theory. In Christopher A. Sims (ed.), *New Methods in Business Cycle Research: Proceedings from a Conference.* Federal Reserve Bank of Minneapolis, Minnesota, pp. 45–109.

———— and Bruce D. Smith. 1995: *Coinage, Debasements, and Gresham's Law.* Unpublished Manuscript. Hoover Institution, University of Chicago, and Cornell University.

———— and François R. Velde. 1995: Macroeconomic Features of the French Revolution. *Journal of Political Economy* 103 (3), pp. 474–518.

———— and Neil Wallace. 1973: Rational Expectations and the Dynamics of Hyperinflation. *International Economic Review* 14 (2), pp. 328–50.

———— and ————. 1975: "Rational" Expectations, the Optimal Monetary Instrument, and the Optimal Money Supply Rule. *Journal of Political Economy* 83 (2), pp. 241–54. Reprinted in Robert E. Lucas and Thomas J. Sargent (eds.). 1981: *Rational Expectations and Econometric Practice.* Minneapolis: University of Minnesota Press, pp. 215–28.

———— and ————. 1976: Rational Expectations and the Theory of Economic Policy. In Robert E. Lucas and Thomas J. Sargent (eds.). 1981: *Rational Expectations and Econometric Practice.* Minneapolis: University of Minnesota Press, pp. 199–213. Reprinted from *Journal of Monetary Economics* 2 (2), pp. 169–84.

———— and ————. 1981: Some Unpleasant Monetarist Arithmetic. *Federal Reserve Bank of Minneapolis Quarterly Review* 5 (Fall), pp. 1–17. Reprinted in Thomas J. Sargent. 1986: *Rational Expectations and Inflation.* New York: Harper & Row, pp. 158–90.

Sent, Esther-Mirjam. 1996a: What an Economist Can Teach Nancy Cartwright. *Social Epistemology* 10 (2), pp. 171–92.

————. 1996b: Convenience: The Mother of All Rationality in Sargent. *Journal of Post-Keynesian Economics* 19 (1), pp. 3–34.

————. 1997a: Sargent versus Simon: Bounded Rationality Unbound. *Cambridge Journal of Economics* 21 (3), pp. 323–38.

————. 1997b: An Economist's Glance at Goldman's Economics. *Philosophy of Science* 64, *Proceedings.*

————. 1998: Engineering Dynamic Economics. *History of Political Economy* 29, *special issue,* pp. 41–62.

————. forthcoming: Sargent's Symmetry Saga: Ontological versus Technical Constraints. In Uskali Mäki (ed.), *The Economic Realm.*

Shaw, Graham K. 1984: *Rational Expectations.* New York: St. Martin's Press.

Sheffrin, Steven M. 1983: *Rational Expectations.* Cambridge: Cambridge University Press.

Shiller, Robert J. 1979: The Volatility of Long-Term Interest Rates and Expectations Models of the Term Structure. *Journal of Political Economy* 87 (6), pp. 1190–219.

Sidrauski, Miguel. 1967: Rational Choice and Patterns of Growth in a Monetary Economy. *American Economic Review* 57 (2), pp. 534–44.

Simon, Herbert A. 1954: Bandwagon and Underdog Effects and the Possibility of Election Predictions. *Public Opinion Quarterly* 18 (3), pp. 245–53.

———. 1956: Dynamic Programming under Uncertainty with a Quadratic Objective Function. *Econometrica* 24 (1), pp. 74–81.

———. 1967: Reply to Professor Binkley's comments. In Nicholas Rescher (ed.), *The Logic of Decision and Action.* Pittsburgh: University of Pittsburgh Press, pp. 32–3.

———. 1976: From Substantive to Procedural Rationality. In Spiro J. Latsis (ed.), *Method and Appraisal in Economics.* Cambridge: Cambridge University Press, pp. 129–48.

———. 1979: Rational Decision Making in Business Organizations. *American Economic Review* 69 (4), pp. 493–513.

———. 1981: *The Sciences of the Artificial,* 2nd ed. Cambridge, MA: MIT Press.

———. 1982a: Election Predictions: Reply. *Inquiry* 25 (3), pp. 361–4.

———. 1982b: "Accurate Predictions and Fixed Point Theorems": Comments. *Social Science Information* 21 (4/5), pp. 605–26.

———. 1982c: *Models of Bounded Rationality,* Volume 1. Cambridge, MA: MIT Press.

———. 1982d: *Models of Bounded Rationality,* Volume 2. Cambridge, MA: MIT Press.

———. 1987: Bounded Rationality. In John Eatwell, Murray Milgate, and Peter Newman (eds.), *The New Palgrave.* London: Macmillan, pp. 266–8.

———. 1991: *Models of My Life.* New York: Basic Books.

———. 1993: The Human Mind: The Symbolic Level. *Proceedings of the American Philosophical Society* 137 (4), pp. 638–47.

Sims, Christopher A. 1971a: Discrete Approximations to Continuous Time Lag Distributions in Econometrics. *Econometrica* 39 (3), pp. 545–64.

———. 1971b: Linear Regression with Non-Normal Error Terms: A Comment. *Review of Economics and Statistics* 53 (2), pp. 204–5.

———. 1972: Money, Income, and Causality. *American Economic Review* 57 (2), pp. 534–44. Reprinted in Robert E. Lucas and Thomas J. Sargent (eds.). 1981: *Rational Expectations and Econometric Practice.* Minneapolis: University of Minnesota Press, pp. 387–403.

———. 1977: Exogeneity and Causal Ordering in Macroeconometric Models. In Christopher A. Sims (ed.), *New Methods in Business Cycle Research.* Minneapolis: Federal Reserve Bank of Minneapolis, pp. 23–43.

———. 1980a: Macroeconomics and Reality. *Econometrica* 48 (1), pp. 1–45.

———. 1980b: Comparison of Interwar and Postwar Business Cycles: Monetarism Reconsidered. *American Economic Review* 70 (1), pp. 250–9.

———. 1982a: Policy Analysis with Econometric Models. *Brookings Papers on Economic Activity* (1), pp. 107–52.

———. 1982b: Scientific Standards in Econometric Modeling. In Michiel Hazewinkel and Alexander H.G. Rinnooy Kan (eds.), *Current Developments in the Interface: Economics, Econometrics, Mathematics.* Dordrecht: Reidel, pp. 317–40.

Smith, Vernon L. (ed.). 1990: *Experimental Economics.* Brookfield, VT: Gower.

Snippe, Jan. 1986: Varieties of Rational Expectations: Their Differences and Relations. *Journal of Post-Keynesian Economics* 8 (3), pp. 427–37.

Snowdon, Brian, Howard Vane, and Peter Wynarczyk. 1994: *A Modern Guide to Macroeconomics.* Brookfield, VT: Edward Elgar.

Sober, Elliott. 1993: Temporally Oriented Laws. *Synthese* 94 (2), pp. 171–89.

Sonnenschein, Hugo. 1972: Market Excess Demand Functions. *Econometrica* 40 (3), pp. 549–563.

Spiegel, Henry W. 1991: *The Growth of Economic Thought.* Durham, NC: Duke University Press.

Takayama, Akira. 1985: *Mathematical Economics.* Cambridge: Cambridge University Press.

Taylor, John B. 1975: Monetary Policy during the Transition to Rational Expectations. *Journal of Political Economy* 83 (6), pp. 1009–21.

——— . 1979: Estimation and Control of a Macroeconomic Model with Rational Expectations. *Econometrica* 47 (5), pp. 1267–86.

——— . 1980: Output and Price Stability: An International Comparison. *Journal for Economic Dynamics and Control* 2 (1), pp. 109–32.

Taylor, Lester D. 1974: Minimizing the Sum of Absolute Errors. In Paul Zarembka (ed.), *Frontiers in Econometrics.* New York: Academic Press, pp. 169–90.

Theil, Henri. 1964: *Optimal Decision Rules for Government and Industry.* Amsterdam: North-Holland.

Tirole, Jean. 1982: On the Possibility of Speculation under Rational Expectations. *Econometrica* 50 (5), pp. 1163–82.

Treviño, George. 1992: An Heuristic Overview of Nonstationarity. In A.G. Miamee (ed.), *Nonstationary Stochastic Processes and Their Applications.* Singapore: World Scientific, pp. 48–61.

Varian, Hal R. 1987: Differences of Opinion in Financial Markets. *Financial Risk: Theory, Evidence, and Implications.* Proceedings of the 11th Annual Economic Policy Conference of the Federal Reserve Bank of St. Louis, pp. 3–37.

Wagner, Harvey M. 1959: Linear Programming Techniques for Regression Analysis. *Journal of the American Statistical Association* 54 (285), pp. 206–12.

Waldrop, M. Mitchell. 1992: *Complexity: The Emerging Science at the Edge of Order and Chaos.* New York: Simon and Schuster.

Weagle, Matthew C. 1995: *Inoculating Neoclassicism against the Genetic Algorithm.* Unpublished Working Paper. University of Notre Dame, Department of Economics.

Weatherford, Roy. 1982: *Philosophical Foundations of Probability Theory.* New York: Routledge.

——— . 1991: *The Implications of Determinism.* New York: Routledge.

Weintraub, E. Roy. 1991: *Stabilizing Dynamics: Constructing Economic Knowledge.* Cambridge: Cambridge University Press.

Weyl, Hermann. 1952: *Symmetry.* Princeton, NJ: Princeton University Press.

Whiteman, Charles, H. 1983: *Linear Rational Expectations Models.* Minneapolis: University of Minnesota Press.

Whittle, Peter. 1963: *Prediction and Regulation by Linear Least-Square Methods.* Princeton, NJ: Van Nostrand.

——— . 1983: *Prediction and Regulation by Linear Least-Square Methods,* 2nd ed. Minneapolis: University of Minnesota Press.

Wiener, Norbert. 1956. *I Am a Mathematician.* New York: Doubleday.

———. 1964: *Extrapolation, Interpolation, and Smoothing of Stationary Time Series.* Cambridge, MA: MIT Press.

Wold, Herman. 1938: *A Study in the Analysis of Stationary Time Series.* Stockholm: Almqvist and Wiksell.

Woolgar, Steve (ed.). 1988a: *Knowledge and Reflexivity.* London: Sage.

———. 1988b: *Science: The Very Idea.* London: Tavistock.

———. 1992: Some Remarks about Positionism: A Reply to Collins and Yearly. In Andrew Pickering (ed.), *Science as Practice and Culture.* Chicago: University of Chicago Press, pp. 327–42.

Wu, De-Min. 1973: Alternative Tests of Independence between Stochastic Regressors and Disturbances. *Econometrica* 41 (4), pp. 733–50.

Wulwick, Nancy J. 1990: The Mathematics of Economic Growth. *Working Paper No. 38, Jerome Levy Economics Institute, Bard College.*

———. 1995: The Hamiltonian Formalism and Optimal Growth Theory. In Ingrid H. Rima (ed.), *Measurement, Quantification, and Economic Analysis.* London: Routledge, pp. 406–35.

Yaglom, A.M. 1962: *An Introduction to the Theory of Stationary Random Functions.* Englewood Cliffs, NJ: Prentice-Hall.

Zarembka, Paul (ed.). 1974: *Frontiers in Econometrics.* New York: Academic Press.

Zellner, Arnold and Franz Palm. 1974: Time Series Analysis and Simultaneous Equation Models. *Journal of Econometrics* 2 (1), pp. 17–54.

Zolotarev, V.M. 1986: *One-Dimensional Stable Distributions.* Providence, RI: American Mathematical Society.

Index